THE PRESIDENT ELECTRIC

D1028714

THEATER: THEORY/TEXT/PERFORMANCE
Series Editors: David Krasner and Rebecca Schneider
Founding Editor: Enoch Brater

Recent Titles:

THE PRESIDENT
ELECTRIC

Ronald Reagan and the
Politics of Performance

Timothy Raphael

THE UNIVERSITY OF MICHIGAN PRESS

ANN ARBOR

2012 2011 2010 2009   4 3 2 1

A CIP catalog record for this book is available from the British Library.

Library of Congress Cataloging-in-Publication Data

Raphael, Timothy.
    The president electric : Ronald Reagan and the politics of
performance / Timothy Raphael.
        p.   cm. — (Theater : theory/text/performance)
    Includes bibliographical references and index.
    ISBN 978-0-472-07073-2 (cloth : alk. paper) —
    ISBN 978-0-472-05073-4 (pbk. : alk. paper)
    1. Reagan, Ronald.   I. Title.
E877.2.R35   2009
973.927092—dc22   2009024927

For Kim

ACKNOWLEDGMENTS

This book has been a long time in the making, and the village that has raised this child is vast. I began writing about Ronald Reagan in Chicago at Northwestern University in a class with Margaret Drewal. It began to take shape through subsequent conversations and classes with Dwight Conquergood, Paul Edwards, and Orville Lee. The conversations continued in Connecticut while I was teaching at Wesleyan University, and the work owes much to the insights of Richard Slotkin, Bill Stowe, Betsy Traube, Khachig Tololyan, Ann Wightman, Patricia Hill, Henry Abelove, Christina Crosby, Gayle Pemberton, Gertrude Hughes, Dick Vann, Sean McCann, Liz McAlister, Maureen Mahon, and Gareth Williams. During the better part of a year in Portugal, while teaching American studies at Universidade Aberta with an infant in tow, I continued the research. Of the many Portuguese friends whose kindness sustained our new family and my research, a special acknowledgment is due Cuca Antonio and Kevin Rose, who opened up their home and lives to us in a way that has bonded us for life.

At Ursinus College, President John Strassburger and Dean Judy Levy provided research support and a leave that made it possible to write. Several of my colleagues at Ursinus—including Dallet Hemphill, Patti Schroeder, Lynne Edwards, Jon Volkmer, Paul Stern, Nzadi Keita, and Charles Rice—contributed thoughts, ideas, and criticisms that improved the book. My friends and colleagues at Rutgers University, Newark, sustained me through the final stages of writing and revising. Fran Bartkowski's reading improved two chapters immensely. Jan Lewis pointed me to several texts that influenced my thinking about the relationships between political and theatrical representation in the early years of the republic. The work and friendship of Sherri-Ann Butterfield, Mara Sabinson, Laura Lomas, Jamie Lew, and Belinda Edmondson are ghosting presences throughout. My colleagues in the sometimes unwieldy but always stimulating Department of Performing Arts—especially Rob Snyder, Edin Velez, John Howland, Paul Sternberger, Nick Kline, Leo Aristmuno, Dan Drew, and Eric Johnson—helped keep me sane at a time when it seemed the book was in perpetual revision. My chair, Ian Watson, was an enthusiastic supporter of the work and facilitated research funding to help make it happen. Through its fabulous staff and the visionary leadership of Clem Price and Charles Russell, the Institute on Ethnicity, Culture and the Modern Experience provided an exemplary cultural and intellectual environment in which to expand the work into the public sphere.

Thanks are also owed to Richard Schechner and Harry Elam, the editors of *The Drama Review* and *Theatre Journal,* respectively, who published excerpts from the work while it was still in development and in the process assigned readers whose comments have strengthened the book. An early exploration of the book's themes appeared in *The Drama Review* as "The King Is a Thing: Bodies of Memory in the Age of Reagan." An earlier version of "The Rights of Memory" appeared in *Theatre Journal* as "Mo(u)rning in America: Hamlet, Reagan, and the Rights of Memory." An excerpt from "The Reagan Brand" was published in *The Drama Review* as "Performing the Body Electric: GE, TV, and the Reagan Brand." Along its lengthy path to completion several other anonymous readers have positively impacted the development of the book. I am grateful to what Benedict Anderson called "the community in anonymity" that has left its traces within these pages. Throughout the book's odyssey at the University of Michigan Press, my editor, LeAnn Fields, has skillfully guided it through the Scylla and Charybdis of the review process.

I must also acknowledge a special thanks and a singular debt of gratitude to Joe Roach, who graciously read the work at virtually every stage of its development and whose observations were invariably dead-on. Whatever the book's flaws are, they would be significantly greater were it not for his input.

Throughout the research and writing my family has provided encouragement and sustenance. This book would not have been written without the support of Ann Wiener, Jenifer Raphael, Chad Raphael, Monique Houston, Gregg Houston, and Judy and Bob Holton. A special shout-out is due to my irrepressible, indefatigable, and incomparable children, Noah and Antonia. The development of this book spans your lifetimes, but its virtues pale in comparison to yours. Finally, to Kim, to whom the book is dedicated, I am eternally grateful for the companionship and support without which this book could not have come to be.

Yet the dynamo, next to the steam-engine, was the most familiar of exhibits. For Adams's objects its value lay chiefly in its occult mechanism. Between the dynamo in the gallery of machines and the engine-house outside, the break of continuity amounted to abysmal fracture for a historian's objects. No more relation could he find between the steam and electrical current than between the Cross and the cathedral. The forces were interchangeable if not reversible, but he could only see an absolute fiat in electricity as in faith.

    —HENRY ADAMS

And we must always remember that the pleasure given by representations of such different sorts hardly ever depended on the representation's likeness to the thing portrayed. Incorrectness, or considerable improbability even, was hardly or not at all disturbing, so long as the incorrectness had a certain consistency and the improbability remained of a constant kind. All that mattered was the illusion of a compelling momentum in the story told, and this was created by all sorts of poetic and theatrical means.

    —BERTOLT BRECHT

He is similar, not similar to something, but just similar. And he invents spaces of which he is the convulsive possession.

    —ROGER CAILLOIS

CONTENTS

INTRODUCTION

The Body Electric

People come to Hollywood from many different places, and certainly are varied in their background and training, but all of them either bring one thing with them or acquire it upon arrival: The desire to see a certain story become a picture.
—Ronald Reagan, *Where's the Rest of Me?*

Ronald Reagan first appeared at the 1984 Republican National Convention on a screen above a stage. From that stage, astride a podium flanked by two American flags, Nancy Reagan raised her eyes to greet the image that dwarfed her. As she turned her notorious gaze on his celebrated image, she extended both her arms upward toward the screen. Rising to their feet beneath and behind her, his delegates held his portrait aloft. Trimmed in the colors of the flag, the convention hall reverberated with their adoration.

Photo: President Reagan's initial appearance at the 1984 Republican Convention.
Photo © Bettman/Corbis.

The rest of us watched him, smiling and waving, on television. We watched as the crowd waved back, while he, "diffused to infinity," disappeared into "an infinitely fragmenting video relay."[1] We watched our televisions as the cameras watched the conventioneers watch Nancy watch the screen, and it was easy to conclude that Ronald Reagan had indeed become, in Michael Rogin's apt phrase, "the image that has fixed our gaze."[2] But why were we watching *this* man? What were the qualities he possessed that enabled him to fix our gaze and define our viewing habits? And why did we keep watching as he became—in the infinitude of his representation—a projection on a screen? What story becomes this picture?

In what follows, I propose that answers to these questions can be found in the increasing importance of *performance* in American political life and the lessons these performances hold for the transformation of American politics in the twentieth century. In the production and reception of Reagan's video greeting, various incarnations of the politician as performer flash together and circulate. These performances illuminate an intricate network of connections between statecraft and stagecraft, political and cultural representation, media and mimesis, the devil and the deep blue sea. Renowned as the first actor to become president of the United States, Ronald Reagan was, more significantly, the product of an exhaustive education in the performance *techne*—the techniques and technologies—of electronic media. His transition from the cultural to the presidential stage nominates Reagan as an avatar of the electronically mediated performance circuit that has ineradicably altered the practice of politics in the United States.

Like Woody Allen's Zelig, Reagan materializes at and on the formative stages of the dominant media technologies of the twentieth century. A decade after the inception of commercial radio, he began broadcasting Chicago Cubs baseball games and listening to Franklin Roosevelt's fireside chats. Through radio he learned firsthand the power of an electronically transmitted voice to entertain and enchant an invisible audience. A decade after the release of *The Jazz Singer* introduced sound to motion pictures, Reagan moved to Hollywood, where over the next twenty-two years he appeared in fifty-two feature films and ten documentaries and short subjects and was the narrator in six others. As a contract player for the Warner Brothers film studio, Reagan acquired the requisite skills for performing before the camera and a lifelong appreciation for the capacity of a state-of-the-art image factory to manufacture and market its commodities.

The erosion of Reagan's career as a movie actor after World War II marks the beginning of his education in the political economy of culture. From 1947 to 1952 and again from 1959 to 1960 he served as president of the Screen Actors Guild during a particularly contentious period for the film industry. As a labor negotiator he was a key figure in constructing a new relationship between Hollywood's unions and management that reflected the new consensus reached between labor and capital after the war. Reagan's negotiation of an unprecedented blanket waiver granting his own talent agency, Music Corporation of America (MCA), the exclusive rights to both produce television shows and represent the labor that created them helped shape the future of the film industry and hastened the transition from film to television as the dominant form of mass entertainment.

A decade after television sets first appeared in American living rooms, Reagan, his film career in decline, took over as the series host, occasional actor, and commercial spokesman for *General Electric Theater*. As host of the program from 1954 to 1962, he became General Electric's (GE's) most visible public persona and a skillful practitioner of corporate branding. As goodwill ambassador for GE, his public relations tours took him to 135 plants across the country where he addressed over a quarter of a million employees. As a corporate spokesman and television host, Reagan honed the public speaking skills and neoconservative rhetoric that would serve him so well in politics.

Like his image on the screen above the stage, Reagan's resume prior to running for governor of California evokes the genealogy of the body electric. "I sing the body electric," Walt Whitman rhapsodized in *Leaves of Grass,* extolling the capacity of a human body to electrify others, to "charge them full with the charge of the soul."[3] The charge Whitman envisions owed something to the antebellum fascination with electricity and something else entirely to what his biographer, David S. Reynolds, called "the carnivalized culture of antebellum America."[4] In Whitman's America political orators, religious evangelists, poets, and musicians shared the same stage, and audiences regularly attended both Shakespearean and minstrel performances, "oblivious to the distinctions between 'high' and 'low' culture that would begin to form after the Civil War."[5] Whitman's poetry and body politic were both charged by the occult forces of electricity, but the current that animated his body electric was that of the performer.

Whitman himself was a performer by sensibility as well as occupation. His friend William Roscoe Thayer described him in admiring terms as "a poseur of truly colossal proportions, one to whom playing a part had long before become so habitual that he ceased to be conscious he was doing it."[6] Whitman's unconscious performances derived from the seemingly limitless repertoire of roles he witnessed from the audience of a wide range of cultural performances that constituted an integral part of daily life in antebellum America. In carrying out his mission to poetically reconstruct the United States, he borrowed heavily from the eclectic array of performances he covered for *The Brooklyn Eagle*. It was from the models provided by these performances that Whitman crafted the multitudes of personae he assumed in his songs of self and nation. For Whitman the very promise of democratic sovereignty was derived from a vision of democracy that valued the theatrical presentation of the self as the definitive measure of both individual representation and national distinction.

In the twentieth century, though, something happened to the charge between bodies as they circulated through the performance circuits that hardwired culture and capital to democracy. The movie *Fame,* released shortly after Reagan was elected to his first term as president, depicts the education of aspiring actors, dancers, singers, and comedians at New York City's High School of Performing Arts from their entry auditions to their final year. At the end of the movie, their education completed, the students perform the graduation number. What the acolytes have learned, and the distance between Whitman's and Reagan's America, is expressed in a song that articulates a distinctly new vision of the charge of bodies. "I Sing the Body Electric" is a paean to the performer as author "of the me yet to come," the embodiment of the "glory in the glow of rebirth," and the creator of "our own tomorrow." Here the vision of the performer extends beyond the political—a sphere in which "we" are already "emperors" and "czars"—to a more exalted dimension, a utopian future in which "we will all be stars."[7]

Ronald Reagan was a devotee of the same electronically magnetized performance circuit that attracted *Fame*'s students to stardom and re-defined the performer as a body electric. During Reagan's presidency the body politic was similarly reconfigured as a collective body electric, a body charged by electronic media. Spanning the realms of star and czar, Reagan's career traces the arc from Whitman's characterization of Abraham Lincoln as the "great star" who "early droop'd in the western sky" to *Fame*'s invo-cation of Hollywood's wilder West, a new frontier that beckoned with the promise of stardom for all.[8] This new body electric—celebrated by the stars of *Fame* and embodied by Reagan at the convention—initiates a new rela-tionship between the body of the performer and the body politic, a rela-tionship that is only possible in a fully dramatized society.

The Dramatized Society

Delivering his inaugural lecture as Professor of Drama at Cambridge Uni-versity in 1974, Raymond Williams identified several reasons for the life-altering impact of mass-mediated performance. In his account of the ef-fects of television's dissemination of a wide variety of performances into virtually every arena of contemporary life, Williams delivered a startling assessment of the role those performances now played in that life. He re-minded his audience that for the vast majority of human history the ex-perience of drama in the West was an occasional activity, a ceremonial event experienced at festivals from the Greek golden age through the Middle Ages and in specially designated sites from Elizabethan England through the nineteenth century. In Williams's analysis, however, the ad-vent of electronic media had radically altered the extent to which these performances shaped individual and collective experience. "We have never as a society," he told the gathered theater professionals and aspiring performers, "acted so much or watched so many others acting." Through these new media, "drama, in quite new ways, is built into the rhythms of everyday life. . . . What we have now is drama as habitual experience: more in a week, in many cases, than most human beings would previ-ously have seen in a lifetime." The result, he concluded, was the first fully dramatized society.[9]

Yet while these new media provide access to a vast array of models for individual identity and social relations on a hitherto incomprehensible scale, the ubiquity of mass-mediated performance is only part of the story. We need also to acknowledge, Williams contended, how the mass dissemination of these performances had altered the structural dynamics of our preconscious relationship to cultural forms and conventions and to consciousness itself. The historically unprecedented consumption of simulations, representations, and dramatizations—of "scenes, situations, actions, exchanges, crises"—had overtaken lived experience as the arbiter of the real. In Williams's estimation, the drama ("a complex opening of ritual to public and variable action; a moving beyond myth to dramatic *versions* of myth and of history") had so saturated social life that "the modes of dramatization . . . which are active as social and cultural conventions" had become the primary way "not only of seeing but of organizing reality."[10]

Ronald Reagan's journey from culture worker to president suggests that the modes and methods of dramatization modeled by the movies, radio, and television have so altered our experience of both geographic space and historical time that they have irreversibly diminished the dimensions of the *un*mediated world. By providing increasingly greater access to events beyond our immediate temporal and geographic space of reception, these media have become our dominant window on the world, our primary frame of reference. Over the course of Reagan's career, dramatization (dramatic conventions, speech, gesture, and genre) and its technological modes (the fade, dissolve, cut, flashback, voice-over, and montage) generated new ways of imagining and enacting individual lives and collective social life. Thanks to Hollywood we all possess the training and desire to make our stories into pictures. By the time Ronald Reagan became president we were all drawing on the same mechanically reproduced repertoire of stories and pictures generated by electronic media to express what we knew of the world or what we wished it to be. It was these forms and conventions, imported from the past and inflected with contemporary reason and rhythm, that inspired our imaginations and whetted our appetites. Viewed within the context of Reagan's education in toto, his political success was normative not aberrant, a paradigmatic expression of the seminal role of the body electric in a fully dramatized society.

This, then, is not a biography of Ronald Reagan. It is not, in the strictest sense, about Ronald Reagan at all. It is an account of Reagan's training in the techne of electronic media (radio, film, and television) and related apparatuses of persuasion (notably advertising and public relations). The premise of the book is that Reagan's education—both the one he received and the one he provided—has something to tell us about how these new modes of cultural production and social reproduction have accelerated and intensified the performative processes by means of which the body electric has altered political discourse and practice. Electronic media, I will argue, have not only changed the way we imagine and engage the political; they have staged a mimetic reformation and instituted a new regime of cultural and political representation. What follows is the mapping of a particular trajectory of that reformation and the regime it produced. Our vector is defined by the arc of the career of the president electric.

I must confess that during the 1980s I was baffled by Reagan's political success. Why, I found myself asking repeatedly as the evidence of half-truths, deceptions, and lies accumulated, was he seemingly universally acclaimed as "the Great Communicator"? How did the career of an itinerant performer culminate in the presidency of the United States? How did this by most accounts mediocre actor develop into a star performer in the political sphere? What was the secret of Reagan's appeal? Probing these questions, I came to believe that Reagan's political achievements were directly attributable to his prior training as a cultural performer; a hypervisible expression of the enhanced role played by the body electric in American life generally and American politics in particular.

That Reagan's training as an actor had something to do with his political success is hardly a new idea. Biographer Lou Cannon subtitled his account of Reagan's presidency "The Role of a Lifetime" while the cultural historian Neal Gabler described Reagan's presidential persona as "entertainer-in-chief."[11] In fact, one would be hard-pressed to find a single account of his life or presidency that does not place a premium on Reagan's skills as a performer in explaining his unparalleled path to political prominence. However a still prevalent antitheatrical prejudice has led most commentators on Reagan to diminish or rationalize his performance skills as effective if somewhat unseemly techniques employed to win elections or achieve ideological and programmatic objectives.[12] Whether lamented or celebrated, the performance elements of Reagan's presidency are still generally perceived to be an epiphenomenon—the smoke and mirrors of stagecraft generated to sell the meat and potatoes of statecraft.

As a theater director and performance historian, however, I was inclined to believe that Reagan's political success had something to do with a range of performance skills inadequately acknowledged and imperfectly understood by the accounts I was reading of his life and presidency. The vast majority of these books—written by political scientists, historians, journalists, and members of his administration—depicted the Reagan Revolution in predominantly ideological terms. They defined Reaganism as either a neoliberal or neoconservative order that formed in response to the dominant liberal consensus that emerged after World War II. While varying in its emphasis, this version of the rise of Reaganism held that the political affiliations that spanned the American Century disintegrated in the 1970s in the wake of Vietnam, Watergate, a stagnant economy, and a host of "special interest" groups emboldened by the social movements of the 1960s. In this account, Reaganism was fomented by the growing resentment of "ordinary Americans" (construed as the white middle class) toward a government perceived to be corrupt, ineffectual, intrusive, and incapable of winning either the cold or culture wars. Aligned in opposition to excessive taxes and entitlements, global communism, a bloated welfare state, and the "new morality," or so the story goes, a disaffected "silent majority"—first identified in the presidential campaigns of Barry Goldwater and George Wallace and named by Richard Nixon in 1968—rejected the tenets of liberalism and formed the vanguard of the Reagan Revolution.

While on the whole I am sympathetic to this explanation of the underlying causes of the deterioration of the liberal consensus, it fails to provide a convincing explanation for the triumph of Reaganism as opposed to another ideological formation critical of liberalism. The Achilles' heel of this body of political thought, it seems to me, was the presupposition that political loyalties and affiliations are predicated on rational decisions consciously arrived at by political consumers who form their allegiances and cast their votes on the basis of their social and economic interests. This analysis of contemporary American politics as a process of conscious, reasoned decision making reflects the standard (and limited) tendency of political analysts to reify rational choice as the sine qua non of modern democracies.

Reagan's infamous remark that "facts are stupid things" points to an alternative site of social struggle in the Reagan era, one more politically potent than that of rational thought or the conscious mind.[13] As Lawrence Grossberg has argued, in the Age of Reagan, "Rather than attempting to win the minds of the nation, there is a struggle over its heart and body. . . . The question is how people's affect—their attention, volition, mood, passion—is organized, disciplined, mobilized and ultimately put into the service of specific political agendas." In this contest, he insists, "*culture leads politics.*"[14] Emphasizing the cultural dimensions of Reaganism, Grossberg would have us imagine a politics in which ideas are themselves epiphenomenal, popular culture is the staging ground for generating political movements and authorizing political power, and affect trumps or at least precedes ideology. Affect, he suggests, may in fact provide the key to understanding how ideology functions by offering

> the possibility of a "psychology of belief," which would explain how and why ideologies are sometimes, and only sometimes, effective, and always to varying degrees. It is the affective investment in particular ideological sites . . . that explains the power of the articulation which bonds particular representations and realities. It is the affective investment which enables ideological relationships to be internalized and, consequently, naturalized. . . . People actively constitute places and forms of authority (both for themselves and others) through the deployment and organization of affective investments. By making certain things matter, people "authorize" them to speak for them, not only as a spokesperson but as a surrogate voice. . . . [P]eople give authority to that which they invest in; they let the objects of such investments speak for and in their stead. . . . To put this another way, affect is the plane or mechanism of belonging and identification.[15]

Rational choice cannot account for the way the electronic media in which Ronald Reagan trained have enhanced the role of cultural production in generating the affective investments—the sites of belonging and identification—that define political affiliations and loyalties in the Age of Reagan.

While conventional wisdom holds that Reagan was the most ideological of presidents, ideology alone is insufficient to explain how he came to be a surrogate voice for the ideologically disparate and often incompatible constituencies mobilized by the Reagan Revolution. As Michael Denning puts it, "[T]he peculiar powers of the 'Great Communicator' demanded a cultural explanation. Whereas Richard Nixon's success seemed sufficiently explained by media debunkers detailing the 'selling' of a president, Reagan confounded manipulation theory. There was a utopian promise in the Reagan narrative, that fantasy bribe, that element of recognition," that turned on "the dialectic of ideology and utopia in popular culture."[16] If, like Marx's architect, we must "raise our structure in imagination" before doing so in reality,[17] then the primary tools at our disposal for constructing the imaginary utopian prototypes that inspire sociopolitical action and affiliation are derived from the cultural forms, conventions, and technologies available to us in our particular historical moment. It is from their techne that we fashion our image of how the world should be.

The utopian visions generated by electronic media rarely assume the form of ideological or systemic models of utopian worlds. Instead, as Richard Dyer has written of entertainment genres such as the movie musical, their charge is contained in "the feelings [they] embod[y] . . . what utopia would feel like rather than how it would be organized." Like the performances they circulate, electronic media produce their effects "at the level of sensibility . . . [through] an affective code that is characteristic of, and largely specific to, a given mode of cultural production."[18] Radio, film, and television are not solely responsible for generating the cultural performances that structure the contemporary imagination. Through their mass-mediated transmission, however, extant performance forms and conventions are (as Bertolt Brecht might put it) "refunctioned," deployed to code and coordinate new political practices and social and cognitive habits. Through their incessant recycling, recombining, and circulation of cultural products and performances, the electronic media generate what Williams has identified as a new and global "structure of feeling," a new kind of "practical consciousness" and sociality derived from "specifically affective elements of consciousness . . . meanings and values as they are actively lived and felt."[19] Arguments about the ideological effects generated by the performances disseminated through electronic media are highly speculative, inevitably limited, and as ideologically inflected as the effects they purport to describe. What is indisputable, however, is that each film and radio or television broadcast generates models of being and belonging, identification and aspiration. The scope and scale of electronic media, the extent to which they suffuse our everyday lives, endow these performances with the capacity to alter human behavior; the way we move and speak, dress and eat, work and play. These media provide the repertoire of resources—scripts and scenarios, tools and techniques—that we draw on to enact our daily life or to imagine how it might be different.

Culture as Politics

"There have been times in this office," Reagan confided to the American Broadcasting Company's (ABC's) David Brinkley a month before he left the White House, "when I've wondered how you could do the job if you hadn't been an actor." "I do not know precisely what he meant," George Will confessed in a rare acknowledgment of uncertainty, "and he probably doesn't either, but he was onto something."[20] The elusive something Will was grasping for is the ubiquity and affective force of electronically circulated cultural products in the latter half of the twentieth century and the new skills required of those who would govern under the new conditions they spawned. The result is that Americans, as Alan Wolfe has written,

> are increasingly oblivious to politics but they are exceptionally sensitive to culture. What constitutes for other countries the meat and potatoes of political conflict—distribution of income among classes, regulation of industry, protectionism vs. free trade, sectional antagonism—captures in this country only the attention of the interests immediately affected. . . . Culture, on the other hand, grabs everyone's attention all of the time. . . . [B]ecause they practice politics in cultural terms, Americans cannot be understood with the tool kits developed by political scientists.[21]

In the aftermath of the 1960s the dissolution of political allegiances in place since the New Deal shattered decades of consensus on a wide variety of social and economic issues. During the Reagan years, culture, grabbing our attention all the time, became the most effective arena for generating the kind of affective investments capable of constructing a tenuous majority from a fragmented electorate. In a nation where no consensus existed on a wide range of ideologically and emotionally charged issues from abortion and affirmative action to gun control and taxes, culture became the contentious forum for constituting political authority through what the public relations impresario Edward Bernays has called "the engineering of consent."[22]

By the time he became president, Ronald Reagan had become an adept of the media responsible for making culture the most ubiquitous and influential product produced in the United States. In 1979, in an influential essay that anticipates the practice of politics during the Reagan presidency, Fredric Jameson observed that "culture, far from being an occasional matter of the reading of a monthly good book or a trip to the drive-in, seems to me to be the very element of consumer society itself. . . . [E]verything is mediated by culture to the point where even the political and ideological 'levels' have initially to be disentangled from their primary mode of representation which is cultural."[23] In *Postmodernism*, a collection of essays written over the span of the Reagan presidency, Jameson extends his claim for the impact of the cultural, arguing that the dissolution of an autonomous sphere of culture has resulted in "a prodigious expansion of culture throughout the social realm, to the point at which everything in our social life—from economic value and state power to practices and to the very structure of the psyche itself—can be said to have become 'cultural' in some original and as yet untheorized sense."[24] Citing culture as the primary site of mediation between (individual and national) subjects and political and economic formations, Jameson suggests that the pervasiveness of cultural production and its products has transformed culture into "a veritable second nature." It is precisely the performative capacity of electronically enhanced cultural production to naturalize its effects that generates what Jameson identifies in *Postmodernism*'s subtitle as "the cultural logic of late capitalism." Among the myriad consequences of his diagnosis is the suggestion that the cultural and the political, historically perceived to be semiautonomous spheres, have become virtually indistinguishable. Our engagement with politics is now thoroughly mediated by culture. And if culture can no longer be construed as a superstructural feature of capitalism but rather its animating logic then anyone seeking to understand American politics today must pay close attention to the cultural predicates of political practice and power.

The cultural logic of the Reagan presidency is emblematized by the discursive shift in the conception of and criteria for "presidential performance." Prior to Reagan's presidency the term most often referred to the ability of presidential administrations to implement political and policy initiatives. During Reagan's presidency, however, assessments of presidential performance most often focused on the process of scripting, staging, producing, and enacting the role of the president of the United States. Journalists, politicians, policy analysts, and lobbyists—the gamut of professionals whose livelihoods depended on conveying authoritative knowledge of government—employed the imagery, language, and evaluative criteria of Reagan's former occupations to depict and critique his presidency. The discourse about Reaganism as a political or social philosophy was conditioned by a widespread fascination with its practice as a performance art. Any genealogist of the so-called Reagan Revolution must trace its lineage through Reagan's training in the arts and crafts of mass mediation, an education that signals a new relationship between culture and politics, sense and sensibility, knowledge and power, and a new emphasis on electronically mediated performance as the defining element of American political life.

Reagan's was not the first presidential administration to employ the body electric, but it was the first to fully exploit the techne of performance and the networks of electronic media as principal modes of governance. The apparent effortlessness of Reagan's presidential performances never fully obscured the traces of the vast machinery and incessant labor required to fix our gaze. During his presidency the man his primary image crafter, Michael Deaver, often referred to as "the talent" was the leading player in a presidency that was produced and promoted like a Hollywood studio production. The Reagan administration's massive communications operation managed and deployed its "star" asset in much the same way studio bosses groomed and promoted film actors during Reagan's tenure in Hollywood. Proposals for potential presidential appearances were titled "scenarios" and were required to have a designated press coverage proposal attached. Advance teams did "walk-throughs" (commonly referred to as "rehearsals") of upcoming events involving Reagan. He was briefed on pending issues through "mini-memos" that were constructed like film treatments.[25] To educate Reagan about foreign affairs, National Security Adviser William Clark screened Defense Department movies on international issues in the White House theater. This approach proved so successful that Clark enlisted the Central Intelligence Agency (CIA) to prepare a "profile movie documentary" on world leaders Reagan was scheduled to meet.[26]

Reagan had been taught to follow a script and was most comfortable sticking to one. Blessed with a photographic albeit selective memory (especially for anecdotes, childhood incidents, and scenes from favorite movies), he had the ability to memorize a script rapidly but usually carried cue cards in the left-hand pocket of his suit coat lest he lose his way. His years in Hollywood had taught him how to take direction. Admonished by Chief of Staff James Baker for telling jokes before preparing to face the press after Secretary of Defense Alexander Haig's resignation, Reagan reassuringly replied, "Don't worry, I'll play it somber."[27] A horrified aide recalls witnessing Secretary of State George Schultz coaching Reagan for his meeting with Soviet premier Mikhail Gorbachev during the 1988 Moscow summit by advising him on what to do "in this scene."[28] As Baker and Schultz demonstrated, with the help of a strong director Reagan could play almost any conceivable scene.

He entrusted the property of his presidential image to Michael Deaver in much the same way he had signed over his movie image to Warner Brothers and his television image to General Electric. In the envious assessment of Jimmy Carter's image packager, Gerald Rafshoon, Deaver was given "total control of the body."[29] Capitalizing on television's impact as a forum for influencing public opinion, Deaver disseminated Reagan's voice and image to the public in sound bites and video clips timed to fit the formats of the networks' nightly news shows. At Deaver's behest, Reagan avoided press conferences, where the news media controlled the agenda, in favor of scripted media events conceived and staged by Deaver and produced by his communications team. According to Deaver's replacement as chief of staff, Donald Regan, Deaver "designed each presidential action as a one-minute or two-minute spot on the evening news" and "conceived every presidential appearance in terms of camera angles."[30] When reporters complained that their ability to cover the White House was limited by lack of access and their coverage buried in a flood of Deaver's broadcast-ready "spots" and sound bites, a plaque on Press Secretary Larry Speakes's desk provided the Reagan team's reply: "You don't tell us how to stage the news, we won't tell you how to cover it."[31] The production of newsworthy audio and video footage was the stock-in-trade of the Reagan administration, leading Regan to describe the president "as a sort of supreme anchorman whose public persona was the most important element of his presidency."[32]

Reagan needed the stage set for him, however, and when it didn't happen he often floundered. As Reagan's former chief of staff, Kenneth Duberstein, explained, an administration oriented around the acting skills of the president required "a very strong stage manager-producer-director" and "very good technical men and sound men at all times." Without the necessary technical support, the production "falls apart because the actor-president isn't prepared." If the director and producer are "not up to speed . . . [President Reagan] can't walk into a situation using his years of experience and function effectively."[33] When the performance was poorly produced or directed, there were problems, as Deaver describes in his criticism of a mismanaged press conference. The president "should have bounced into that press conference. [Instead] he *walked* down that hall. Somebody probably told him, 'Now, be serious tonight.' Absolutely wrong coaching!"[34] But when everyone did their job Reagan's training kicked in. He had learned how to ignore bad reviews and hostile critics and how to face press cameras and questions. He knew how to hit the toe marks that Deaver placed for him and how to play to the camera. He knew how to make an entrance, how to suck in his breath and stomach, straighten his shoulders, and puff himself up till his body grew to its film shape. Then "he would walk that smooth walk."[35] Reagan knew how to do all this because he had trained for the role for half a century.

Mapping

Over the course of his lifetime, Ronald Reagan apprenticed in virtually all of the dominant twentieth-century paradigms of performance as a means of knowing the world and acting in it. Analyzing a wide range of primary and secondary sources and radio, film, and television performances, as well as videotapes and documents made available for the first time through Freedom of Information Act requests submitted through the Reagan presidential archives, *The President Electric* documents how the training Reagan received answered Henry Adams's call at the dawn of the twentieth century for a "new education" that would address the conditions produced by the rise of corporate capitalism, mechanical science, and mass culture.[36] As president, drawing on skills he acquired over a lifetime of enacting an astonishing range of cultural performances, Reagan's body electric embodied Adams's new education as an exemplar of what Foucault has termed the "governmentality" of the neoliberal state.

Chapter 1 traces the genealogy of the body electric, providing a historical overview of the culture of performance into which Ronald Reagan was initiated. Here I make the case that since the inception of the republic the techne of performance have provided the most influential paradigms for imagining and negotiating the idea of America, the identity of the national subject, and the ideology of American Exceptionalism.[37] While political and cultural representations have been inextricably linked from the beginning of the American experiment, I argue that the development of electrical technologies at the end of the nineteenth century generated new modes and methods of representation that reconfigured the culture of performance. I examine this development against the backdrop of *The Education of Henry Adams,* Adams's jeremiad against the failure of his "eighteenth century education" to prepare him for the modern world. His education culminates in Paris at the Great Exposition of 1900. There, confronted by the dynamo in the Gallery of Machines, his "historical neck broken by the sudden irruption of forces entirely new," he finds "only an absolute *fiat* in electricity as in faith."[38] What Adams refers to as the fiat of electricity encompasses the growing sociopolitical and numinous power of three forces (mechanical science, corporate capitalism, and mass culture) whose emergence in the decades immediately preceding Reagan's birth was made possible by the widespread availability of electricity. I propose that if Adams had scripted a model childhood education for acquiring the "social and political habits" and generating the "ideas and institutions to fit the new scale and suit the new conditions" produced by the fiat of electricity it would have looked much like Ronald Reagan's.[39] As a corollary, I suggest that this new education placed a premium on skills that could only be acquired through the codes and practices of a historically specific culture of performance. If, as Adams surmised, the dynamo was to electricity what the cross was to Christianity—

the "supersensual" symbol of a new class of forces poised to rule the coming century—then electronic media would become the church of the dynamo and mass-mediated performance the rock upon which that church was built.

Reagan's training in radio, film, and television only enhance the impression that performance was his epistemology and mass mediation his ontology. Chapters 2–5 analyze the formation of the body electric under the fiat of electricity. Covering his training in radio, film, and television, they describe the skills Reagan acquired as a performer in each medium and relate these vocal, corporeal, and representational techne to the political practices they mediated. Chapter 2 examines Reagan's radio days as an incubator for the rhetorical and oratorical practices that would culminate in his anointment as "the Great Communicator." Assessing the formative influences on Reagan during these years, the chapter argues for the impact of radio as an instrument for shaping what Roland Barthes has termed "the grain of the voice."[40] Chapter 3 addresses Franklin Roosevelt's use of radio as a political technology and explores how radio linked politicians to other cultural performers during the Great Depression as representatives of a national voice. Here I make the case that recognizing Roosevelt's influence as the first political voice of the electronic age is essential to gaining an understanding of the way Reagan employed the grain of his voice to topple the New Deal order. Chapter 4 assesses Reagan's years in Hollywood as a tutorial in the arts and crafts of mechanical reproduction and the political economy of cultural production. Chapter 5 focuses on three avatars of the fiat of electricity—television, General Electric, and Ronald Reagan—and their contributions to the rebranding of the imagined community of the nation.

The final chapter explores the subtext of the previous ones: the triangular relationship between the practice of politics, the culture of performance, and the representation of the body politic. It narrows the focus to one particular theatrical "line of business" enacted by Ronald Reagan—the mediator of cultural memory—as a means of analyzing how mass-mediated performance functioned as a principal techne of government during the Reagan presidency and the new relationship his presidential performances established between cultural and political actors as co-creators of national identity.

As should be apparent by now, the term *performance* in my usage encompasses not only acting but also a related array of cultural practices and discourses concerned with the representation and reinvention of social life. At times when I use the term I am referring to a role in a movie, television show, or radio broadcast. At other times it describes the ways a political administration represents its claim to power or a corporation promotes its image. Performance also refers to the way the charged bodies of performers embody historically and culturally specific modes of knowing and being through conscious and unconscious performances of various kinds. This definition of performance engages with the concept of *performativity* to reference the way in which language constitutes what it connotes or the way in which social values, sedimented in human bodies, materialize in expressive or ritualized behavior. In the widest sense in which I employ the term, performance describes the processes by which we audition, rehearse, stage, and enact our individual and corporate identities.

Garry Wills suggests that the length of Reagan's career and the breadth of his immersion in the industries that mediate contemporary culture and politics lend him a unique status as "a link between the pioneering era of broadcast technology and the sophisticated politics of our modern communications industry."[41] Assessing Reagan as an adept of the principal techne linking popular culture, corporate capitalism, and American politics, I propose that over the course of the twentieth century mass-mediated performances became the primary mode for educating Americans. It was through these performances that Americans rehearsed and represented, reproduced and reconfigured their individual and collective identity. By the time Reagan entered politics in the 1960s, the discourses and practices of performance had become fundamental components of the struggle for political authority and legitimation, a constitutive feature not only of the cultural economy but of the political economy as well. *The President Electric* asks what we might learn by assessing the career of the former radio announcer, film actor, union leader, TV star, corporate spokesman, governor of California, and president of the United States as a map of the territory colonized by the body electric in a culture of performance.

CHAPTER ONE

The Culture of Performance

The image of Ronald Reagan at the 1984 Republican National Convention has been characterized by Michael Rogin as symbolic of Reagan's "claim to embody the nation" by "exploiting the boundary confusion between the president's body and the body politic."[1] As such, Rogin contends, it is a virtual restoration of the sixteenth-century French and English monarchies' doctrine of legitimation. The doctrine of the king's two bodies—which held that the king possessed both a *body natural* and a *body politic*—derives from medieval Christology. "Theologically," explains Rogin, "the death of Christ's mortal body created a mystic body, the regenerate Christian community. Sixteenth century political leaders sought, like divine

Photo: President Reagan's initial appearance at the 1984 Republican Convention.
Photo © Bettman/Corbis.

kings, to reabsorb that mystic community into their own personal bodies."[2] This transformation from a "Christian to a statist world view" traces
a trajectory of substitutions, from the *corpus mysticum*'s sanctification of
the mystic community formed in Christ's name to the assimilation of
that community into the king's body politic, making the monarch, in the
words of Pierre Bourdieu, "an entirely real substitute for an entirely symbolic being."[3]

Rogin cites the frontispiece of Thomas Hobbes's *Leviathan*—in which
Hobbes's head sits atop a body composed of tiny, fully rendered homun-
culi who gaze up at his/their head—as the emblematic visual metaphor
for this social fiction of the body politic. In Reagan's debut at the convention, Rogin finds an invocation of *Leviathan*'s frontispiece in which
Nancy Reagan, representing the television audience, stands in for the
body politic. According to Rogin, the political body that Hobbes authors
in *Leviathan* and his head sits atop in the frontispiece are transformed in
the political theater of the Reagan era by replacing the head of the author
with that of the actor. Just as the doctrine of the king's two bodies
"marked a shift in the locus of sacred power from the church to the state,"
so Reagan's presidency marks the culmination of a second reformation in
the theology of power whereby the movies and television replace the state
as the dominant force in the production of sacred value.[4]

The trajectory of Ronald Reagan's career illuminates in fine detail the
evolution of electronic media's status as the church of contemporary politics. By way of historicizing the political effects of media techne on the
presidency, there are two corollaries to Rogin's account that are worth emphasizing. The first is that what the Leviathans authored by Hobbes and
embodied by Reagan have in common is a dependence on the actor's craft
to naturalize their social fictions. For Hobbes, the body politic was constituted through a process of representation by substitution. The self's au-
thoring of its *Person* ("the *disguise* or *outward appearance* of a man, coun-
terfeited on the stage") was mirrored in the political sphere by the self's
act of consent authorizing the sovereign to be its representative.[5] In
Hobbes's formulation, the person and the sovereign were both performed
identities, staged characters that represented the social and political subject respectively. Subjectivities and subjects alike were enacted through a
mimetic process whereby both self and sovereign were represented
through the performance of a surrogate body.

Hobbes's theatrical metaphors for self and political representation reflect the growing influence of the actor as a paradigm for conceptualizing the individual and national subject at a time when the monarchy's aura of invincibility had begun to crack under the weight of the Enlightenment. In 1710—a century after the twenty-one-year-old Hobbes first absorbed the teachings of the European Enlightenment on his inaugural tour of the continent—an actor was interred for the first time amid the royal dead in Westminster Abbey. The death of Thomas Betterton provided the occasion for at least one longtime observer to speculate on the doubling of actors and kings—"the Imaginary and Real Monarch"—in a society of "Free-Born people."[6] Joseph Roach proposes that the hagiographic accounts of Betterton's life that followed his death cast the actor in the role of the mimetic double of the sovereign, a "shadow king, a visible effigy signifying the dual nature of sovereignty, its division between an immortal and an abject body." As the shadow king of the "mimic state" of the London stage, Betterton served as a "performed effigy" whose burial enacted "the memorial constitution of the body politic." Betterton's funeral, Roach concludes, "constitutes an epitomizing event in the early development of a particular kind of secular devotion" in which "performers become the caretakers of memory through many kinds of public action." The narrative construction of "a fiction like 'Betterton' defines a cultural trend in which the body of an actor serves as a medium"—an *effigy*—"in the secular rituals through which a modernizing society communicates with its past."[7] As the expression of a cultural trend, Reagan's presidency also constituted an epitomizing event; one in which the mimic state gained ascendancy over the state it mimics, reconfiguring the triangular relationship between the performer, the head of state, and the body politic they both strive to represent.

The second corollary I propose is that while Rogin is no doubt correct in identifying Reagan's appearance on a screen above a stage as emblematic of the new role to be played by the actor in American politics his formulation ignores the political impact of the much wider range of cultural media and performance forms in which Reagan trained. During his presidency the skills Reagan mastered working in radio, film, television, advertising, and public relations formed the basis for a presidential character fully equipped to exploit the dominant cultural media of the day. Reagan's administration crafted its political authority by scripting and producing electronically disseminated narratives and images featuring the talents of its leading actor, employing mimetic techne and cultural media as the practice of politics by other means. As Reagan speechwriter Peggy Noonan observed, "[T]he president's top aides who planned the day were no longer just part of the story—it was as if they were producers of the story. They were the line producers of a show called *White House,* with Ronald Reagan as the President." However, as Noonan reminds us, this particular mode of political representation "wasn't particular to that White House, *it was simply a trend that achieved its fullness in the Reagan era.*"[8] The trend to which Noonan refers is the enhanced status of the politician as performer in a fully dramatized society. This development, in turn, reflects a broader trend toward the expansion of the impact of performance generally, as what Jon McKenzie has characterized as "an emergent stratum of power and knowledge."

In *Perform or Else,* McKenzie proposes that the sociotechnical systems that organized the reciprocal constitution of knowledge and power in the latter half of the twentieth century became increasingly performance driven. Invoking Michel Foucault's formulation of discipline as the primary regime of statements and visibilities through which power was exercised in Western Europe in the eighteenth and nineteenth centuries, McKenzie identifies a shift in emphasis from discipline to performance in the proliferation of discourses and practices of performance in the United States after World War II. He characterizes the emergence of these new paradigms of cultural, technological, and organizational performance as "the becoming-performative of knowledge itself."[9] The education of Ronald Reagan, however, suggests that the emergence of the performance stratum described by McKenzie can be traced to the end of the nineteenth century when the body electric first begins to flicker on the motion picture screen.

Natural Theatricality

Before assessing Reagan's presidency as a manifestation of this new culture of performance in the political sphere, it is worth noting that politics in the United States has always been a performance art. The United States was "the first new nation," the first modern form of political association[10] As Christopher Looby has observed, unlike previous national communities, its image of communion was forged not from blood or kinship or a shared myth of origin but from a historically contingent social vision and a self-conscious process of nation building.[11] As the first nation to be conceived without historical precedent or a preexisting script, from the outset the task of forming it was intertwined with the process of expressing a persuasive rationale for its existence. As a consequence, the founding documents and rituals of the United States express a shared perception of the unprecedented task of performatively enacting an authoritative basis for revolution. Once independence was achieved it was generally understood that in a nation without a king new modes of political authority would need to be constituted for governance.

Despite a residual antitheatrical prejudice inherited from their Puritan ancestors, American patriots understood their task in theatrical terms. They were products of their education, which emphasized the arts of political rhetoric and stagecraft as much as those of political philosophy and statecraft. Whether struggling to generate consensus for independence from Britain or to express their vision for the new nation, the founders were as likely to employ the language of *theatrum mundi* as that of the Scottish Enlightenment. The founders' familiarity with the venerable tradition in Western thought of conceptualizing the world as theater stemmed from their reading of the accounts of the societies that exerted the strongest influence on their political imaginations: Plato's *Laws*, in which human existence is represented as a puppet show staged by the gods; Petronius's *Satyricon*, in which all social life is figured as theater; or Shakespeare's plays, in which all the world was a stage and all of society was represented on that stage and in the audience of his Globe theater.[12] The utopian social and theological promise of "America" was, in fact, often depicted by the founders through the trope of the nation as a stage "designed by Providence," as John Adams forcefully proclaimed, "on which Man was to make his true figure."[13] The theater to which Adams referred is, of course, history. Yet the "true figure"—the figure bequeathed to America and its people—was understood by the founders to signify both a historical destiny and a contingent identity. The new national subject was conceived as a *role* that needed to be individually and collectively enacted if the nation's destiny was to be realized.

The founders' conception of the role of theatricality in the making of

America and Americans resonates with the derivation of *drama* from *dran,* the Doric word for "to do" or "to accomplish." As Adams maintained, while the nation may have been designed by providence, Americans were required to make their true figure. "The American war [against England] is over," wrote Benjamin Rush in 1787, "but this is far from being the case with the American Revolution. On the contrary, nothing but the first act of this great drama is closed."[14] From the beginning, the figures who would thrive on the American stage believed that their status as social actors was inextricably linked to the other kind of acting, the kind in which their skills in the arts of rhetoric, oratory, elocution, and stagecraft constituted their political capital. "The Declaration of Independence I always considered a theatrical show," Adams wrote to Rush, in which "Jefferson ran away with all the stage effect . . . and all the glory of it." Despite a lingering distrust of theatricality and his jealousy over what he described as Jefferson's "coup de theatre," Adams exhibited a savvy actor's understanding of the importance of billing and mise-en-scène in arguing that as president of the United States George Washington should be given the title of "Majesty" and possibly a throne in order to command the respect of the European powers, which placed great value on the theatrical dimensions of politics.[15]

Washington shared Adams's conviction that the United States had been assigned a leading role on the world and providential stage. In the letter resigning his commission as commander in chief of the Armies of the United States of America in 1783, Washington proposed that America's new status as an imperial power offered new opportunities and responsibilities for its citizen actors. "The Citizens of America," he wrote, "are now, by the late satisfactory pacification, acknowledged to be possessed of absolute freedom and Independence. They are from this period to be considered as actors on a most conspicuous Theatre, which seems to be peculiarly designed by Providence for the display of human greatness and felicity."[16] As the founders foresaw, the *idea* of America dictated that the power of performance and the performance of power would be inextricably linked in the formation and governance of the new nation.

The making of America and Americans—the persuasive performance of a divinely scripted destiny—would require a historically unprecedented intimacy between stagecraft and statecraft. Jay Fliegelman identifies the Declaration of Independence as the quintessential example of the productive tension between scripted destiny and performed identity in the making of America and Americans. Positing the mysterious diacritical accent marks on Jefferson's rough draft of the declaration as rhetorical pauses and accentual stresses, Fliegelman characterizes it as the product of a symbiotic relationship formed in the eighteenth century between new and related ideals of elocutionary and political representation that led American patriots to frame independence "as a rhetorical problem as much as a political one."[17] As Fliegelman infers, the declaration was not simply a political document. It was also, and as importantly, a performance manifesto, a script written to be published aloud on village greens and in town meetings throughout the colonies as a means of enacting a new nation and calling forth the political actors required to manifest the nation's destiny.

As Fliegelman documents, the Declaration of Independence derived its political efficacy not solely from the revolutionary political ideals it espoused (the political philosophy of John Locke or the communitarian thought of Frances Hutcheson) but also from new ideas about individual expression and social behavior propagated by elocutionary revolutionaries who advocated a paradoxical aesthetic of an unconscious naturalism *and* the cultivation of a studied artifice. This paradox was exemplified in the naturalistic acting style introduced on the English stage by David Garrick, embodied in the eerily lifelike busts theatrically fashioned by the American sculptor Patience Wright, and articulated through the new elocutionary paradigms that coalesced around the ideal of "natural theatricality." The trope of natural theatricality materializes the ideology of American Exceptionalism through the figure of the American as a performer chosen to enact a preordained role. For the founders, natural theatricality was a quintessential expression of the tensive paradox of national formation. For the utopian vision of the new nation and national subject to be "true," and thus ideologically compelling, it needed to be "natural," yet to generate affective investments in its providential design required its expression to be theatrical.

The "truths" the declaration held to be self-evident were clearly not so to King George III nor to a significant number of the colonists residing in the would-be republic. These truths had to be persuasively articulated in such a way as to compel allegiance to their epistemology over and above that of the British monarchy. Oratorical performances of the declaration, Fliegelman theorizes, played a critical role in achieving consensus for dissolving the bonds that connected America to Britain. By appealing to the auditor's *sensibility,* a keyword in both revolutions, the orator bonded with his audience by evoking a mutuality of feelings. This bond, Fliegelman argues, envisioned at the level of the nation, provided a compelling alternative to the filial bonds that shackled the colonies to the fatherland.

> If, as [Thomas] Paine summarized it, the essential British argument was that the colonies have no relation to each other but through the parent country . . . [as] sister colonies . . . sensibility articulated a higher bond that transcended both the bonds of descent through the father and, by its involuntarism, the nullifiable bonds of contract and consent. At the heart of sensibility, as Paine made clear, was its insistence on the subordination of government ("a necessary evil") to the higher claims of society ("in every state a blessing")—not the Rousseauian society of common interest, but the society of common feeling.[18]

The task of convincing a colonial population separated by different and often conflicting geographic, economic, and social interests to imagine itself as a collective entity—a "society of common feeling"—required a communications technology capable of creating a common imagination. Elocutionary training supplied a pedagogy rooted in theatrical techniques for developing a voice and body capable of reproducing a common language of expression and generating an affectively compelling theology for a new nation and national subject.

The enduring power of elocution to enact the society of common feeling is evoked by Abraham Lincoln in his inaugural address as president. On the verge of civil war, Lincoln tried to hold the country together with words. He began by emphasizing the contractual bonds that united the states—the Articles of Association, the Declaration of Independence, the Articles of Confederation, the Constitution—as a guarantor of the nation's perpetuity. As a contractual union, Lincoln argued, the nation could not be unmade without the agreement of all parties to the contract.

In his peroration, however, Lincoln abandons the legal arguments against recognizing the rights of the southern states to secede. Instead, in a language Paine would have approved, Lincoln invokes "the mystic chords of memory" constitutive of "our bonds of affection" that "passion may have strained" but "must not break." Situating himself squarely within the elocutionary tradition that initiated the society of common feeling, he identifies these musical *chords* as emotional *cords,* the connective tissue of national memory that "will yet swell the chorus of the Union, when again touched, as surely they will be, by the better angels of our nature." In these concluding sentences, as Michael Kammen notes, Lincoln echoes two passages written by "Publius" (James Madison) in the winter of 1787–88. The first passage cements the rhetorical link between Lincoln's union chorus and Paine's society of common feeling: "Hearken not to the *unnatural voice* which tells you that the people of America, knit together as they are by so many chords of affection, can no longer live together *as members of the same family.*"[19] Lincoln mimics Madison in order to silence the unnatural voice that would unravel a national family joined together not by birth, armed struggle, institutions, or government but by the expressive chords of affection that constituted the primary affiliation of the national family. Like the founders, Lincoln believed that the indissoluble bond of national identification was a society of common feeling activated by a culture of performance.

The Fiat of Electricity

While political and cultural representation had been inextricably linked from the beginning of the American experiment, Lincoln's failure to avoid war gave rise to a series of developments at the end of the nineteenth century that transformed the role of performance as mediator of the imagi-nation. In the wake of the Civil War, new structures of accumulation accelerated the pace of industrialization and transformed American capitalism. New technologies of transportation and communication revolutionized the productive capacity of industry. And new performance media accelerated the development of mass culture, generating new modes and methods of representation that would electrify the culture of performance.

In order to understand how this new performance culture prepared the way for Ronald Reagan, I turn now to an account of a life lived on the cusp of the dominant and emergent performance pedagogies in the latter half of the nineteenth century. At the dawn of the twentieth century, in the twilight of a remarkable but, by his own reckoning, disappointing life, Henry Adams set out to chronicle what he had learned about the world he had been trained to lead and the world that was eclipsing it. Born in 1838 into the ruling class of the egalitarian oligarchy that governed the nineteenth-century American liberal democratic order, Adams's observations offer a glimpse into the dominant social vision of the day. His relatives were American revolutionaries and republic builders: ministers, presidents, merchant aristocrats, the closest American equivalent to European royalty. In *The Education of Henry Adams,* Adams recounts what it was like to be raised as a Boston Brahman, "christened by his uncle the Minister of the First Church," who, "had he been born in Jerusalem under the shadow of the Temple and circumcised in the temple by his uncle the high priest under the name of Israel Cohen . . . could scarcely have been more distinctly branded."[20] The book describes how Adams was selected by birth and groomed by training to assume the mantle of his illustrious forebears, including his great-grandfather, John Adams; his grandfather, John Quincy Adams; his uncle, Edward Everett; and his father, Charles Francis Adams.

Adams's breeding and education marked him as an exemplary individual of the modal type celebrated by his fellow Bostonian Ralph Waldo Emerson in *Representative Men:* a figure whose life was representative of the training and values that defined the dominant American social formation in the middle of the nineteenth century. The lessons documented in *The Education of Henry Adams,* however, deviate dramatically from those Emerson draws from the representative figures he identifies as models for the development of a social order capable of producing a citizenry of moral character and achievement in a democratic society. The book's distinctive third-person narrative voice recounts the travails of its fragmented subject and his fruitless quest to discover the unity and order that cohere in Emerson's understanding of the culture of character. Its pages chart Adams's growing disillusionment with his "eighteenth century education" and its contribution to the decline of the social class into which he was born.[21]

Adams's account of his early years reads like a textbook for the self-education prescribed by Emerson. His childhood training culminates during his senior year at Harvard when he is chosen as the class orator, an honor that anoints him as a representative of his class and marks him for future achievement. When he delivers the class oration of 1858, his candidacy for one of Emerson's representative men is further enhanced by the acclaim he receives for his speech and his "perfect self-possession." He was, it would seem, an exemplar of the elocutionary and American revolutions' ideal subject: the self-evident self. Adams, however, characterizes both his performance and his casting in the role as indices of a dominant social order in decline. While at Harvard he reaches the sobering conclusion that his "social advantages were his only capital in life." The acknowledgment of his skills as a writer and orator—"the last remnant of the old Unitarian supremacy"—and his social connections marked him for success. Yet he remained skeptical of both his training and his class: "What no one knew was whether the individual who thought himself a representative of this type, was fit to deal with life."[22]

Adams's political education begins promisingly enough. Following the traditional postgraduate European tour, he serves as his father's secretary during Charles's tenure as a congressman in Washington and minister to England. On his return from London in 1868, however, Adams's resolve is immediately shaken by the inability of his outmoded education to prepare him for comprehending, much less thriving in, a country he no longer recognizes. "Had they been Tyrian traders of the year B.C. 1000, landing from a galley fresh from Gibraltar," he writes of his arrival on New York's Desbrosses Street ferry, "they could hardly have been stranger on the shore of a world, so changed from what it had been ten years before." The technological innovations, entrepreneurial energies, and new capital unleashed at the conclusion of the Civil War had dramatically altered the physical and social landscape. The "great mechanical energies—coal, iron, steam," he observed, now possessed "a distinct superiority in power over the old industrial elements—agriculture, handiwork, and learning." Reconstruction of the South and the rapid colonization of the continent west of the Mississippi now occupied "the energies of a generation, for it required all the new machinery to be created—capital, banks, mines, furnaces, shops, power-houses, technical knowledge, mechanical population, *together with a steady remodeling of social and political habits, ideas and institutions to fit the new scale and suit the new conditions."* The education of Henry Adams had outfitted him with the attributes Emerson had defined as essential for a man of character. Yet this "American of Americans, with Heaven knew how many Puritans and Patriots behind him, and an education that had cost a civil war," judges his breeding and education irrelevant to a nation that now required "new Americans" capable of creating "a world of their own, a science, a society, a philosophy, a universe, where they had not yet created a road or even learned to dig their own iron."[23]

Adams's attempts to reconcile the knowledge and values his education had provided with a world now being shaped by men of steel and science and finance capital ultimately leads him to France in pursuit of that most American of vision quests: historical understanding as self-mediation. In France he immerses himself in the thirteenth century (Amiens' cathedral, Mont-Saint Michel and Chartres, the works of Thomas Aquinas and the medieval cult of the Virgin), searching for the origins of the vanishing world of order and unity—the world for which his education had prepared him—that was born at "the point in history when man held the highest idea of himself as a unit in a unified universe." But not even the Virgin retains the power to reassure Adams of his place in a world and universe no longer comprehensible through the optic of an antiquated metaphysics. By 1900, at the age of sixty-two, despite having "dabbled in fifty educations all over the world," a despairing Adams judges his education, and indeed the entire history of Western scientific knowledge and Judeo-Christian belief, to be insufficient for comprehending the new world of perpetual motion and multiplicity identified by mechanical science, represented by mass culture, and governed by market capitalism.[24]

Adams's epiphany occurs in Paris, where, with the physicist and aeronautical engineer Samuel Pierpont Langley as his guide, he tours the Great Exposition of 1900. Finding little to teach him about the new century in the art or industrial exhibits, he follows Langley into the Gallery of Machines, where his education takes an unexpected turn.

> To [Langley], the dynamo was but an ingenious channel for conveying somewhere the heat latent in a few tons of poor coal hidden in a dirty engine-house carefully kept out of sight; but to Adams the dynamo became

a symbol of infinity. As he grew accustomed to the great gallery of machines, he began to feel the forty-foot dynamos as a moral force, much as the early Christians felt the Cross. The planet itself seemed less impressive, in its old-fashioned, deliberate, annual, or daily revolution, than this huge wheel, revolving within arm's length at some vertiginous speed. . . . Before the end, one began to pray to it; inherited instinct taught the natural expression of man before silent and infinite force. Among the thousand symbols of ultimate energy, the dynamo was not so human as some, but it was the most expressive.[25]

The dynamo, that most expressive symbol of infinity, eradicates any lingering doubts Adams may have harbored that a metaphysical unity or an animating will still retained its explanatory power as the prime mover of human history. Not since Constantine erected the cross, Adams reckons, had there been a historical rupture such as this. In the shadow of the dynamo every organizing principle, every material and metaphysical theory Adams's education could provide falls apart, and he finds himself "lying in the Gallery of Machines at the Great Exposition of 1900, his historical neck broken by the sudden irruption of forces entirely new."[26]

Adams's ironic impulse to bow down and pray before the "moral force" of the dynamo reflects his understanding of the pulsing machine as a synecdoche for the Dynamic Theory of History he lays out in the final pages of his book. For him, the dynamo is the exemplar of "a new class of supersensual forces" that signal a rupture in historical time comparable to Constantine's fateful decision in 303 C.E. to admit Christianity into the "Trust of State Religions," an event that would ultimately yoke the Roman Empire to the Catholic faith and inaugurate the historical continuum that stretched from the raising of the cross straight through to 1900.[27] Ever the contrarian, Adams rejects the orthodox view that the initial impulse to embrace Christianity was rooted in the belief in a Christian God: "The laity, the people, the million, almost to a man, bet on the gods as they bet on a horse." Christianity, he notes, was only one of many religious practices legalized by Constantine's Edict of Milan in 313, a pragmatic political doctrine that sought to incorporate potential rivals in the imperial domain in order, as Constantine declared, "that whatever exists of divinity or celestial power may help and favor us and all who are under our government." It was not its theology, Adams insists, but the affective lure of its symbology that led the Holy Roman Empire to adopt Christianity as its state religion. Roman society "was drawn to the Cross because, in its system of physics, the cross had absorbed all the old occult or fetish power."[28] The power of the cross, like that of the Virgin in Adams's beloved thirteenth century, was as a "supersensual" symbol of the Civitas Dei, a material sign of the human capacity to transform disparate individuals into a coherent empire, chaos into order, and the many into one.

Adams's gloomy conclusion is that the alliance between Christianity and empire initiated by Constantine had withstood the assault of every alternative form of social organization in the West for 1700 years until "in 1900, the continuity snapped."[29] The dynamo finally rendered untenable the affirmation of unity and coherence that had endowed the allegiance of Christianity and empire with the power to structure the Western world and mind. For Adams, the dynamo encapsulated the indisputable denial of unity that every scientific theory and discovery of the day appeared to point toward, and which he expresses in one halting, awestruck sentence: "Matter was Motion—Motion was Matter—the thing moved." Electrical energy, as exemplified in the figure of the dynamo, was the new supersensual force to be reckoned with, and its defining characteristics were not order and unity but motion and multiplicity.

As strange a force as electricity seemed to Adams in 1900, it was its uncanny familiarity that convinced him of its power to topple the cross.

> Yet the dynamo next to the steam-engine was the most familiar of objects. For Adams' objects its value lay chiefly in its occult mechanism. Between the dynamo in the gallery of machines and the engine house outside, the break of continuity amounted to abysmal fracture for a historian's objects. No more relation could he discover between the steam and electric current than between the Cross and the cathedral. The forces were interchangeable if not reversible, but he could see only an absolute *fiat* in electricity as in faith.[30]

Here was a god a mechanical population could worship, a force capable of remodeling social and political habits, ideas, and institutions. For Adams, just as the cross replaced the legion and the Civitas Dei the Civitas Romae as the organizing principle of the Roman Empire, so, too, in the electrified world of the twentieth century, the dynamo would over-power the synthesis of God and empire, shattering the unity and conti-nuity of thought and belief that had guided the Western world since the Holy Roman Empire.

His education completed by the dynamo, Adams avows that "the only honest alternative to affirming unity is to deny it, and the denial would require a new education."[31] An argument could be made that other con-temporary ideas and discoveries Adams mentions (Ernst Mach's mechan-ics or Marie Curie's radium) and some he does not (Freud's psychology, Max Planck's quantum physics, or Einstein's special theory of relativity) would have as great an impact as the dynamo on the coming century, but it is hard to imagine anything that could enable Adams's new education better than electricity. From the home to the school to the workplace, from communication to transportation to militarization, there was not an arena of American life that remained the same once it had been electrified. Even as Adams despaired that the old synthesis of science and religion had lost its capacity to organize, unify, and educate Americans, the new mechanical sciences and the nascent empires of capital that would fund and profit from them began to forge alliances with the emer-gent forms of a newly electrified mass culture. Over the course of the next century, the media and the market would absorb the old occult and fetish power now fallen from the cross, and Whitman's charged body, like Frankenstein's monster, would prove to be electrifying in ways its inven-tor never envisioned.

Of the multiple progeny of the dynamo, the ones I am most con-cerned with here are radio, film, and television, which from Adams's rev-elation through the Reagan presidency were the primary technologies for constructing the body electric. The speed at which these media entered American lives is astonishing. The effect on those lives was unparalleled. Together with the network of related industries and professions that grew with them, their penetration of the public and private sphere and their re-modeling of social and political habits, ideas, and institutions was virtu-ally absolute. The task here, then, is to describe the new education pro-vided by an electrically generated faith, and the new selves and political formations it produced.

The Pedagogy of Performance

> The child born in 1900 would, then, be born into a new world which would not
> be a unity but a multiple. Adams tried to imagine it, and an education that
> would fit it.
>
> —Henry Adams, *The Education of Henry Adams*

On 3 June 1928, Ronald Reagan's childhood sweetheart and frequent acting partner, Margaret "Mugs" Cleaver, in her capacity as president of the senior class at North Side High School in Dixon, Illinois, addressed the audience at their commencement ceremony. In her speech, entitled "A Chair for the New Home," Mugs spoke of the educational opportunities afforded by the new high school that was scheduled to open in Dixon the following year. She also offered some suggestions for its design. In order to "train the citizens of tomorrow," she advised, the "new home" would "require new furnishings." The chair with which she proposed to outfit the new home, however, was not a piece of furniture but a "Chair, or Department, of Public Speaking and Dramatics." The modern world, she decreed, "was a social world. Every person, to be the fullest success, must be able to mingle with people." To be a skillful mingler, she added, it was not as important to learn facts, most of which were quickly forgotten, as it was to learn "how to convey an idea clearly and forcefully, and, in general, how to conduct oneself before an audience." The new chair was practical, but it was also magical. While providing training in socially useful performance skills it would also offer a means of shrinking the dimensions of space and time. The ideal way to study history would be "to visit the world's famous spots, and get the setting and facts at the same time." This, Mugs acknowledged, was not possible for most people. Instead she extolled the virtues of "dramatization and pageant work" as an "excellent substitute."[32] Her pedagogical dictums—public speaking and "dramatics" as requisite training for social life, oral communication and public presentation as the keys to self-realization, and theatrical representation as a substitute for lived experience—depict a world in which the social realm is a stage, and society an audience for the performing self.

Mugs's speech was a clarion call for a new education capable of providing access to and knowledge of a rapidly changing and increasingly interconnected world through the "excellent substitute" of performance.

Descriptions of Ronald Reagan's early years, including his own, echo this model of self-development by describing a childhood in which most of the seminal lessons learned derived from some form of public performance. Reading through these accounts it is hard to ignore the remarkable degree to which the important figures in Reagan's childhood exhibited a similar understanding of performance as the most significant way to know oneself and one's world. "I don't know," Reagan answered during his first political campaign when asked what kind of governor he would be, "I've never played a governor."[33] It would not be overstating the case to suggest that from his earliest days performing was Ronald Reagan's epistemology.

If Henry Adams could have imagined an education ideally suited for thriving in the new world that so bedeviled him, it would have looked much like Ronald Reagan's. Unlike Adams, who until he set sail for Berlin at the age of twenty lived in the same house on Mount Vernon Street in which he had been born, Reagan, born in 1911, grew up in a world defined by motion and multiplicity. During the first thirteen years of his Illinois childhood he lived in eleven homes, moving from Tampico to Chicago to Galesburg to Monmouth and back to Tampico before finally settling in Dixon. Adams's roots were firmly planted on the Eastern Seaboard, the political, religious, and commercial fount of American power. The ocean was his conduit to Europe and his skeptical vision of America and its future, but it was rivers that shaped the horizon of the landlocked, cockeyed optimist Reagan's earliest vistas. "Dutch"—a nickname acquired at birth when his father declared "for such a little bit of a fat Dutchman, he makes a hell of a lot of noise"—grew out of the prairies of the Middle West, where the West begins to exert its attraction as the other side of the river. Throughout his peripatetic childhood, Dutch Reagan never wandered more than a hundred miles from the east bank of the Mississippi, the spinal column of America's mythic geography.

What connected Reagan's prairie upbringing to both the utopian myths of the West and the ideological legacy of the East was an education steeped in the culture of performance. His education began in earnest at the age of nine when the Reagans moved to Dixon, a midwestern hamlet on the banks of the Rock River, a hundred miles west of Chicago, with a population of eight thousand. It was Reagan's home until he graduated from college. He later wrote that this was where "I really found myself," the place "that shaped my mind and body for all the years to come after."[34] The education that he received during the Dixon years spans the cusp of two distinct but overlapping epistemologies of performance. The first pedagogical model that shaped his mind and body as a youth derived from the still dominant ideals of what Emerson defined as the culture of character. The second was an expression of what Warren Sussman has termed the "culture of personality."[35]

As Reagan's childhood education attests, the performance pedagogies of the two cultures are not unrelated. Sussman, examining the advice manuals written in the early years of the twentieth century, identifies a challenge to Emerson's culture of character in their depiction of "another vision of self, another vision of self-development and mastery, another method of the presentation of self in society." He locates the seeds of the new modal type representative of the culture of personality "in the very bosom of the old culture . . . the other side of Emerson—his vision of a transcendent self."[36] In his formulation, the character-oriented self strove for fulfillment through self-control, self-mastery, and self-sacrifice while the new, personality-driven self stressed self-fulfillment, self-expression, and self-gratification. Sussman's account of this new self is consonant with that expressed in Mugs Cleaver's commencement address. "The social role demanded of all in the new culture of personality," writes Sussman, "was that of a performer. Every American was to become a performing self. Every work studied stressed the importance of the human voice in describing methods of voice control and proper methods of conversation or public speaking. Everyone was expected to impress and influence with trained and effective speech."[37] In its vision of the self and its relationship with society, the culture of personality Sussman describes represented a consumer-oriented society that challenged the dominant production-driven model of the self espoused by the culture of character. The order with which the culture of character sought to harmonize was that of the expanding producer-oriented society of the nineteenth century. But Mugs's call for a pedagogy of performance that would provide the tools with which to assert one's individuality while simultaneously learning how to function as a member of a group is a pedagogical imperative for a self in a society in transition from scarcity to abundance, from the imperatives of production to those of consumption.

The dominant model of performance as knowledge during Reagan's early years was exemplified in the Christian pedagogy of the Chautauqua movement. From shortly after the Civil War until the Great Depression, Chautauqua constituted the leading edge of the cultural front of evangelical Protestantism's bid to naturalize its claim as "the national religion, a religion of civilization."[38] The original Chautauqua institution, or "assembly," was established in 1874 by the inventor and businessman Lewis Miller and the future Methodist minister John Heyl Vincent on Lake Chautauqua in western New York. The founders' initial goal for Chautauqua was to train teachers in the best pedagogical methods for teaching Sunday school.[39] Chautauqua proved so popular, however, that in less than a decade it was transformed from "a summer assembly of Sunday School teachers on a camp meeting ground to a monster institution of popular education, embracing many realms of human inquiry and study."[40] Chautauqua's growing influence was propagated by the Chautauqua Literary and Scientific Circle (CLSC), which provided "Chautauqua all the year" through a course of study that included classes on both religious and secular subjects, lectures by prominent public figures, and the first correspondence degree program in the United States. The CLSC spread Chautauqua's influence by promoting its democratic philosophy of "education for everybody, everywhere in every department, inspired by a Christian faith" and stimulated the creation of independent Chautauquas throughout the country.[41] By the end of the nineteenth century, thirty-one states had their own assemblies and the movement had blanketed the Midwest, stretching as far west as Kansas and as far south as Missouri.[42]

Chautauqua's influence in shaping the mind and body of the young Ronald Reagan has been largely ignored by Reagan scholars. The only mention of Chautauqua I have been able to find in the numerous accounts of Reagan's childhood is by Anne Edwards, who writes that "in the summer [his mother] dragged Dutch with her to Chautauqua." Edwards provides no further information about Chautauqua or its influence on the future president.[43] The impact of Chautauqua ideals and pedagogy on the young Reagan, however, is indisputable and wide ranging.

When Chautauqua first came to Dixon in 1889 it redefined the cultural and civic life of Lee County. The Rock River Assembly, established by a Special Committee of the Northern Illinois Lutheran Synod, was initially conceived, like the original Chautauqua, as a "Sunday School Institute." Its stated purpose was to teach "such subjects as may be of interest and value to Sunday School teachers and students of the bible."[44] Almost immediately, however, the founder of the assembly, Rev. John Mosheim Ruthrauff, perceiving Chautauqua's "sphere of usefulness" to be greater than its intended function, expanded its operations to include a "summer resort where rest and recuperation can be secured for the body and where the highest mental, moral, and spiritual associations can be enjoyed."[45] By 1892, in addition to instruction for Sunday school teachers, the assembly offered classes in mental philosophy, language, public school teaching, physical culture, cookery, elocution and oratory, geology, music, and art. Inspirational and religious lectures vied for the growing audience's attention with more practical addresses on the virtues of "agricultural citizenship" and travel lectures with such titles as "Southern Norway, the Wonderland of the North."[46] By 1895 no less an authority than John Heyl Vincent, in his keynote address at the inaugural Recognition Day for the assembly's newly established Chautauqua Literary and Scientific Circle, declared that the "Rock River Assembly comes nearer the Chautauqua ideal than any other Assembly I have visited."[47]

Dixon's Chautauqua quickly became arguably the leading cultural attraction between Chicago and the Mississippi, and its popularity soon required the construction of a new facility to house its multifaceted offerings. In 1899, with Vincent on hand to celebrate the opening of "The Great Auditorium," the assembly dedicated what its members declared to be "the finest and most completely adapted building for Chautauqua purposes on this continent." Designed by a Dixon resident and transplanted Chicagoan, Morrison Vail, the circular auditorium boasted a perimeter measuring 500 feet and a diameter of 160 feet and featured a platform stage that was 64 feet wide and 20 feet deep. Reflecting the Chautauqua ideal of communing with nature, Vail ringed the building—with the exception of the stage—with doors that could be raised upward to a height of 7 feet to provide light, ventilation, and easy access. Arrayed around the sides and front of the platform were seats for an audience of five thousand. Behind the platform Vail provided amphitheater-style seating capable of accommodating an additional four hundred. Every seat had an unobstructed view of the stage thanks to Vail's invention of a new form of truss construction that eliminated the need for center posts.[48] From the platform stage of what came to be known as "The Dome" an astonishingly eclectic mix of speakers and performers entertained and enlightened the citizens of Dixon during the early years of the twentieth century. The impact of the education Chautauqua bestowed on its audience can be gleaned from Mugs Cleaver's commencement address, which she delivered, like the three decades of commencement addresses that preceded it, from the stage of the great auditorium.

Mugs's speech reflects the influence of Chautauqua's blend of education and entertainment, and its emphasis on the pedagogical efficacy of public oratory and performance as tools of instruction in the rituals of national belonging and the education of a Christian citizenry. Inspirational speakers such as Booker T. Washington and William Jennings Bryan taught their listeners "how to convey an idea clearly and forcefully, and, in general, how to conduct oneself before an audience." Mugs's call for "dramatization and pageant work" as an "excellent substitute" for studying other cultures was answered by assembly programs such as "The Hiawatha Indian Play" performed by a company of Ojibway Indians from Canada, the "Polynesian" play presented by the Raweis of New Zealand, and the Alpine Singers and Yodelers, who performed attired in "the picturesque costumes of the mountains of Tyrol."[49]

With the proliferation of independent assemblies like Rock River's, it was only a matter of time before someone figured out how to market the growing demand for Chautauqua. In 1904, an enterprising veteran of the burgeoning knowledge business and manager of the Redpath Lyceum Bureau, Keith Vawter, launched the first Circuit Chautauqua. The lyceum movement, a predecessor of Chautauqua, originated with Massachusetts farmer Josiah Holbrook in 1826 as a "voluntary association of individuals disposed to improve each other in useful knowledge."[50] As the movement expanded, local lyceums began to import celebrity lecturers, including Emerson, Mark Twain, and Susan B. Anthony. During the second half of the nineteenth century, lyceum bureaus emerged as the commercial vehicle for booking speakers who would address local communities on the pressing national and international issues of the day. The most successful of the bureaus was the one founded by James Redpath in 1868. In 1904, Vawter was managing Redpath's territory west of Pittsburgh and believed he could apply the circuit model employed by Redpath to efficiently and profitably meet the increasing demand for useful knowledge regarding self-improvement, cultural awareness, and spiritual development stimulated by the growing Chautauqua movement. By 1910, the Circuit Chautauqua system reached throughout the West and Midwest, and by 1920 its scope was national, with twenty-one companies operating ninety-three circuits throughout the United States.

Every summer during Reagan's childhood the Circuit Chautauqua would roll into Dixon and take over the grounds of "Governor" Charters's old estate along the banks of the Rock River, the site where the Rock River Assembly first convened in 1889. For two weeks in early August, Dixonians would forsake work and play to absorb the offerings of a uniquely American brand of education and entertainment that inspired Theodore Roosevelt to call Chautauqua "the most American thing in America."[51] As Charlotte Canning documents in her indispensable history of the Circuit Chautauqua: "All of the relevant concerns of the time—citizenship, race, community, gender, politics, government, quality of life, foreign affairs, family—were debated and examined by Chautauqua."[52] The gravity of these topics was leavened by the motley crew of musicians, actors, lecturers, elocutionists, humorists, magicians, animal trainers, yodelers, and whistlers who appeared together with the politicians, educators, and inspirational speakers on the typical Chautauqua bill.

In contrast to other popular touring performance forms of the day—vaudeville shows, medicine shows, and circuses—Chautauqua was commended by clerical and secular leaders alike for its capacity to "inspire cultural, community, and individual improvement through performances of various kinds."[53] Chautauqua advertising and programs trumpeted the moral and educational value of their product with endorsements from the likes of Lyman Abbot, a noted minister and Chautauqua speaker, who declared that it "was next to the church and the public school system among the forces that are making for the elevation and ennobling of the American people."[54] Abbot's endorsement of Chautauqua as an educational institution on a par with churches and schools was critical to the image of a business that required clerics to encourage their congregations to sell tickets to Chautauqua events and to ensure maximum participation and future audiences by convincing parents such as Reagan's mother

Nelle to bring their children with them. The success of Chautauqua's business model was staggering. Under a big brown tent, Dixonians were initiated into a pioneering form of a fledgling mass culture through the auspices of a performance-based pedagogy that at its peak in the mid-1920s served more than ten thousand communities in forty-five states with audiences totaling as many as forty-five million people.[55]

While statistics can convey the scope of Circuit Chautauqua, they cannot measure the impact of the new education it provided for rural and small-town Americans. "The town was never the same after Chautauqua started coming," recalled Sue Humphrey of Havensville, Kansas. "The Chautauqua brought a new touch of culture which we immediately applied to our lives: new ways of speech, dress, ways of entertainment."[56] Through both time-tested and pioneering forms of infotainment, Chautauqua performers provided a model of mimetic education endorsed by Mugs Cleaver in her advocacy of dramatics and public speaking as a cornerstone of public education. The impulse of children to act out and orate their emotions, she insisted, was a "natural trait of childhood" that should be preserved and developed by the public schools as a "remedy" for the lack of "ease and poise" that typified the "self-conscious period of adolescence." The promise of Chautauqua was that through exposure to its performance-based pedagogy rural Americans could, like Mugs's self-conscious adolescent, overcome their "silliness and awkwardness" by acquiring new forms of speech, dress, and entertainment that would outfit them with the ease, poise, and self-reliance they craved.[57]

Self-reliance was a key component of the ideology of the self-made man, and it would become a central component of Ronald Reagan's personal and political philosophy. In Mugs's speech, and throughout Reagan's political career, the health of the nation and the welfare of its citizens were rhetorically linked through a philosophy that promoted individual self-sufficiency as a guarantor of personal and national prosperity. Chautauqua promised to benefit both the individual and the nation through its cultivation of citizens equipped with the tools for achieving self-reliance, while simultaneously fortified by their participation in the shared rituals of community and nation. As one Chautauqua advocate is said to have told the performers staying in her home, "[Chautauqua] is our oasis—our life belt. The music we hear during assembly week is the music we sing and play all through the year. The lectures we discuss for months. My husband remembers all the jokes and the politics and I try to remember . . . all the new ideas set forth. . . . Sometime I think we could not endure the privations and loneliness of this new land if it were not for the Chautauqua."[58] By incorporating the lessons learned from the cultural performances witnessed on the Chautauqua platform into their everyday lives, rural Americans embodied the cultural performances and theatrical reenactments Mugs identified as an excellent substitute for experiencing the country and the world beyond their isolated communities. Chautauqua was the most American thing in America because its modeling of personal conduct and social behavior enabled isolated Americans such as the young Ronald Reagan not only to imagine but to enact the image of their communion with a nation they experienced most immediately through the excellent substitute of Chautauqua performances. These performances ameliorated the privations and loneliness of rural Americans by initiating them into a new set of cultural beliefs and practices that connected them to the imagi-nation that formed in the early years of the twentieth century.

The conviction that cultural instruction and religious instruction are mutually beneficial components of a modern education was reinforced by the religious beliefs and practices shared by Dutch's and Mugs's families. Like the founders of Chautauqua, Nelle Reagan was raised a Methodist and attended the Methodist Episcopal Church as a child in Clyde Township, Illinois. Although she agreed to have her children baptized and educated as Catholics when she married Jack Reagan in 1906, she only followed through on her promise with her eldest son, Neil. On Easter Sunday in 1910, the year before Dutch was born, Nelle adopted a new faith and was baptized as a Disciple of Christ in the Hennepin Canal in Tampico.

The Disciples of Christ, known also as the Christian Church, was the product of a merger in 1832 between the followers of Alexander Campbell and Barton Stone, two liberal Presbyterians who had rejected both the creedal dogmatism of the Protestant church and the emotional excesses of the Second Great Awakening. Originating in rural America, the Disciples reflected the dominant beliefs of the Anglo-Saxon South and Midwest, as well as the ideology of Chautauqua: faith in progress, Providence, and Anglo-Saxon superiority; a reverence for farmers and laborers; and a suspicion of urban life and the people who lived it. As the frontier expanded westward after the Civil War, so, too, did the Disciples. By the time Nelle was baptized there were 682 Christian Churches in Illinois alone.[59]

The one urban value that mitigated the Disciples' ruralism was an emphasis it shared with the urban settlement movement on self-improvement through cultural uplift. Like the founders of Chautauqua, the inspirational architects of the Christian Church were the products of a particular strain of nineteenth-century Protestantism that rejected the emotionalism of camp-meeting evangelism and believed that reason applied to scripture offered the best route to salvation. The Disciples' commitment to a faith informed by reason manifested itself in a fondness for oratory and polemical debate and the prolific creation of schools, colleges, and theological journals. The Disciples valued education for its spiritual utility but also for the cultural enrichment it offered. As Garry Wills notes, after the Disciples founded Ronald Reagan's alma mater, Eureka College, in 1855, "the first extracurricular group was the Edmund Burke Society, established to discuss literary works."[60] In lieu of creedal orthodoxy, the Disciples professed an "undenominational spirit" that placed a premium on the cultural affiliations that bound the community of believers together. The image of their communion was cultural as well as spiritual, a product of the same conviction that animated the Pilgrims, the Founding Fathers, and Chautauqua. They believed that American Protestants of British descent were duty bound to become evangelists for a belief system that encompassed the spiritual, the secular, and the national and that they were destined to establish their system of belief as the law of the land.

The growth of the Christian Church owed much to its emphasis on the same tenets of spiritual and cultural self-improvement through education that fueled the spread of Chautauqua. The Disciples' rejection of all human creeds and their reliance on the Bible as the only true source of faith were summarized in the maxim "Where the Scriptures speak, we speak; where the Scriptures are silent, we are silent." In 1906, in a dispute over the interpretation of this central tenet of the faith as it applied to incorporating instrumental music in worship, the Disciples separated into two factions. A group of conservative churches, primarily located south of the Ohio River, changed its denominational affiliation to the Church of Christ. The advocates of the spiritual efficacy of instrumental music retained their identity as the Disciples of Christ. Four years later it was with the supporters of cultural performance as an integral expression of faith that Nelle Reagan cast her spiritual lot.[61]

Nelle's conversion to the Christian Church was a spiritual matter, but the role she played as a soldier of the faith suggests that being a Disciple fed her cultural aspirations as well. As a Disciple, Nelle would forswear her love of dancing. Unlike Methodism, however, her new religion had no strictures against the theater. In small-town Tampico (population 1,276), the Reagans were the first family of the stage, having founded an amateur theater company that performed at the grandly named Burden's Opera House (actually a small room with a stage above the town bank). In 1913 alone, the Reagans appeared in three full-length plays, one of which provided Nelle with the highlight of her acting career when on Thanksgiving night she appeared in the title role in *Millie the Quadroon; or, Out of Bondage,* a five-act bodice ripper characterized by its author as a "play of antebellum trueness." By all accounts, Nelle acquitted herself well in meeting the challenge of her multiple roles "as, successively, a genteel Northern matron, a French nun in green glasses, and a Southern field hand." Beside her, Reagan's father Jack was corked and carmined in his role as an escaped slave.[62]

That Nelle viewed theater as a suitable family activity is evidenced by her casting of the four-month-old Neil, Dutch's only sibling, as a dying infant, his face calcimined to make him appear ghostly, in *The Dust of the Earth.* Describing his subsequent acting experience, "Moon"—the nickname Neil acquired from his resemblance to the comic strip character Moon Mullins—recalled only his role as a teenage "song and dance man" in the Knights of Columbus annual benefit show at the Dixon Theater.[63] The pages of the *Dixon Evening Telegraph* tell a different story, documenting Moon's high school acting career in roles that ranged from the "promising young lawyer" Richard Tate in *His Uncle's Niece* to Nimble Wit in the operetta *Blue Beard.*[64] The paper's reviews of his performances support his younger brother's appraisal that as a child Moon "could sing or dance with the best of 'em." Ronald Reagan's observation in his memoirs that many of the Reagan boys' childhood acquaintances were surprised that it was he and not his brother who ended up in show business underestimates the formative and enduring influence of his brother's performances.[65] Neil Reagan's selective memory regarding his thespian past may have been a product of his lifelong attempt to assert his independence from his mother's faith and his brother's fame. But while Moon did not become an actor, he did utilize his theatrical training by following his brother into radio broadcasting, paving the way for a long career in advertising, a trajectory that situated him squarely within the professional ranks of the new culture of performance.

Unlike his brother, Dutch embraced Nelle's religious beliefs, love of the stage, and belief in the persuasive potency of performance. Nelle initiated Dutch into the culture of performance at the age of nine, shortly before the Reagans moved to Dixon, an experience Reagan retrospectively credits as shaping his future goals and aspirations. Shy and apprehensive at first, he resisted his mother's initial attempt to help him memorize a short dramatic reading and present it before the congregation. In his memoirs, he describes how he overcame his fears and the benefits he received from learning how to conduct himself before an audience.

> Summoning up my courage, I walked up to the stage that night, cleared my throat, and made my theatrical debut. I don't remember what I said, but I'll never forget the response: *People laughed and applauded.* That was a new experience for me and I liked it. I liked that approval. For a kid suffering childhood pangs of insecurity, the applause was music. I didn't know it then, but, in a way, when I walked off that stage that night, my life had changed.[66]

Performing a homiletic reading entitled "About Mother" from the "stage" of the Christian Church of Tampico, the awkward nine year old discovered the ease and poise to be acquired from acting, his first and most enduring love. Throughout his childhood both Nelle and the Christian Church encouraged the aspirations of the young performer as a means of achieving a moral and cultural education.

Nelle's embrace of the ethos of performance as consistent with her religious beliefs and cultural aspirations speaks to the endurance and adaptability of cultural performance forms in the making of America and Americans. While social and religious mores precluded Nelle from pursuing a professional acting career, both church and Chautauqua sanctioned the channeling of her theatrical aspirations into a wide variety of religious and secular performances. As a member of the First Christian Church of Dixon, Nelle became president of the Women's Missionary Society, a member of the Ladies Aid Society, secretary of the Bible School Workers Conference, a delegate to the state convention of the Christian Church, and song director for the choir. In all these roles she found the opportunity to incorporate her love of performing. In his first autobiography, Reagan characterized his mother as "the dean of dramatic recitals for the countryside. It was her sole relaxation from her family and charitable duties" and "she executed it with the zeal of a frustrated actress. She recited classic speeches in tragic tones, wept as she flung herself into the more poignant, if less talented passages of such melodramas as *East Lynne*, and poured out poetry by the yard."[67] Commenting on Nelle's performance of a selection of readings at the Christian Church in nearby Prairieville, one observer described her as "most versatile, and . . . equally happy in tragic, comic, or descriptive readings."[68] Over the course of Dutch's childhood he bore witness to his mother's faith in the pedagogy of performance through her participation in dramatic recitations, Sunday school plays and pageants, and musical and elocutionary recitals in venues as varied as churches, prisons, schools, hospitals, mental institutions, private homes, and public clubs. Civic and religious gatherings at which Nelle gave dramatic or inspirational readings, performed in plays, or sang included events hosted by the Ladies Aid Society, the Christian Endeavor Club, the Women's Christian Temperance Union, the Pine Creek Revival, the American Legion, and the Kiwanis Club.[69] Judging by accounts in the Dixon newspaper, from "scramble suppers" to Bible school banquets it was the rare public gathering Nelle Reagan attended at which she did not perform.

Mugs Cleaver's belief in the efficacy of public speaking and dramatics as pedagogical tools owes something as well to the influence of Nelle Reagan. Mugs often sang and acted with Nelle and accompanied her on piano at church functions. As a Sunday school student in Nelle's True Blue class, and subsequently in her teacher-training classes, Mugs absorbed Chautauqua pedagogy by participating in inspirational readings, music recitals, and educational plays under Nelle's direction. As president of the Dixon High School Parent-Teacher Association during the mid-1920s, Nelle was also in a position to influence the decision to expand the scope of dramatics through the plans for the design of the new high school Mugs referred to in her commencement address. Thanks in part to Nelle's advocacy, the new high school, unlike the old one, would contain a rehearsal room with a fully equipped stage and an auditorium for public performances.

The belief that religion and performance are interconnected elements of a well-rounded education permeated Dutch's childhood. Much of his youth when he was not at school or playing sports was spent at church and church-related events. Nelle attended prayer meetings with her children on Wednesday and Sunday nights, and on Sunday mornings the Reagan boys attended Sunday school.[70] Church functions where Dutch gave dramatic readings and acted in church sanctioned plays—often written and staged by Nelle—were the first venue to shape the voice and body of the future president. According to Anne Edwards, "[T]he congregation was much taken with his voice, which they believed owed a great deal to the private elocution lessons Nelle gave him."[71]

Perhaps the best example of the intertwined influence of religious and cultural performances on the young Reagan is the oft-told story of how he came to be baptized as a Disciple. For the Disciples, religious belief was a matter of rational choice as well as spiritual commitment. Conversion to the faith required the believer to make a conscious decision, and thus the Christian Church prohibited pedobaptism. At the age of eleven, Dutch picked up Nelle's copy of Harold Bell Wright's novel *That Printer of Udell's*. The prologue must have been what grabbed his attention first. In it a scared young boy, Dick Falkner, watches his father, intoxicated and unconscious on the floor of a cabin, eerily mirroring Dutch's own recent experience of discovering his own father, drunk and "dead to the world," lying in the snow outside their home.[72] As the novel begins, sixteen years have passed and the young boy has become a young man and "a printer by trade." Broke and adrift, Dick stumbles into a Christian church in a midwestern industrial town. Through his association with the church, he acquires a sense of community, a social conscience, and a new wardrobe. It is also at church that Dick, in an effort to impress a girl, gives an impromptu speech that dazzles her with its eloquence, providing him the confidence to become an influential public speaker and local reformer. He ultimately joins the church, wins the girl, and in the last scene prepares to depart for Washington as an elected official to apply his gifts for political oratory, social charm, and snappy dressing in "a field of wider usefulness." The parallels to Reagan's subsequent political awakening are striking, as is the role of the church in providing a formative venue for self-development through performance. The novel, like the Christian Church and Chautauqua, modeled a pedagogy of performance that emphasized the interconnectedness of spiritual and cultural training.

Shortly after reading the book, Dutch told Nelle that he was ready to declare his faith and be baptized as a Disciple. On 21 June 1922, the Reagan boys were part of the first group of Disciples to be baptized at the newly rebuilt First Christian Church of Dixon. On the eve of the presidential election in 1980, Reagan would tell Rev. Adrian Rogers, president of the Southern Baptist Convention, that he had felt "called" at the time of his baptism, adding, "I had a personal experience when I invited Christ into my life." When Reverend Rogers asked him if he knew Jesus or just knew about him, Reagan replied, "I KNOW him!"[73] As was most often the case with Ronald Reagan, what he "knew" derived from an affective connection to a cultural product that had performatively mediated his experience and beliefs.

Despite the fact that it is never mentioned by name, the practical Christianity that motivates Dick Falkner to translate his oratorical prowess into an active involvement in social reform and politics derives from the teachings of the Christian endeavor movement, another one of Nell's religio-cultural affiliations. The Christian Endeavor Society was founded in Maine in 1881 by a Congregationalist minister, Dr. F. E. Clark, to provide Christian youths "the opportunity for self-expression by means of words and service for Christ and church." Christian Endeavor sought to provide impressionable Christians with the knowledge of other cultures in order to develop an image of their communion with their brethren in an increasingly global faith. Its message proved so popular that by the 1920s the interdenominational, international, and interracial organization boasted thirty-six thousand individual societies with a membership of approximately four million from thirty different denominations. Christian Endeavor was also credited by contemporary church leaders with training the cultural vanguard of recruits for pastoral and missionary work.

The teachings of the Christian Endeavor Society were soon reinforced for Ronald Reagan by a more immediate source. Shortly after Dutch was baptized, the First Christian Church appointed Mugs's father, the Rev. Ben Cleaver, as its new minister. According to Dixonite Isabelle Newman, Reverend Cleaver was "an old-time pastor with much rhetoric," and one of his first initiatives was to encourage greater participation of the children of the church in the Christian Endeavor Society.[74] The Reagan and Cleaver families were among the most ardent church members in answering the reverend's call. Two months after Ben Cleaver's appointment, Nelle Reagan became the leader of Christian Endeavor's midweek prayers. Over the course of their childhood, the Reagan and Cleaver children were all active in Christian Endeavor, and both Mugs and Dutch assumed leadership roles.

The adult counterpart of Christian Endeavor was the Women's Missionary Society, which also flourished under the Reverend Cleaver's pastorate. As president of the Missionary Society, Nelle modeled the virtues of Christian Endeavor's performative epistemology of "self-expression" through Christian words and service by producing plays such as *The Pill Bottle,* a play about missionary work in India, in which Nelle and Mugs also performed. Nelle also worked closely with the Girls Missionary Triangle Club for which Mugs served a term as president.[75] Sponsoring missionary talks on topics such as "Filipino life and customs," Nelle spread Christian Endeavor's message of world brotherhood and understanding as a bulwark against international conflict in the modern world. The education offered by Christian Endeavor and the Women's Missionary Society suggests that the isolated, independent America in which evangelical Protestantism could aspire to be the religion of civilization was on the wane. The new world in which Ronald Reagan would come of age was one in which—according to a participant in "The Large World: My Neighborhood," another program Nelle hosted—"newspapers, moving pictures, radio, steamship, and aeroplane . . . tie the world together."[76] Members of new religious organizations such as the Christian Endeavor Society and the Women's Missionary Society sought to reconcile their faith with these new modes of communication and transportation, which would shrink the large world to the proportions of a neighborhood. Over the course of the twentieth century, however, these new technologies would increasingly undermine the teachings of evangelical Christian culture and themselves become icons of a new faith.

Before the fiat of electricity transformed the way Americans were educated and to what end, certain early-twentieth-century educational philosophies prepared the way by redefining the pedagogical mission of the culture of performance. Many of the ideas that influenced Mugs's design for Dixon High's new home originated with the Chicago school of the Progressive movement. It was in 1896 in Chicago, less than a hundred miles from Dixon, that John Dewey, influenced by Charles Darwin's theories of evolution and the nascent science of psychology, founded his Laboratory School at the University of Chicago. Mugs's criticism of the inadequacy of a fact-based education and her advocacy for a curriculum that would teach students "to work together as a unit" and provide training in communication and socialization resonates with Dewey's philosophy that a school should be a laboratory for developing the practical and adaptable social skills that would enable students to become both autonomous individuals and engaged citizens.

Dewey believed that the various modes and forms of human activity evolved as instruments for solving individual and social problems. Human beings, he asserted, were creatures of custom and habit who, when faced with new conflicts or challenges, required the ability to adapt their behavior to meet them. Like Henry Adams, Dewey held that conventional education, with its emphasis on the teaching of perpetually outmoded facts, did not provide students with the tools required to meet the challenges of a changing world. At the Laboratory School, which Dewey ran with his wife Alice, the emphasis was on the integration of cultural and vocational training, cooperative learning, and learning by doing. These educational tenets formed the basis of a pedagogy oriented toward providing students with the practical skills they needed to become, as Mugs insisted they must, both self-reliant and socially adept.

While Dewey has been criticized for neglecting the imaginative in favor of the pragmatic dimension of human experience, one of the first practical experiments to combine all the major pedagogical tenets of the Laboratory School occurred in 1901 with the building of a "Playhouse" constructed entirely by the students. Cultural performance in general and theater in particular were integral components of the Progressive social reform movement, which embraced many of the tenets of Dewey's educational philosophy. Shannon Jackson, in her "performance historiography" of Jane Addams's Hull House, chronicles the role of a performance-based pedagogy in the Progressive movement's vision of early-twentieth-century social settlements. Jackson coins the term *reformance* to describe how the wide range of cultural performances at Hull House—including theatrical presentations, storytelling festivals, living museums, and children's games—instructed recent immigrants in cultural assimilation and expression by utilizing the mimetic capacity of performance to reform individual conduct and social behavior.[77]

In addition to borrowing the rhetoric of the Progressive pedagogy that emphasized the pragmatic, real-world applications of training in dramatics and public speaking, Mugs's rationale for the new chair also echoed an influential revisionist view of drama as a vital form of Christian education. "There has always been an instinct in man," she declared, "to express his emotion in dramatic form. Most of the ancient religious ceremonies," she added, "were only a response to the dramatic urge."[78] Her depiction of the formative role of the dramatic urge in religious ritual resonates with the writings of the "Cambridge Ritualists," a loosely associated group of mostly British classicists from a variety of academic disciplines who shared an interest in the current ideas of anthropology and evolutionary science and their application to the study of classical civilizations. Like Dewey, the Ritualists believed that the acquisition of knowledge was a transformative process rooted in practical experience. In *Themis*, the Cambridge anthropologist Jane Harrison, influenced by James Frazer's *The Golden Bough* and its view of the origins of classical religion and art in "primitive" ritual, made the Ritualists' case for the impact of dramatization on both artistic and religious expression. Citing the sociologist Émile Durkheim's concept of "imitative rites," Harrison described how "primitive" people reenacted the most intensely emotional events in their lives: birth, adolescence, marriage, and death. When these emotions were collectively expressed, she argued, they became codified as mimetic rituals. Artistic and religious expression shared their origins in the same commemorative or anticipatory rituals in which the desired result was acted out so that the experiences depicted might be incorporated or realized.[79]

The influence of the Ritualists' view of drama as the mimetic basis for religious and artistic expression is evident in Mugs's advocacy of a performance-based pedagogy as the cornerstone of a modern Christian education. A decade earlier this same perspective had shaped the declaration of imagi-nation that accompanied the premier of theater on the Chautauqua stage. When contemporary drama entered the Chautauqua repertoire in 1915, circuit operators justified its inclusion by virtue of drama's historic connection to religion: "In the beginning the drama was the handmaiden of the church. Since then it has wandered afar. . . . The church today recognizes [drama's] power and force for good when rightly directed and looks forward to the time when it will come into its own."[80] As Charlotte Canning points out, Redpath's brochure answered the objection that theater threatened the epistemology of religion by insisting that "rather than endangering religious standards and practices, theater was essential to maintaining them."[81] By situating the dramatic urge at the origins of religious expression, Mugs, Chautauqua, and the Ritualists sought to reverse the historical antipathy of Protestantism toward the drama and, much as the founders did, to champion theatricality as a crucial component in the development of American character.

In its early years, guided by an evangelical Protestant vision of a Christian nation, the Circuit Chautauqua offered fare drawn largely from the same late-nineteenth-century performance culture found on the platforms of the independent assemblies. When the Reagans moved to Dixon commercial radio was still a dream, film was in its infancy, and its impact was most pronounced in urban America. Circuit Chautauqua had developed into an embryonic form of mass culture as responsive to the imperatives of mass entertainment and market forces as it had been to those of Christian doctrine. By introducing mass culture to the heartland, Chautauqua altered the discourse and practice of evangelical Protestantism. This development is evident in the response of the church to changes in

Chautauqua programming, most notably its position on the introduction of theater to the Chautauqua stage.

The arrival of actors on the Chautauqua stage marks a defining moment in the history of the social and professional status of the American actor. In 1887, three years after the founding of the original Chautauqua Institution, the same Methodist Episcopal Church that had developed Chautauqua issued a comprehensive ban, barring its members from attending certain "amusements," including theater. Chautauqua performances, however, would increasingly push back the boundaries of the theatrical taboo. In a scenario that would be repeated with subsequent mass cultural media, the popularity of theater on the Chautauqua stage ultimately triumphed over the objections of the church. Victoria Case and Robert Ormond Case describe the process whereby a variety of Chautauqua performance forms paved the way for theater by immunizing audiences against the church's antitheatrical prejudice.

First came the impersonators and dramatic readers. Who could object to them? Then came lecturers reading extracts from great plays in resounding, musical, frightening voices. This was still above reproach, but with each passing season the dramatic offering—always reflecting an increasing public demand—came closer to crumbling the walls of prejudice. Soon there were bits of opera and Shakespearean excerpts; and finally, without squirming, Chautauqua audiences were sitting through a real play in which up to a dozen actors appeared, and the curtain actually rose and fell between acts. . . . These were the successive steps whereby the stage reached the cornbelt.[82]

When Chautauqua introduced theatrical productions, they quickly proved, as Chautauqua producer Charles Horner observed, "so popular and drew so well, that when we had begun to offer them there was no way to stop."[83] By 1924, at the peak of Chautauqua's popularity, the Methodist church acknowledged the futility of resistance and rescinded the ban on attending theater.[84] By 1927, when theater had become a staple of Chautauqua programming, the *New York Times* observed, "This season's plays have drawn larger audiences than other program items. Religious opposition to the drama has ceased in rural America and the growth in the appreciation of good music and plays has been phenomenal."[85] By the end of the 1920s, theatrical productions had become the primary attraction on the Circuit Chautauqua stage.

Chautauqua's embrace of theater marks a watershed moment in the development of the new culture of performance. In *Actors and American Culture,* Benjamin McArthur documents the remarkable transformation in the social perception of actors from 1880 to 1920. In the late nineteenth century actors were still routinely denied a Christian funeral and were deemed unfit to appear on the Chautauqua stage.[86] By 1916, the change in fortune of the American actor was so dramatic that it prompted one acting teacher, Arthur Hornblow, to observe that the actor was "no longer a social outcast. The stage is a recognized profession. Society no longer despises the actor, but greets him with open arms."[87] McArthur summarizes the multiple and complex reasons for this transformation in the social status of the American actor by concluding that actors were "prophetic figures in the shift from the Victorian ethic of self-discipline and restraint to the twentieth-century celebration of self-realization."[88] Hornblow's assessment of actors' new status reflects the transition from the performance culture of the nineteenth century to that of the twentieth, from a production-driven to a consumer-oriented economy, and from the culture of character to the culture of personality.

Hornblow's characterization of actors as prophets of a cultural transformation that occurred around the turn of the century implies a heightened significance of the social role that actors have always played. While it wasn't until the twentieth century that actors and their craft became socially acceptable in the United States, actors have always played a prominent role in the ongoing production of individual and national identity. Trained in what Roach describes as "the frequently contradictory ideals of calculated effect and sincerity of spontaneous expression" that define the paradox of natural theatricality, actors have historically served as surrogates for resolving, however tenuously, the conflicted ideology of American character. Actors can do this because they represent contemporary and memorial ideas about personal character through the performance of theatrical characters. Roach cites the Astor Place Riot of 1848—which occurred two years prior to the publication of Emerson's *Representative Men*— as the seminal event in the emergence of a distinctively American actor.

From the middle of the nineteenth century, he argues, observers began to extrapolate from the performances of the American actor an ideal of character they then "generalized to the social performances of every citizen. . . . a core identity at the heart of every real American, against which the authenticity of performances in a variety of roles could be measured."[89] In their performances actors embodied this contradiction at the heart of American character, and thus, a half century before gaining social respectability, actors served as "the avatar of authenticity in the culture of performance."[90] Actors played this role because in the years following the Civil War, when racial, ethnic, and class boundaries became more fluid, the shifting balance between the natural and the theatrical in the shaping of American identity tipped toward the theatrical. In a world of "self-made men"—in which authenticity ceased to be a criteria for assessing the content of one's character and became a measure of the social efficacy of the different characters one played—actors provided practical models for generating performances capable of navigating the roiled social waters.

In the early years of the twentieth century the formalization of acting training, the establishment of acting schools and studios, and the professionalization of the craft through the establishment of actors' unions and societies all contributed to the growing respectability of the actor. As the Cases' account suggests, the inclusion of theater in the programming of popular and respectable cultural venues such as the Circuit Chautauqua institutionalized the role of the actor as a cultural bellwether. No longer required to assume a disguise, the actor shed the protective cloak of oratory and elocution and took the stage decked out in the respectable guise of pedagogy. On Chautauqua stages actors introduced audiences to the new breed of American characters that were transforming the nation from the homogeneous Anglo-Saxon Protestant society in which Henry Adams was born to the increasingly urban and ethnically diverse mass society that he lamented was rendering his world obsolete.

Ronald Reagan's description of the town that shaped his mind and body as a "typical Midwestern America [*sic*] melting pot" is an example of how, when the stage reached the Corn Belt, theater altered Chautauqua audiences' image of their communion with a changing nation.[91] A smash hit on Broadway in 1909, Israel Zangwill's *The Melting Pot* was first presented on the Chautauqua stage in 1915 in a solo version by the play "enactor" Arthur Kachel, and subsequently in a fully mounted form. *The Melting Pot* quickly became a perennial circuit favorite. Its protagonist, the Russian Jewish immigrant David Quixano, dreams of composing a symphony about America. In contrast to the early Chautauqua's evangelical Protestant rhetoric rooted in the Anglo-Saxon errand in the wilderness, Quixano's American symphony strives to represent a contemporary urban vision of America as "God's crucible, where all the races of Europe are melting and reforming."[92] Translating *The Melting Pot*'s narrative of immigrant assimilation and acculturation into Chautauquaese, circuit publicists trumpeted its "new vision of America," in which the urban crucible forged diverse races and ethnicities into a "common brotherhood and civilization."[93] The metaphor of the melting pot as a new model for the making of Americans in an increasingly heterogeneous nation was born on Broadway, but it grew to maturity on the Chautauqua stage through its dissemination in countless performances along the circuit. It is a testament to the enduring impact of cultural performance that a play that ceased touring in 1919—which means that Reagan probably never saw it performed—would provide the language in which the grown man would describe his childhood home, a relatively homogeneous small town that bore little resemblance to Zangwill's New York. Like Reagan's description of his childhood as "one of those rare Huck Finn–Tom Sawyer idylls," his characterization of Dixon as a melting pot tells us less about the material conditions of his childhood than it does about the capacity of cultural products to constitute the American imagi-nation.[94]

The development of the Circuit Chautauqua marks the commercialization of the Chautauqua ideal, and its passage into modernity as a nascent form of mass culture. As a popular cultural representation of the image of national communion, Chautauqua contributed to reconstituting the affective basis of American identity in response to the new social, political, and economic forces unleashed by the Civil War, immigration, and the fiat of electricity. The education Chautauqua provided naturalized this new vision of the American imagi-nation through the performative processes of repetition and reproduction. In towns and villages across the country, circuit performances—like the public proclamations of the Declaration of Independence—announced a new imaginary relationship between Americans and their real conditions of existence. Chautauqua audiences embodied its offerings in the language they spoke, the songs they sang, and the behavior they adopted. Operating on the cusp of a dominant and emergent performance culture, Chautauqua combined performance forms from both to provide a new education for isolated Americans such as the young Ronald Reagan. In the 1920s, Chautauqua programming represented a new image of communion for connecting individuals to family, community, and an increasingly heterogeneous nation. By the end of Reagan's childhood, however, Chautauqua performances were depicting a nation in which Chautauqua itself was becoming irrelevant. By the early 1930s, the Circuit Chautauqua was all but extinct, a casualty of the Great Depression, the expansion of a mass audience for film and radio, and its dependence on a largely rural, agriculturally based audience in a nation that was increasingly urban and industrial.

The connections Chautauqua modeled between the pedagogies of performance and religion helped legitimate the new culture of performance. These connections were reinforced throughout the early education of Ronald Reagan. Chautauqua's influence is also evident in Mugs's depiction of dramatic training as a unique tool for shaping the emotional and bodily conduct required for adolescents to become more self-reliant, socially adept, and culturally aware. Mugs was no doubt correct when she insisted that her proposal to emphasize public speaking and dramatics in the curriculum of the new high school was "not a new and fanatical idea" but a mimetic impulse "as old as man." But the new performance technologies that emerged during Mugs's and Dutch's childhood would multiply Americans' exposure to mimetic models and media to a hitherto unprecedented degree.[95] Radio, film, and television—the dominant media of the fiat of electricity—would expand the sway and dominion of mass culture. Over the course of the twentieth century they would generate an increasingly formidable challenge to the pedagogical hegemony of the evangelical Protestant culture that built a nation and gave birth to Chautauqua.

CHAPTER TWO

The Voice of the Electronic Age

> The story begins with the close-up of a bottom in a small town called Tampico in Illinois, on February 6, 1911. My face was blue from screaming, my bottom was red from whacking, and my father claimed afterward that he was white when he said shakily, "for such a little bit of a fat Dutchman, he makes a hell of a lot of noise, doesn't he?"
>
> —Ronald Reagan, *Where's the Rest of Me?*

The opening sentences of Ronald Reagan's first autobiography merge the languages of legend ("The story begins") and film ("the close-up of a bottom") to evoke his mythic origins "in a small town called Tampico." The theatrical description of his noisy debut—the infant's blue face and red bottom and the father's claim to whiteness—inscribe the image of Reagan's

---

Photo: The sky reflects in the bulletproof glass protecting President Reagan as he addresses the crowd gathered to witness the 1981 reenactment of the British surrender at Yorktown. Photo © Bettman/Corbis.

Americanness on the scene. The representation of his birth as a red, white, and blueprint of the birth of the nation is reinforced in the second paragraph, in which he is nurtured by ideals imbibed from his mother's milk: "[M]y breast feeding was the home of the brave baby and the free bosom."[1] In this playful account of his arrival on the American scene, Reagan retrospectively scripts the birth of what would become his presidential character, his role of a lifetime. Published in 1965 on the cusp of his transition from entertainment to politics, *Where's the Rest of Me?* depicts Reagan as a seasoned veteran of the culture industry poised to claim his missing parts in the political sphere. This liminal condition, betwixt and between statecraft and stagecraft, forms the irreducible basis of his presidential character. The actor's performance strategy as president is prefigured in the narrative of his birth: the deployment of mass-mediated cultural forms to represent an idealized America through the performative evocation of a mythic past, a bodying forth of an American identity that is animated vocally.

While numerous commentators have addressed the development of Reagan's public image, to fully appreciate the production and consumption of his presidential performance requires an investigation of the genealogy of his public voice. The presidential character Michael Rogin identifies as *"Ronald Reagan,* the image that has fixed our gaze," began his career in public life on the radio as a disembodied voice.[2] Garry Wills makes a convincing case that:

> Reagan's use of his voice has been his most valuable professional skill. It took him into radio. It gave dignity to his movie appearances even when his body was stiff and unconvincing. He played a radio announcer in his first two films, and in two more over the next year. . . . In the Air Force he was the narrator of training films. . . . On television, he was host and announcer. . . . He acted as master of ceremonies for a nightclub act in Las Vegas and for charitable and civic banquets. As an elected official his speeches were the high point of his campaigns and administrations. After his retirement as governor, his voice was on the air with syndicated political opinion five times a week for five years.[3]

From the time he began his career in radio in 1933 through the end of his presidency in 1989, Ronald Reagan earned his living and hailed his audience through the public use of his voice, the primary instrument for articulating his embodiment of American identity.

The story I pursue in this chapter is the vocal development of the screaming infant into "the Great Communicator." To assess the relationship between Reagan's voice and public image I listen to what Roland Barthes calls "the grain of the voice." In defining the "grain," Barthes distinguishes between the *pheno-song* and the *geno-song*. The former operates at the level of communication, representation of feelings, expression, while the latter "has us hear a body which has no civil identity, no 'personality,' but which is nevertheless a separate body. Above all this voice bears along *directly* the symbolic, over the intelligible."[4] Wills's assessment of the significance of Reagan's voice is a testament to his mastery of the pheno-song. Here, however, I am more interested in Reagan's use of the geno-song and the clarion call it sounded for the Reagan Revolution. According to Barthes, the response the geno-song elicits from its audience is individual but not "'subjective' (it is not the psychological subject in me that is listening)."[5] But Barthes also emphasizes that the symbolic realm articulated by the grain is not cultural per se. The grain of the voice functions as a mediating term that, like behavioral psychology's conception of *affect*, inhabits the liminal space between cognition and behavior, between something experienced and the formulation of a reaction to that experience. In this middle ground belief supersedes reason and affective investments trump or precede ideological affiliations.

Crucial to an appreciation of the grain of Reagan's voice is that the symbolic body sounded by the geno-song is constituted by affective stimulus rather than ideological interpellation. The geno-song does not carry an ideological message. It captivates by stimulating the same affective investments that authorize political actors to speak in our stead, act in our name, and situate us in relation to an abstract entity such as a nation. In this regard, politicians and cultural performers play a shared role in representing the body politic and articulating what the nineteenth-century actor and elocutionist James E. Murdoch called "the national voice."[6] Both championed and attacked as the most ideological of presidents, the appeal of Ronald Reagan's presidential character derived instead from the capacity to inspire powerful affective investments capable of generating the symbolic currency that underwrote the Reagan Revolution.

By the time Reagan became president, nearly half a century after he began working in electronic media, his voice was hardwired into the American psyche. Listening to Reagan address the 1980 Republican National Convention, the novelist Robert Stone observed that "it is not entirely facetious to speak of his voice as dear and familiar." What caught Stone's ear was not the words Reagan spoke but the music he produced through the grain of his voice and the effect it had on his audience: "He was giving the assembled delegates and their guests enormous pleasure, making them laugh, bringing them to their feet with fierce patriotic cries, and occasionally bringing them to tears . . . [through] a happy mating of *ursprache* and muzak." Listening to Reagan, Stone concluded that what he heard was "the voice of the electronic age . . . the voice of American popular culture."[7] How the new culture of performance shaped the voice of the body electric is the subject of this chapter.

On the eve of the 1964 presidential election, Ronald Reagan gave a nationally televised address in support of Barry Goldwater's candidacy. What would come to be referred to simply as "The Speech," launched Reagan's political career. The journalist David Broder described it as "the most successful national political debut since William Jennings Bryan electrified the 1896 Democratic convention with the 'Cross of Gold' speech."[8] In comparing Reagan to Bryan, Broder was situating Reagan within a rhetorical tradition that has always played a seminal role in defining the governmentality of the United States. When Reagan told his audience that in the battle against totalitarianism it had "a rendezvous with destiny," he was invoking the memory of Franklin Roosevelt, who at the Democratic National Convention in 1936 had used the very same trope to inspire his audience to stand firm against the tyranny of "economic royalists" in "a war for the survival of democracy." Whether exhorting an audience of citizens to resist the Soviet Bear, unfettered capitalism, or crucifixion on a cross of gold, the formative rendezvous invoked by the orator is the Puritan errand in the wilderness.

In his writings on Puritan rhetoric, Sacvan Bercovitch proposes that the ability of protonationalists such as John Winthrop and Cotton Mather to convince the faithful to enact their sacred destiny was due in large part to the language they employed to generate consensus for the ideology of American Exceptionalism. The *expression* of their faith, Bercovitch argues, was so critical to the Puritan mission that the foundational basis of their "America" was neither religious nor institutional. It is in the utopian rhetoric of the Puritans that Bercovitch locates their contribution to the coherence and perpetuation of "the idea of America." Puritan oratory—what Bercovitch characterizes as "the music of America"—achieves its affective force in the "realm of symbology" by forming and performing "a compelling fantasy of American identity." As an audible representation of both ideology and utopia, of assimilation and dissent, Puritan oratory paradoxically harmonized these seemingly dissonant strains by sounding them together within the "symbolic *field* that is 'America.'"[9]

The journalist Nicholas Lemann heard the same music watching Reagan initiate his rendezvous with destiny on television over three centuries later: "If you were then an American inclined in your heart and mind to think of yourself as a conservative, and you saw [the speech], it stayed with you—not the precise words, but the feeling and the message, they were impossible to forget."[10] Sounding the music of the new conservatism, Reagan, like the Puritans, gave an oratorical performance that underscored the capacity of language to do more than merely connote its referent. Reagan's speech—which he continued to give in various incarnations through the end of his presidency—exemplifies the performative role spoken language has played historically in constituting the imagination and the national subject. Christopher Looby, acknowledging that all nations "are made, ineluctably, in language," notes that the unprecedented conditions of American nation building placed a particular stress on the performative capacity of the spoken word: "Precisely because the new nation's self-image was characterized by its difference from a traditional (quasi-natural) conception of the nation, indeed by the conscious recognition of its historical contingency that was produced by the abrupt performativity of its inception, vocal utterance has served, in telling instances, as a privileged figure for the making of the United States." Reading a representative sample of eighteenth-century texts, Looby finds an abiding preoccupation with the way, as James Wilson expressed it in 1793, "Republican America was spoken into existence."[11]

The political imperative to speak the nation into existence was addressed by a new elocutionary ideal that, in contrast to classical rhetoric's stress on the construction of logical arguments, emphasized the performative aspect of speech. In his *Lectures on Elocution* (1762), Thomas Sheridan, the self-professed founder of the English elocutionary movement, declared, "Our greatest men have been trying to do that with the pen, which can only be performed by the tongue; to produce effects by the dead letter which can never be produced but by the living voice, with its accompaniments"[12] Sheridan's rejection of "the dead letter" as a vehicle for social and political reform is emblematic of a new understanding of rhetoric predicated on the performative act of declaring independence from a subjugation and subjectivity enforced as much by the King's English as by the king's army. "True eloquence," advised James Burgh in *The Art of Speaking* (1764), would elevate the "tongue of the orator" to a position on a par with "the *sceptre* of the monarch."[13] In the founding ideology of the new republic, the tongue—the orator's instrument of affective persuasion—was capable of generating political symbols for a new body politic as powerful as the one the scepter—the material sign of the monarch's ruling authority—represented for the body it signified. To acquire the vocal "accompaniments" to which Sheridan referred, and that elocutionary manuals stressed in the exercises they prescribed, elocutionists called for rigorous physical training in a newly codified language of gesture, a semiotics of the body that would visually engage an audience's passions. The primary model for this body language was the theater, invoked not simply as a metaphor for governance but as a training ground for government, a laboratory for the development of effective methods for teaching the conduct of conduct.

In his first career, as actor-manager of the Dublin Theater, Sheridan, the father of playwright Richard Brinsley Sheridan, was a theatrical reformer who strove to discipline the unruly behavior of theater audiences and actors alike. Addressing the problem of rowdy audiences by removing them from the stage and insisting they refrain from throwing food at the actors and attend to the play, he also compelled his actors to learn their lines, enter and exit on cue, and stick to the script.[14] On retiring from the stage in 1757, Sheridan attempted to form an academy with an educational philosophy derived from his theatrical practice. His proposal to potential subscribers "suggested that a proper theater might supply helps to

the right kind of educational institution."[15] Polite Dublin society was outraged by the idea of entrusting their children's education to theater
people, and Sheridan was forced to flee to England to pursue his pedagogical vision. There, in a series of books devoted to reforming the British
education system, he disseminated his method in which the theater
bandmaster would serve as music instructor, the scene designer as drawing master, and the actor as the model of eloquence.[16] Sheridan's association with the theater doomed his attempts to establish an academic institution that would transform British education. However, his elocutionary
tracts, which were widely read in the colonies, influenced a generation of
American revolutionaries struggling to define a new language capable of
expressing a vision of Lockean liberalism sufficiently compelling to establish a new nation. Sheridan's writings served as a user's guide for American revolutionaries by addressing what he believed Locke had left out in
his treatment of language: "The nobler branch of language, which consists of the signs of internal emotions."[17]

While Sheridan's elocutionary ideals were fashioned from a pedagogy
based on his training in the theater, Burgh's interest in elocution
stemmed directly from his prior involvement in politics. As a Scottish
Presbyterian living in England, Burgh could not hold political office, but
his eclectic political interests made him an activist for election reform, relief for the poor, and opposition to colonial taxation. Through the
influence of his writings, Burgh became, in Isaac Kramnick's estimation,
"literally the schoolmaster for a whole generation of bourgeois radicals."[18]
Burgh's contribution to eighteenth-century educational reform also included running an academy near London that, in addition to "practical"
professional training, provided instruction in modern languages, history,
and elocution, an education Kramnick characterizes as providing "a
preparation peculiarly appropriate for the new age."[19] The connecting
thread Kramnick identifies in Burgh's instructional writings, pitched to a
bourgeoisie aspiring to enter the still "closed world of rank, privilege, and
power," was his insistence on "a thoroughly Protestant regimen of individual improvement and achievement through rigorous management of
the self."[20] Like Sheridan, Burgh turned to the theater as inspiration for an
education capable of teaching the tools required for both self-manage-
ment and self-expression. The fact that as a young man he had equated
"playhouse culture" with "idleness, gluttony, drunkenness, lewdness,

gaming" makes it all the more remarkable that three decades later, as an advocate of the new elocution, he lists theater among the entertainments "a set of able statesmen might make use [of] in reforming and improving" public manners.[21]

Reagan's nationally televised political debut in 1964 harkened back to Burgh and Sheridan's vision of a social education rooted in the techne of acting and elocution. From the inception of the republic, the crafting of a national identity has been intimately linked to the imperatives of natural theatricality and its paradoxical embrace of a studied spontaneity. Paul Edwards points out that elocutionary manuals enjoyed a prominent place in the libraries of so many American revolutionaries for the same reasons that "books on net surfing, web-page construction, and 'Windows for Dummies' belong in the libraries of communications-savvy politicians (or their staffers) at the end of the twentieth century. The oratorically extended body of the revolutionary era, like the cybernetically extended body of our own, was a major communications technology."[22] From the birth of the republic the body of the actor has modeled the kind of body required for the exercise of power. As Edwards points out, the more than a dozen pages in *The Art of Speaking* that describe how an orator should visually and aurally render the emotional content of a speech in order to engage the passions of an audience are not drawn from books on rhetoric but from Burgh's observations of David Garrick's legendary performance in *Hamlet*.[23] While the actor was not yet ready to join the world of rank, privilege, and power, through the teachings of the new elocution performers influenced those who would transform that world by teaching them a new language of representation.

Scratching the Crystal

> You know—none of the developments that came after, talkies, and television and so forth, were ever such a revelation as that day I first scratched that crystal with a wire whisker, under the bridge at Dixon.
>
> —Ronald Reagan, quoted in Edmond Morris, *Dutch*

Before the movies, before television, Ronald Reagan's training in the body electric commenced with radio. The nine-year-old's epiphany under the Galena Avenue bridge in Dixon derived from the same source as Henry

Adams's in the Gallery of Machines: the occult and fetish power generated by the fiat of electricity. Until the day he tuned in "The Skater's Waltz" on a borrowed crystal rectifier, Reagan's only experience of transmitted sound had been via the telegraph or telephone. "Now," as his biographer Edmond Morris describes it, "through some magic trembling of the ether, what was distant and strange became near and familiar; the invisible became the audible."[24] Years later, in words that echoed Mugs's description of performance as an excellent substitute for experience, Reagan would recall how radio's "magic" enchanted him, transporting him "to glamorous locales around the world" by engaging his imagination through a "theater of the mind."[25] Radio gave the young Dutch Reagan access to the world beyond Dixon, just as on graduation from Eureka College it would provide his ticket out of Dixon, and five years later his entrée to Hollywood. Radio is also where he began to develop the grain of his voice.

In retrospect, perhaps the most remarkable thing about radio is that it was so unexpected. In contrast to the much anticipated arrivals of the movies and television, radio burst on the American scene with little warning. The scientific groundwork for making the invisible audible was laid as early as the 1860s by James Clerk Maxwell's study of electromagnetic waves, but it wasn't until 1897 that Guglielmo Marconi developed the first commercially viable application of radiotelegraphy. In 1900, while Henry Adams was in Paris marveling at the mechanical force of the dynamo, Marconi was in Britain patenting a tuning dial that enabled radio reception to distinguish signals at different frequencies. While hardly the restoration of unity Adams was searching for, the tuning dial was one of the first of a series of technological innovations that channeled the forces of multiplicity unleashed by the new century's insatiable appetite for electricity. Marconi's Wireless Telegraph and Signal Company soon succeeded in communicating across the Atlantic, and until the end of World War I, following Marconi's example, technological innovations in radio were largely focused on improving its capabilities as a wireless telegraph and telephone.

The application of wireless telegraphy as an extension of the telegraph to places unreachable by wire was readily apparent. Until World War I ended, however, almost nobody perceived the possibilities of radio as a broadcast medium. In the early years of the twentieth century, broadcasting in the United States was still a cult phenomenon, a hobby practiced by a handful of radio enthusiasts. As the media historian Paul Starr relates, it took a fortuitous encounter between a Westinghouse vice president and a department store advertisement for radio sets to generate the conceptual realization that a consumer market for radio receivers could be created if broadcasting became a regular service.[26] By most accounts it was Westinghouse's station KDKA in Pittsburgh that initiated the radio boom on 2 November 1920 when it broadcast the results of the presidential election.

It was KDKA that first caught Dutch Reagan's ear the following year, and it was tuned to KDKA that he first began to experiment with radio announcing. Reagan's parents did not own a crystal set, but his aunt and uncle, whom they visited at Christmastime on their farm near Morrison, Illinois, did. There, Reagan would recall, with "breathless attention, a pair of earphones attached tightly to my head, scratching a crystal with a wire," he listened to "raspy recorded music and faint voices saying, 'This is KDKA, Pittsburgh, KDKA, Pittsburgh.'" When the signal became too faint, he rose and, in front of a roomful of people, mimicked the announcer. When everyone laughed, he repeated the performance.[27] While the Christian Church gave the young Reagan his first public stage, it was radio that encouraged him to imagine a world beyond Dixon, aspire to be a part of it, and provided the opportunity to do so.

Almost overnight, radio—which, like Chautauqua and the movies, was a national media that did not rely on a literate audience—redefined the scope and impact of mass cultural forms through an aural medium that transformed the role of what Arjun Appadurai has called "the imagination as a social practice."[28] Even those who could not afford to buy their own set could easily build a receiver, as Moon Reagan did, by winding copper wire around a round oatmeal box and attaching a slide bar. Moon also built a shortwave Morse code transmitter with which he conducted conversations with a friend across town. "It didn't mean anything," he recalled years later, "but we thought we were on the same list as Marconi and the rest of the great brains who brought radio into existence."[29] As it did for the future president, radio would provide Neil Reagan's livelihood during the Depression and his initiation into the new class of mass-mediated dream merchants who would define the American Century. After graduating from Eureka College, Moon visited Dutch, who by that time was working at the station WHO in Des Moines. With his brother's help, Moon landed a regular Friday night slot in which the Reagan brothers predicted the outcome of Saturday's college football games. Eventually Moon became an announcer and then the program director at WHO. Later, having followed his brother to Los Angeles, he became a director, producer, network executive, and ultimately a vice president at McCann-Erickson, one of the largest advertising agencies in the country. It was in that capacity that he was able to repay Dutch by hiring him as a replacement for the Old Ranger on television's *Death Valley Days* in 1964.[30]

Although Chautauqua would not survive the rapid dissemination of radio in the late 1920s, its spirit flourished atavistically within radio's new circuits. Like Chautauqua, early radio offered an eclectic mix of cultural education, information, and entertainment, exposing families outside the cultural mainstream to the new world emerging from the fiat of electricity and stimulating their desire to be a part of it. In the living room, the car, or the barbershop, radio linked disparate audiences through broadcasts of news, sporting events, political speeches, and audio versions of the same performances that appeared on the Chautauqua stage. Capable of updating its content more rapidly and efficiently than either Chautauqua or print media, radio cannibalized the extant performance forms of popular culture to provide an inexhaustible supply of new stories and characters to imitate and emulate. Serializing these forms like the magazines did with novels, radio became a part of Americans' daily routine. By the 1930s, the most popular shows were cultural touchstones, and radio stars were as familiar to their listeners as their own families. "When 'Amos and Andy' came on the air," Reagan recounts in his autobiography, "the whole world stopped. If you were at a movie theater, they'd shut off the projector, turn on the lights, and a radio set would be placed on the stage while everybody sat quietly in their seats for a half hour listening to the latest episode."[31] As the number of sets sold and stations licensed increased, so did the variety of programming, and the radio became part of the common cultural language.

Woody Allen's *Radio Days*—a Reagan era film that situates the formative origins of electronic media's impact on social life in early radio—humorously captures the ways in which radio taught Americans what to think, dream, and feel about their lives. *Radio Days* demonstrates how quickly radio programming in the United States varied its content to appeal to every segment of the population and how its pervasiveness colored the events and memories of the day. Allen's narrator describes a childhood in Rockaway, Queens, in which every member of his extended family had an intimate relationship with radio. His father, a failure at business, fantasizes about striking it rich on a quiz show; radio's bastardized version of the immigrant ideal of education as the quickest route to assimilation and wealth. His mother represses their poverty and indulges her goyische fantasies of sophistication and upward mobility by listening to *Breakfast with Roger and Irene* and fantasizing about a world in which witty repartee is carried out in palmy diction by men and women clothed in peignoirs and silk robes. Uncle Abe's favorite program is *Bill Kern's Sports Legends,* which profiles athletes such as Kirby Kyle, a one-legged, one-armed, blind pitcher with "lots of heart" who after being run over by a car was able to win eighteen games in "the big league in the sky." Dotty Aunt Ceil listens to ventriloquists while love-starved Aunt Bea's big date with Mr. Manulis ends in disaster when his car "runs out of gas" on Breezy Point. Just as Manulis begins to make his move, the seduction music on his car radio is interrupted by Orson Welles's infamous broadcast of *The War of the Worlds*. Manulis runs screaming from the car, abandoning Bea to walk home alone seven miles in the fog.

The only character who realizes her radio-fueled dream of deliverance from Brooklyn is the starstruck Sally White. After several unsuccessful attempts to seduce her way into radio, "the voice of God" advises her to take diction lessons to improve her voice and prospects. Making the vocal and social leap from Canarsie to upper Manhattan, Sally lands her own gossip show, *Sally White and the Gay White Way.* It is by speaking rather than sleeping her way to the top that Sally punches her ticket to radioland.

The Theology of the Ether

After graduating from Eureka College, Ronald Reagan—who, like Sally White, was convinced that a job in radio was more attainable than a movie career—set out to speak his way to a better life. The voice that first spoke to Reagan as he scratched the crystal under the bridge in Dixon, Illinois, assumed a new intimacy in Davenport, Iowa, in 1933. It was there that he landed his first job as a radio announcer. The man who hired him was Pete MacArthur, the station manager and top announcer at WOC. MacArthur, a vaudeville and music hall veteran with a Scottish burr, had arrived in Davenport to seek relief from crippling arthritis that required him to be lifted from a wheelchair in order to walk with the assistance of two canes. Davenport's Palmer School of Chiropractic had not eased his pain, but its radio station had provided a job that made MacArthur the most familiar voice in the region.

The impresario of WOC was Col. Bartlett Joshua Palmer, who in one of his many self-published books billed himself as "B. J. of Davenport— philosopher, scientist, artist, builder, hobbyist, musician, author, lecturer, publisher, art connoisseur—a little bit of a moral human being whom In- nate Intelligence developed."[32] B. J.'s eclectic interests and moral philoso- phy derived from his father, D. D. Palmer, who is often credited as the founder of chiropractic medicine. At the end of the nineteenth century, D. D. fell under the thrall of vitalism and mesmerism, two of the most influential spiritual schools of the early electrical era. He became a mag- netic healer, and subsequently founded the Palmer School of Chiroprac- tic, one of the first chiropractic schools in the United States. Following in his father's footsteps, B. J. became a key figure in the development of the science of chiropractic and an adherent of an educational philosophy that rejected the theological and scientific tenets of Adams's eighteenth- century education in favor of a material and spiritual training focused on the body electric.

Under B. J.'s leadership, the Palmer School's chiropractic training fea- tured an eclectic blend of pioneering technology and new age spiritualism. One of the first practitioners to use X-rays in chiropractic, B. J. also swore by the curative powers of the "INNATE." Rejecting the "so-called 'sci- entific'" medical profession's conception of sickness as the invasion of the body by an external disease and its emphasis on treatment of disease through medicine—which he called "medi-sin"—B. J. viewed sickness as an internal state of mind and promoted the development of INNATE IN- TELLIGENCE as the key to a healthy body through the cultivation of a healthy mind. An "individualized portion of the All-Wise usually known as spirit," the INNATE was "the same capable INNER VOICE that is capable of getting any sick organ well."[33] He taught that healthy-mindedness, was the direct result of learning the language of one's inner voice. Espousing a vitalist model of human biology in which electrical impulses originating in the brain were conducted by the nerves throughout the body, he held that what he termed "dis-ease" was the result of pressure exerted on the nerves that interrupted the transmission of electrical currents from the INNATE BRAIN to the EDUCATED BRAIN. Crediting innate intelligence rather than formal education for his moral and spiritual development, B. J.—like Mugs—rejected the pedagogical model of a fact-based education, which he described as "the thing you get from outside and put inside; the thing somebody else has thought; the thing some-body else tells you, has put into print for you to read; something somebody else shows you."[34] B. J.'s disdain for conventional education was summarized in one of the many wall legends that decorated the "World of Chiropractic" compound: "THE HIGHEST MERIT WE ASCRIBE TO MOSES, PLATO AND MILTON IS THAT THEY SET AT NAUGHT BOOKS AND TRADITION."[35]

B. J.'s beliefs situated him within a therapeutic movement that began to take shape after the Civil War in response to the widespread diagnosis of a new affliction that was affecting the American psyche, an illness that struck at the heart of the national character as well as individual bodies. This movement, dubbed "mind cure" by William James in 1899 and cited by him as America's "only decidedly original contribution to the systematic philosophy of life," was propagated by an eclectic assortment of social scientists and medical and religious figures, many of whom rejected the appellation.[36] What connected them all as practitioners of mind cure—and connected them to Adams's belief that the modern world could not be comprehended through antiquated epistemologies—was the perception that modern civilization had introduced a new disease that medical science and religious theology were equally ill-equipped to address. In *American Nervousness* (1881), the neurologist George Beard diagnosed this new illness as a neurological affliction, a weakening of the nerves induced by modern society. To explain the pathology of neurasthenia, Beard employed a favorite analogy of nineteenth-century neurology, Edison's electric light. "The force in the nervous system can," he wrote, "be increased or diminished by good or evil influences . . . but nonetheless it is limited; and when new functions are interposed in the circuit, as modern civilization is constantly requiring us to do, there comes a period sooner or later, varying in different individuals, and at different times of life, when the amount of force is insufficient to keep all the lamps actively burning; those that are weakest go out entirely, or, as more frequently happens, burn faint and feebly—they do not expire, but give an insufficient and unstable light—this is the philosophy of modern nervousness."[37]

While Adams's response to the inadequacy of theology and science to illuminate the modern world was to call for a new education, B. J.'s diagnosis for the overloading of circuits that led to American nervousness was his "Hole in One" theory, which addressed "dis-ease" by aligning the upper three cervical vertebrae and restoring the continuous flow of current through the body.[38] His Barnumesque promotion of "the chiropractic Fountainhead" suggests that modernity—at least in Iowa in the 1930s— was a capacious movement that encompassed science and magic, reason and belief, and was powered by an abiding faith in the spiritual and material benefits of commerce.

Perhaps the most significant lesson Ronald Reagan learned from B. J. Palmer was that the skill set required to exploit the new technologies and social relations of modern capitalism were those of the somnipractor, Garry Wills's moniker for people like B. J and the Reagan brothers, who were "salesman, advertisers, product spokesmen. The arrangers of others' dreams."[39] Somnipractors are the magicians and metaphysicians of salesmanship—tent show hucksters and Madison Avenue pinstripes, picture people and public relations impresarios, stage and state crafters. They work in film, television, radio, advertising, public relations, politics, and in church, and as the twentieth century unfolded they were increasingly (to paraphrase the movie trailer) appearing soon at a theater, on a television, or in a pulpit near you. Somnipractors are the dream merchants of the age of mechanical reproduction. They are image makers, maestros of the moving picture and the artful sound bite, wizards of the "optical unconscious" (Walter Benjamin's term for the new "physiognomic aspects of visual worlds" revealed by the still and motion picture camera).[40] Somnipractors were the adepts of the new technologies that retooled the mimetic faculty and underwrote the new mimetic economy of mechanical reproduction.

It was while working for B. J. Palmer that Reagan first came to appreciate the power of somnipractic. Fired from his job at WOC for forgetting to mention that his radio broadcast of *Drink to Me Only with Thine Eyes* was sponsored by a local mortuary, Reagan reproached Pete MacArthur for not having given him proper training, was reinstated, and never forgot the lesson.

The disillusioned deputy White House press secretary Lesley Janka, who resigned in protest when the press was excluded from the Grenada invasion, identified the lesson learned in his appraisal of the Reagan administration's approach to governance: "The whole thing was PR [public relations]. This was a PR outfit that became president and took over the country. And to the degree then to which the Constitution forced them to do things like make a budget, run foreign policy and all that, they sort of did. But their first, last, and overarching activity was public relations."[41] In the domain of the somnipractor it was all about developing product lines and figuring out how to pitch them. Sitting in a budget communications meeting in March 1981, Reagan speechwriter Ken Khachigian stopped doodling long enough to jot down a terse note: "need a sales manual for this campaign." As president, a few months prior to the 1984 Republican convention, Reagan popped his head into the first meeting of his campaign advertisers to announce, "Since you're the ones who are selling the soap, I thought you'd like to see the bar."[42] Ronald Reagan held many jobs but nary a one that did not emphasize somnipracty. In the words of one longtime observer, he "took advertising far more seriously than he took himself."[43] If, as Michael Rogin suggests, "the idol of consumption is the salesman or the object he sells," then surely Reagan qualifies on both counts; his career and his presidency testify to his ability to play either role.[44] During the Reagan presidency the relationship between political and cultural representation, the performance of politics and the politics of performance, was transformed by a student of the somnipractic arts of mechanical reproduction.

Equipped "with a genius for promotion and an abiding interest in its techniques,"[45] B. J. Palmer was the first in a long line of somnipractors to whom Reagan hitched his star, and it was somnipracty, not chiropracty, that made Reagan an adherent of the healing powers of mind cure. In addition to the school and radio station, B. J.'s entrepreneurial ventures included a newspaper, printing press, roller rink, dance hall, root beer stand, "cowboy lounge," and insane asylum. On the grounds of his estate, which connected his home and his commercial complex, he built "A Little Bit O'Heaven," an oriental garden complete with alligators and furnished with the worldly treasures he had collected on his extensive travels, including a Buddhist shrine, a Japanese temple gate, and Greek statues. The fifty-cent admission fee, like the radio station, helped subsidize the cost of the school.[46] B. J.'s cottage empire was a miniaturized vision of where the culture industry was heading. The roller rink, root beer stand, cowboy lounge, and Little Bit O'Heaven would achieve their corporate apogee in video arcades, shopping malls, fast food franchises, and theme parks.

The Palmer School of Chiropracty dispensed rational scientific instruction and Mississippi River tent show hucksterism in equal measure, combining old-style faith healing and newfangled medicine in a syncretic blend of nature and technology, science and magic, that anticipated many contemporary New Age practices. B. J.'s model of human biology, in which the unimpeded flow of electrical currents throughout the body ensured efficient interaction among the vital organs, informed the management of his business empire. The media operation was its core holding, functioning (as it would today in our era of hyperdiversified corporate conglomerates) as the means of promoting, advertising and integrating the various lines of business generated by the incessant boom of cultural production under capitalism. Just as he slept with his head facing the North Pole to ensure that the Earth's currents would flow through him, B. J. oriented his empire around its electronic head, wiring the various organs of his commercial body to the radio station perched on the roof of the school. Radio programs were broadcast in the classrooms, and chiropractic lectures aired on the station. School band concerts, broadcast from the studio, were piped into the auditorium, where B. J. charged admission for dancing.

B. J.'s belief in electricity as a vital life force was reflected in his understanding of radio as a communications technology. Having purchased station WOC of Rock Island, Illinois, in 1922, he moved it to Davenport and employed its call letters to trumpet the "Wonders of Chiropractic." It was the first commercial broadcasting station in Iowa and likely the first station licensed west of the Mississippi River. B. J. boasted that the station was the "strongest, loudest, and clearest radio-phone installation in America," that its signal had been picked up in Stockholm, Paris, Rome, and Manila, and that members of the North Pole expedition of 1923 listened regularly. He held that the remarkable distances reached by WOC's signal resulted from its grounding in the city's water mains, which emptied into the Mississippi River. "Many now believe that the ground is the real antenna and that the air antenna is the counterpoise. If that is true," he boasted, "then WOC has the best possible antenna, miles long and plenty wide."[47] Conflating the river's storied history of transmission and communication with that of his powerful new antenna, B. J.'s explanation of the strength of WOC's signal is an exemplary expression of the quasi-mystical vision of radio's earliest adherents. Like mesmerism, vitalism, chiropractic, and other nascent forms of the body electric, early radio was a hybrid medium that combined the folkways of a still largely rural society and an emergent modernism that trumpeted the promise of Adams' unholy trinity of corporate capitalism, mechanical science, and mass culture.

The imperative to mitigate the potential anxiety produced by a box of wires from which emanated a disembodied voice was addressed in part by the metaphor adopted for radio transmission—*broadcasting*—borrowed from a farming term for scattering seeds across a field. The station's sign-off captured early broadcasting's complex relationship to modernity.

> This is station WOC, owned and operated by the Palmer School of Chiropractic, the Chiropractic Fountainhead, Davenport, Iowa, where the West begins, and in the state where the tall corn grows, broadcasting by the authority of the Federal Radio Commission, using a frequency of 1000 kilocycles, signing off at exactly five seconds of twelve o'clock, Central Standard Time. Good Night.[48]

The invocation of a new and powerful technology ("using a frequency of 1000 kilocycles") with its scientifically precise temporality ("signing off at exactly five seconds of twelve o'clock, Central Standard Time") is married to the mythic geography of the Midwest as both America's abundant breadbasket ("the state where the tall corn grows") and the crossover point from the old world to the new ("where the West begins"). Here radio functions as a chronotopic technology. Time thickens into the mobile space of its reception. Space stretches back in time to the memory of the frontier and forward to the promise of the promontories to be scaled by science and technology.

It was at WOC that Reagan began his training as a somnipractor. The medical profession's hostility toward chiropractic had not diminished much since B. J.'s father was arrested for practicing medicine without a license in 1904. In B. J.'s estimation this necessitated operating the Palmer School on a business rather than professional model. He taught his students that chiropractic healing was a "life BUYING objective for the sick" and a "health SELLING objective" for the chiropractor. "We manufacture chiropractors," B. J. boasted, and the school offered a course in salesmanship in addition to chiropractic training.[49] If in the 1920s, as Anne Edwards proposes, "salesmanship was one of the greatest of the performing arts," then advertising provided cutting-edge training for the salesman as performance artist.[50] "Only the mints can make money without advertising," B. J. declared in one of his many maxims on the subject, and radio, he assured his students, was the future of advertising. What Paul Starr terms the "constitutive choices" that determined the material and institutional framework of radio—retaining the airwaves in public ownership and creating a licensing system for use by private broadcasters—had ensured that "the system created was overwhelmingly commercial, dependent on advertising revenue, and driven by competition for listeners."[51] By the time Reagan began working at WOC, the comedian Red Skelton was already satirizing the pervasiveness of advertising on the radio, informing his audiences that "the single longest word in the English language is as follows: 'And now a word from our sponsors.'"[52]

B. J. was not alone in his conviction that electricity was the key to unclogging the circuits of industry and that radio was the best medium for doing so. In addition to its obvious benefits as a communications technology, radio provided access to a realm that philosophers, scientists, and theologians had long speculated about, what one of radio's inventors described as "the invisible empire of the air."[53] Early proponents of radio expressed the belief that it rendered the invisible audible by channeling the fourth dimension, which—until the popularization of Einstein's theories reconceived it as time—was thought to be a "higher space, quite real, yet existing invisibly in relation to our three-dimensional world somewhat as the cube relates to the two dimensional square."[54] In *Broadcast Advertising: The Fourth Dimension* (1931), Frank Arnold, head of development at the National Broadcasting Company (NBC), touted radio as an unparalleled advertising technology by virtue of its capacity for tapping the commercial potential of the fourth dimension. The solely visible medium of newspapers, magazines, and billboards, he argued, limited advertising's ability to sway the consumer, but then came radio broadcasting, which utilized the very air we breathe, and "with electricity as its vehicle [it] enter[ed] the homes of the nation through doors and windows, no matter how tightly barred. . . . For the first time in the history of mankind, this dream of the centuries found its realization."[55] Echoing Arnold, the chairman of Westinghouse declared broadcast advertising to be "modernity's medium of business expression," the medium that "made industry articulate."[56] Radio projected the inner voice of corporate capitalism into the domestic sphere, and advertising made it irresistible.

By his own account, it was the advertising part of the job that gave Reagan the most difficulty at first. He had been hired on the basis of his ability to make the invisible audible by improvising an account of a football game that successfully met Pete MacArthur's mandate to make him *see* the game as if he were at the stadium listening to the radio. As a staff announcer, however, he proved less successful working from prepared scripts. Reagan's initial attempts to read advertising copy resulted in what he described as "a delivery as wooden as a prairie oak." Fired for omitting the plug for the mortuary that sponsored his show, Reagan complained to MacArthur that his "on-air bumbling" and ignorance of the importance of advertising was due to lack of instruction. Given a second chance, he would never again underestimate the importance of vocal technique or the seminal role of advertising in his professional success in electronic media or politics. With the help of "a crash course on radio announcing," he improved his skills by "reading over the commercials before airtime" and practicing his delivery "to get the right rhythm and cadence and give my words more emotion."[57] "Smile your voice," B. J. coached his employees, a lesson Reagan learned well enough to be promoted to WHO, the NBC affiliate in Des Moines, when B .J. acquired the station shortly after Reagan began working for him.[58]

In Des Moines, Reagan joined the "Advertising Club," where he supplemented his broadcasting training at talks given by guest speakers at the club's "gridiron" lunches. The impression these speeches made on Reagan is evidenced by his detailed reenactment for Edmond Morris a half century later of one of the "routines" he remembered. Employing the inflated rhetoric of 1930s advertising with its exaggerated claims for the products it promoted, Reagan extolled the virtues of "Boffo" toilet paper. "You've heard about the Harvard Classics and the shelf of books of learning for fifteen minutes a day toward college education. Boffo does a college course printed on every roll." For less refined and more practical readers, Boffo's seven pastel shades also offered "the 'Boffo Thrillers,' with a detective story and a climax guaranteed to do away with compound cathartics."[59] Promoting Boffo as a delivery system for the benefits of cultural uplift and entertainment, the speech mimics in a satirical vein the principal claim Chautauqua made for its circuit and that advertisers were making for their profession. To distinguish themselves from the nineteenth-century hucksters and con artists to which they were inevitably compared, Depression era advertisers portrayed themselves as consumer educators, as essential a component of the utopian promise of consumer capitalism as a Harvard education or the entertainments of popular culture. In a society that had learned to efficiently produce vast amounts of consumer goods, advertising was also a form of business insurance; a means of minimizing the risks of overproduction by stimulating the desire for and modeling the behavior of a consumer ethos that would guarantee a profitable and efficient market for these goods. Addressing the American Association of Advertising Agencies in 1926, President Calvin Coolidge praised the pastoral role of advertising. As the church ministers to the soul, and government to human conduct, so advertising, he explained, "ministers to the spiritual side of trade."[60]

The Dead Wire

The grain of Reagan's public voice begins to develop during his early years in radio. Growing up, Neil Reagan had been fascinated by the science of radio. Dutch had always been more interested in the sports announcers. Sports played a significant role in Reagan's childhood. He was an accomplished swimmer who had gained his first taste of celebrity for pulling seventy-seven swimmers out of the Rock River while working as a lifeguard for seven summers at Dixon's Lowell Park. As an avid reader and moviegoer, his favorite genres featured athletic heroes who—as he wrote for the *Eureka Progress* in his enthusiastic review of movie cliffhangers starring sports figures such as Babe Ruth, Jack Dempsey, and Red Grange—"strutted, grimaced, thrashed the villains, kissed the heroines and, not incidentally, showed off their athletic prowess." Among Reagan's favorite books were those in Burt L. Standish's Frank Merriwell series, many of which he checked out more than once from the Dixon Library. Merriwell was, as his name suggests, a candid, happy, and healthy youth, a Yale-educated football star whose combination of brains and brawn inevitably led him to overcome adversity, foil evildoers, and get the girl.[61]

In high school the short and skinny boy grew enough to become the starting offensive tackle on the varsity football team. Reagan's passion for football, and his belief in its capacity for character building, owed a great deal to the literary and cinematic heroes whose personality traits and adventurous exploits were embodied by Garland Waggoner, Dixon's own Frank Merriwell. Reagan attributes his early interest in football to his "hero worship" of Waggoner, "the husky son of one of the ministers who preceded Margaret's father at our church." Waggoner was the star fullback of the Dixon High School football team and subsequently at Eureka College, where he became "an even bigger football celebrity." Mugs and Waggoner were the principal reasons why Dutch ended up at Eureka. In later years, Reagan would attribute his decision to attend college not to a "burning desire" to get an education but in Merriwellian terms, because of his "love for a pretty girl and a love for football."[62]

In his various accounts of the education he received at Eureka, Reagan barely mentions academics. "I've been accused of majoring in extracurricular activities at Eureka," he was fond of saying, and "[my] principal academic ambition was to maintain the C average I needed to remain eligible for football, swimming, track, and the school activities I participated in."[63] When he contemplated dropping out after his freshman year, it was a partial scholarship orchestrated by the football coach, Mac McKinzie, that enabled him to stay. He justified McKinzie's faith in him by earning a starting position on the team. Upon graduating, it was his memories of the reception he had received from his fraternity brothers at Tau Kappa Epsilon when he imitated well-known radio sportscasters by using a broomstick to conduct "mock locker-room interviews" that Reagan credited with giving him the confidence to pursue a job in radio.[64]

The advent of radio broadcasting was the critical factor in making Reagan's childhood years "the golden age of sport." Radio coverage of football, baseball, and boxing matches drew some of the largest audiences and helped establish radio listening as a social habit. In turn, radio broadcasts of athletic events made local heroes into national sports icons. The money Americans spent attending sporting events in the 1920s funded the construction of massive stadiums for professional sports franchises, including the 18,000-seat indoor arena at Madison Square Garden, the 62,000-seat Yankee Stadium, and university football stadiums such as the one at the University of Michigan, which held 100,000 people. The audience for sports played an important role in the shift from a producer- to a consumer-oriented culture. "We pin our hopes to the sporting public," Bertolt Brecht wrote in 1926 in "Emphasis on Sport." "Make no bones about it, we have our eye on those huge concrete pans, filled with 15,000 men and women of every variety of class and physiognomy, the fairest and shrewdest audience in the world. There you will find 15,000 persons paying high prices, and working things out on the basis of a sensible weighing of supply and demand."[65] For Brecht, the terms and conditions of mass culture demanded a new relationship between artist and audience in which cultural events competed with prizefights for consumers' attention. Reagan's experience as a baseball announcer, however, suggests the possibility of a different relationship between capitalism and culture, the culture worker and the mass, artist and audience, in a society in which 15,000 people attending a game represented a slow night at the box office.

Sports announcers were among the most influential of the new professionals created by the growth of radio, and by the early 1930s they had become a new breed of celebrity. They were "as famous as some Hollywood stars," Reagan proudly recalled, "and often more famous than the athletes they reported on."[66] By imaginatively describing a game their audience could not see, these "pioneers" of the airwaves served as "the visualizer for the armchair quarterback." For popular sportscasters such as

Graham McNamee, whom Reagan cites as an early influence, the sporting event itself merely provided the raw materials for their accounts. After sitting alongside McNamee during his broadcast of a World Series game, Ring Lardner concluded that the "Washington Senators and the New York Giants must have played a double-header this afternoon—the game I saw and the game Graham McNamee announced."[67] In an interview with Vin Scully televised while he was president, Reagan said, "I think I liked doing radio better than TV because the audience had to depend on you for the picture."[68] While Reagan's "dramatic instinct" may have "rebelled" at plugging the Runge mortuary while broadcasting romantic organ music, it leaped at the opportunity to picture a game for an audience whose only access was through his voice.[69]

Although his knowledge of football landed Reagan a job, it was baseball, that most mythically charged of American pastimes, that gave him his first taste of mass-mediated celebrity. The biggest audiences at WHO were for its broadcasts of Chicago Cubs baseball games. Unlike many team owners, who worried that broadcasting games would decrease attendance, William Wrigley, the chewing gum magnate and Cubs owner, encouraged radio coverage, believing it stimulated interest in the game and attendance at the park. Because Wrigley initially charged nothing for broadcasting rights, as many as seven Chicago radio stations and several smaller stations throughout the Midwest carried the games.[70] Consequently, it was the appeal of the announcer that determined which radio station audiences would tune in to listen to the national pastime.

While Reagan professed a belief in the sportscaster "locating himself" in relation to the event described, "so that the audience can see the game through his eyes," he had never actually been to a major league ballpark when he began broadcasting Cubs games in 1934.[71] Since he would never see the games he broadcast "live" off a telegraph relay, this was not as big a detriment as his lack of experiential knowledge of the game. As a football announcer he was a method actor, drawing on his personal experience and sense memory of "how it felt to be on the field, and the smell of sweat and the taste of blood."[72] Reading up on baseball, a sport he had never played as a child, enabled him to sound knowledgeable on the air, but his job required him to convey more than facts and figures. To acquire the knowledge required to serve as a surrogate for his listeners he was sent to Chicago. His first stop was not Wrigley Field, the home of the Cubs, but the office of Pat Flanagan, an NBC sportscaster who had pioneered the telegraphic report process. Flanagan advised Reagan that seeing a game was not as important as gathering mental pictures of the ballpark, observing the players' habits, and listening to them talk. Heeding Flanagan's advice, Reagan familiarized himself with the mise-en-scène and dramaturgy he would call on to convey the sounds, images, and behavioral rituals that would enable his audience to visualize the game.[73]

From the first time he scratched the crystal, Reagan intuitively grasped that radio—like chairs in dramatics and Chautauqua performances— could serve as an excellent substitute for firsthand knowledge of the world and its objects. Radio satisfied what Walter Benjamin characterized as the primal urge of mass society, "to bring things 'closer' spatially and humanly . . . to get hold of an object at very close range by way of its likeness, its reproduction."[74] This "urge," which Benjamin identifies as characteristic of mass culture, was sated—at least in Iowa in the 1930s—by a voice describing an event its owner had never seen.

So what *did* Reagan see from his broadcast booth? "Looking through the window," he recalled in his autobiography, "I would see 'Curly' (complete with headphones) start typing. This was my cue to start talking."[75] Sitting in his cubby-sized booth in the WHO studios on the ground floor of the Stoner Piano Building in Des Moines, Reagan's voice was cued into action by Curly's cryptic abbreviations of the game's events conveyed by the teletype operator from the press box at Wrigley Field three hundred miles away. To enhance the illusion of a live broadcast, Reagan used a crowd applause record played on a turntable that allowed him to manipulate the volume with a foot pedal.[76] The radio, teletype, turntable, foot pedal, Curly's headphones, and Reagan's voice were all elements of a space-compressing technology designed to create an illusion of intimacy by broadcasting a "live" event at which none of the participants (Reagan, Curly, or the radio audience) were present. Unable to speak until he received his cue, Reagan's narration was not so much dependent on the events of the game he described as on the technology that reproduced the game he reenacted.

Reagan's most famous radio story is emblematic of what Benjamin termed "the shriveling of the aura" of the work of art in what he famously referred to as "the age of mechanical reproduction."[77] Contemplating the same manipulation of motion and matter that broke Adams's historical neck, Benjamin hailed photography, film, and radio for substituting "a plurality of copies for a unique existence," thereby effecting a "shattering of tradition" that resulted in "the liquidation of the traditional value of the cultural heritage."[78] Also liquidated by mechanical reproduction was the "aura" of the work of art—"its unique existence at the place where it happens to be"—effectively undermining the concepts of uniqueness, authenticity, and presence as relevant criteria for assessing the status and value of the art object.[79]

Reagan's account of his broadcast of a game between the Cubs and the Cardinals, however, problematizes Benjamin's optimistic vision of the democratization of culture that he believed would follow the eclipse of the cult value of an elitist art steeped in ritual, magic, theology, and metaphysics: "I saw Curly start to type so I finished the windup and had Dean send the ball on its way to the plate, took the slip from Curly, and found myself faced with the terse note: '*the wire has gone dead.*' I had a ball on the way to the plate and there was no way to call it back. At the same time, I was convinced that with a ball game tied up in the ninth inning was no time to tell my audience *we had lost contact with the game* and they would have to listen to recorded music."[80] Why, one might ask, was Reagan so concerned to maintain the illusion that he was reporting a game he was actually seeing? As Wills makes clear, Reagan's audience knew he was not at the game. On occasion he would even broadcast from the Crystal Palace at the Iowa Fair Grounds, where people were invited "to watch him as he invented the game from scraps of paper."[81] Wills's explanation is that Reagan was unwilling to break "the continuity of pretense," to violate the suspension of disbelief that is the compact between actor and audience in the theater.

But what if it was a different illusion that was threatened to be revealed by the dead wire; the illusion of Reagan's "contact" with the game, the mimetic authority that authorized his contact with his audience. Reagan was more concerned with maintaining the aura of the work of art than the pretense of theatrical illusion. More precisely, his career as a performer began during a changing of the mimetic guard whereby the erosion of the aura of the work of art is signaled by the simultaneous ascendance of the aura of the mass-mediated celebrity. It was Reagan, not Dizzy Dean, who "finished the windup," it was Reagan who "had Dean send the ball on its way to the plate," and it was Reagan who "had a ball on the way to the plate" with "no way to call it back." He knew that the audience ("my audience") was listening to *his* call, *his* voice, and not the game itself. It is what Reagan describes, how *he* sees it and feels it, that his audience consumes. In this sense, the celebrity stands in for the art object or sporting event and is invested with all the value Benjamin attributes to the copy, bringing the object or event closer to the masses and the masses closer to the real.

It was not the illusion of his performance that Reagan was concerned with maintaining but rather his status as a work of art, the reification of his celebrity, now endangered by the dead wire.

> I knew of only one thing that wouldn't get in the score column and *betray me*—a foul ball. So I had Augie foul this pitch down the left field line. I looked expectantly at Curly. He just shrugged helplessly, so I had Augie foul another one, and still another; then he fouled one back into the box seats. I described in detail the red-headed kid who had scrambled and gotten the souvenir ball. He fouled one into the upper deck that just missed being a home run. He fouled for six minutes and forty five seconds until I lost count. I began to be frightened that maybe I was establishing a new world record for a fellow staying at the bat hitting fouls, and *this could betray me*. Yet I was into it so far *I didn't dare reveal that the wire had gone dead*. My voice was rising in pitch and threatening to crack—and then, bless him, Curly started typing. I clutched at the slip. It said: "Galan popped out on the first ball pitched." Not in my game he didn't—he popped out after practically making a career of foul balls.[82]

Reagan's fear of being betrayed by the revelation that the technology of his celebrity had short-circuited stemmed from the stakes of his masquerade, not the outcome of a baseball game but the income derived from the cultural capital that accrued to him due to his ability to speak for the game and the fans who listened to his call. It is the cultural capital derived from his body electric that connects Reagan's radio days to his presidential politics of performance through the grain of his voice.

CHAPTER THREE

Sounding the Nation

> For the first time in world history, mechanical reproduction emancipates the work
> of art from its parasitical dependence on ritual. To an ever greater degree the work
> of art reproduced becomes the work of art designed for reproducibility. From a
> photographic negative, for example, one can make any number of prints; to ask for
> the "authentic" print makes no sense. But the instant the criterion of authenticity
> ceases to be applicable to artistic production the total function of art is reversed.
> Instead of being based on ritual, it begins to be based on another practice—politics.
>
> —Walter Benjamin, "The Work of Art in the Age of Mechanical Reproduction"

In the mid-1930s, while Walter Benjamin pondered the effect of mechanical reproduction on the work of art, "Dutch" Reagan was acquiring regional celebrity on the radio and dreaming of Hollywood. Among the myriad consequences of the new techne of mechanical reproduction identified

Photo: President Reagan broadcasts an address to the Soviet people in 1985.
Photo © Bettman/Corbis.

by Benjamin and mastered by Reagan were the new possibilities they created for the mingling of art and politics. By altering the means and modes of artistic production, mechanical reproduction transformed both the use and the exchange value of the art object. For Benjamin, this meant that the mechanically reproduced image afforded the opportunity for a mimetic reformation; a performative mimesis he anticipated would "emancipate" aesthetic representation. While Benjamin is here primarily concerned with the impact of mechanical reproduction on the work of art, what are the implications for the other term in his equation, the political? How does this new modernist function of aesthetic representation ("based on another practice—politics") affect political representation? What effect would mechanical reproduction have on the relationship between statecraft and stagecraft?

Benjamin offers a partial answer to these questions in a lengthy footnote to his discussion of the similarity between the experience of confronting one's own image in the mirror and the estrangement felt by the film actor performing for the camera. Here he contemplates the impact of mechanical reproduction on the "function" of cultural and political performers.

> Since the innovations of camera and recording equipment make it possible for the orator to become audible and visible to an unlimited number of persons, the presentation of the man of politics before the camera and recording equipment becomes paramount. Parliaments, as much as theaters, are deserted. Radio and film not only affect the function of the professional actor but likewise the function of those who also exhibit themselves before this mechanical equipment, those who govern. Though their tasks may be different, the change affects equally the actor and the ruler. The trend is toward establishing controllable and transferable skills under certain social conditions. This results in a new selection, a selection before the equipment from which the star and the dictator emerge victorious.[1]

Benjamin's account of the imminent danger posed by the evacuation of the public spaces of cultural and political representation (theaters and parliaments) and the power of radio and movies to create both stars and dictators is a sobering counterpoint to his utopian vision of the decline of the aura of the work of art and the democratizing potential of mass culture.

While "the selection before the equipment" helps explain the rise of Hitler and Hollywood, Ronald Reagan's career offers a counternarrative for the effects of mechanical reproduction on the "tasks" of the actor and the politician. In the American context the new modes of performance that circulated through electronic media would, as Henry Adams predicted, remodel social and political habits, ideas, and institutions to such a degree that they would join the actor and ruler together in a more intimate relationship than the one described by Benjamin. While Benjamin was completing his spirited, albeit ambivalent, defense of the industrialization of art, an American work of art designed for reproducibility, and no longer based on the rituals of a few but on a politics for the many, was just emerging from the prairies of the American Midwest. Assessing the culture of performance that formed the backdrop to Reagan's education and presidency, and the controllable and transferable skills he acquired from the culture industry, it is hard to resist the conclusion that in the United States the tasks of actor and ruler would not prove to be as different as Benjamin anticipated.

The National Voice

. . . I never saw him—
But I knew him. Can you have forgotten
How, with his voice, he came into our house,
The President of the United States,
Calling us friends . . .[2]

When Peggy Noonan was hired as a Reagan speechwriter, she went "looking for the grammar of the presidency, the sound and tone and tense of it." And she knew where to go, "to the modern president who had sounded most like a president, the one who set the standard for how the rest should sound. I went to FDR."[3] While the Reagan administration set about systematically dismantling the New Deal, Noonan studied Franklin Delano Roosevelt's speeches to craft Reagan's presidential voice. But Noonan already knew how FDR *sounded* before reviewing his rhetoric. Like the rest of us she grew up listening to radio addresses and newsreels from the 1930s that made his voice the most recognizable in the nation, a voice that still circulates through our classrooms, televisions, and the

Internet. In her belief in and approach to the way Reagan should sound, Noonan took her cue from his long history of borrowings from the vocal legacy of the first national voice of the electronic age.

As was the case for many members of his generation, FDR was Reagan's first political hero. When he was running for governor of California, Reagan told *Time* magazine that he was a "child of the Depression, a Democrat by upbringing and very emotionally involved" in Roosevelt's presidency.[4] Reagan's attraction to FDR was personal as well as political. His father, Jack Reagan, campaigned for FDR during his first run for the presidency and Ronald cast his first presidential ballot for Roosevelt that same year. During the Depression, Reagan witnessed the beneficial effects of the New Deal firsthand. His father's job with the Works Project Administration (WPA) provided food and relief to Dixon's needy and helped keep the Reagans afloat. Reagan's passionate belief in FDR was still very much in evidence during his years in Hollywood. Jack Dales, who recruited Reagan to join the board of the Screen Actors Guild, remembered Reagan as "an unbelievably strong Roosevelt supporter. He idolized him as some people would idolize a film star—he thought he was almost a godlike man."[5] Describing Reagan's reaction when, while working in the local media, they watched FDR's motorcade roll through Iowa City, his friend Howard Chase recalled more than fifty years later that Reagan was mesmerized by Roosevelt. According to Chase it was not the president's policies or political vision that captivated Dutch but FDR's "empathic and strikingly accessible presence," a magnetism that Reagan found "electrifying."[6] While Reagan's enthusiasm for the New Deal had waned by the time he entered politics, his reverence for Roosevelt's star quality would inform his own mass-mediated ministering of political life through the expanded electronic church that televised his own political revolution.

As with many of the other figures Reagan emulated throughout his life, he expressed his admiration for FDR through mimesis. As a novice radio broadcaster in the early 1930s, Reagan memorized passages of FDR's first inaugural address and entertained his coworkers with impersonations of the president. From the first rehearsals of his political voice while barnstorming for General Electric in the 1950s through his tenure as governor of California and his anointment as the Great Communicator, Reagan borrowed Roosevelt's words, employed his techniques, and adapted his strategic use of radio to television, the dominant electronic medium of his era. Whether political exigencies demanded that Reagan "be willing to be Roosevelt" (an imperative that covered a range of tasks from restoring the New Deal's electoral coalition to adopting an inspirational rather than programmatic style of presidential leadership) or be willing *not* to be Roosevelt (defined as the exemplar of liberalism's excesses and failures), the abiding standard for performing the presidency in the Reagan years was FDR.[7]

The evolution of FDR's political persona illustrates how the grain of the voice generates its effects. According to Roland Barthes, the affective connection the grain of the voice establishes between orator and auditor is generated by *"the encounter of a language and a voice."*[8] The grain of FDR's voice was a product of his encounter with the new languages of mechanical reproduction that emerged over the first four decades of the twentieth century. Elected to the New York State Senate in 1911, he quickly positioned himself as a reformer by opposing the Democratic Tammany political machine. In September of the following year, facing reelection and the unified opposition of Tammany Hall, Roosevelt contracted typhoid with the election just two months away. Confined to bed, a desperate FDR asked Louis McHenry Howe, a former newspaperman and political operative, to devise a strategy that would compensate for his inability to run a conventional campaign. Howe, who suffered from a heart murmur, asthma, bronchitis, and a penchant for chain-smoking Sweet Caporal cigarettes, knew a bit about overcoming physical adversity and a lot about newspapers and the nascent industries of advertising and public relations. He employed the available technologies of mechanical reproduction to produce the first large-batch direct mail campaign, sending thousands of "personal" letters from Roosevelt to farmers throughout his district. He provided local newspapers with ready-to-print boilerplate articles emphasizing issues targeted at specific regional audiences and spent an unprecedented percentage of Roosevelt's campaign funds on print advertising.[9] Howe's strategy won the election and Roosevelt's admiration, and he would remain FDR's chief political strategist through the end of his presidency. In the decades that followed, the techniques Howe employed to disseminate Roosevelt's message and name—repetition, saturation, and segmentation—would form the basis for marketing everything from politicians to movies to soap.

Thanks to Howe, FDR's vision of the political potential of advertising and public relations went beyond their mere utility as tools for marketing political candidates. Like Calvin Coolidge, FDR believed the new industries of persuasion had a critical role to play in educating Americans. Unlike Coolidge, who believed "the business of America was business" and advertising's role in the secular religion was to "minister to the spiritual side of trade," FDR perceived advertising as a force for reinvigorating democracy. It was the pedagogical potential of the new industries of persuasion that led FDR in the year before he became president to tell *Printer's Ink*, "If I were starting life over again, I am inclined to think that I would go into the advertising business in preference to almost any other. . . . It is essentially a form of education; and the progress of civilization depends on education."[10]

In the 1920s, the twin obstacles of a debilitating illness and the concerted opposition of a powerful political constituency again confronted Roosevelt, and again he triumphed by learning a new language of mass communication. Stricken by poliomyelitis in 1921 at the age of thirty-nine, Roosevelt was presented with enormous political and personal challenges. There was little precedent for a physically disabled politician and none for the offices to which he aspired. In addition, his reformist tendencies, attacks on big business, and progressive social policies had earned him the enmity of the conservative magnates who controlled the majority of the country's newspapers. To mitigate the hostility of the press, Howe and FDR exploited one of the seminal lessons they had learned from advertising, public relations, and film: the visual image was fast overtaking the printed word as the arbiter of public opinion.

Prior to the late 1920s, with the development of a national radio network and the introduction of sound to film, the print medium was the communications technology that exerted the strongest influence on American politics. Despite overwhelmingly negative editorial critiques of Roosevelt and his politics, Howe was able to assert almost total control over the visual image of FDR's body in print. According to Hugh Gregory Gallagher, who chronicled what he calls FDR's "splendid deception," as governor of New York Roosevelt had an implicit agreement with the press corps not to be photographed "looking crippled or helpless." The White House photographic corps also adhered to this "unspoken code" when he became president. Astonishingly, of the more than "thirty-five thousand still photographs of FDR at the Presidential library," Gallagher reports, "there are only two of the man seated in his wheelchair. No newsreels show him being lifted, carried, or pushed in his chair. Among the thousands of political cartoons and caricatures of FDR, not one shows the man as physically impaired."[11] Controlling the visual representation of his body to a degree unimaginable in today's politics, Roosevelt's public body only existed from the waist up.

When FDR ran for president, however, the scribes who wrote for many of the nation's largest publishing houses were not as willing as press photographers to burnish his public image. In a letter to Merlin Aylesworth, president of the NBC network, Roosevelt identified a new medium capable of challenging the political hegemony of the printed word: "[N]othing since the creation of the newspaper," he wrote, "has had so profound an impact on our civilization as radio."[12] That Roosevelt was able to generate electoral coalitions and political affiliations strong enough to overcome the opposition of much of the mainstream press is directly attributable to radio's impact on American politics and his mastery of the new medium. Beginning with KDKA's first broadcast—reporting the Cox-Roosevelt ticket's defeat in the 1921 presidential election, FDR's only unsuccessful national campaign—radio would redefine the practice of American politics and the career of its most able practitioner.

Roosevelt's tenure as president spans a period of dramatic transformation in the social impact of technologies of mechanical reproduction in general and radio in particular. In 1929, the year the stock market crashed and the Great Depression began, Robert and Helen Lynd published *Middletown: A Study in Contemporary American Culture*. In the Lynd's middle town of Muncie, Indiana, reading, automobile riding, and gramophone music dominated leisure time while radio was hardly mentioned. In 1936, just seven years later, the Lynds returned to Muncie. During their first visit only one in eight homes had a radio. Now the ratio was one in two. Listening to the radio had become "the area of leisure where change in time spent has been greatest."[13] Nationally the penetration of radio was even more pronounced. When the Lynds returned to Muncie there were thirty million radio sets in use in the United States. By the following year, an estimated 91 percent of all urban and 70 percent of all rural households in America contained at least one radio.[14] In the two decades between FDR's first and last presidential campaigns, radio overtook the newspaper as Americans' primary source of news, and radio listening became the most popular daily leisure activity in the United States.[15]

Roosevelt was not the first president to recognize the political potential of radio. Woodrow Wilson was the first to speak on the radio, Warren G. Harding installed the first radio in the White House, and Calvin Coolidge gave his final campaign speech and took the oath of office over the radio. During the presidential campaign of 1928, Herbert Hoover's advisers announced that he was throwing his hat in the "ethereal ring'" by campaigning "mostly on radio and through the motion pictures." The Hoover campaign's assessment of radio's promise as a political technology was shared by a *New York Times* reporter who asserted that "brief pithy statements as to the positions of the parties and candidates which reach the emotions through the minds of millions of radio listeners, will play an important part in the race to the White House." FDR, however, was the first president to fully exploit the political potential of radio—what E. B. White called its "pervading and somewhat godlike presence"—as a technology for governance.[16]

The rapid growth of radio was fortuitous for FDR, who needed what the medium offered more than any other politician of the era. To fully appreciate the significance of radio in FDR's political career we need to imagine it as not so much a political tool as a technological prosthetic for a political cyborg. Faced with the consistent opposition of the majority of the national press and an inability to withstand the physical rigors of barnstorming and whistle-stop tours, Roosevelt needed another vehicle for communicating with the electorate. Radio was the medium that enabled him to bypass the press and take his body where his legs were unable to carry him. As "the greatest force for molding public opinion," he would write to his secretary of the Federal Radio Commission, radio was an invaluable tool for "promoting policies and campaigning."[17] The first family's identification with radio was so pervasive that it earned them the moniker "the Radio Roosevelts." During the Depression, FDR's son Jimmy was a commentator for Boston's Yankee Network, and his other son, Elliot, was vice president of the Southwestern radio group and part owner of the Texas State Network. Eleanor Roosevelt hosted her own commentary show from 1934 to 1940 and appeared on a wide variety of programs throughout FDR's presidency. Howe had a weekly radio show, and many cabinet members regularly addressed the public on pressing issues. But it was FDR who was the administration's biggest draw.

Through the radio, FDR addressed a larger audience at one time than anyone else had been able to speak to in a lifetime. Even by the standards of the day, his audience was unprecedented. Thanks in part to his Rural Electrification Administration's expansion of centrally generated electricity into previously unreachable rural areas, he was the first president to reach the vast majority of the American people in a single broadcast. During his twelve years in office, he delivered over three hundred radio addresses and fireside chats. These were the only broadcasting events during the Depression for which national and regional networks would preempt regularly scheduled programming and link themselves together into a single network numbering as many as six hundred stations. In the fireside chat aired on 11 September 1941, FDR spoke to 53.8 million listeners, an astonishing 72.5 percent of the population, an audience that exceeded the number of people who attended the movies in an average week.[18]

The ability to address an audience of unprecedented size does not, however, account for FDR's effect on that audience. At the onset of his illness, he was on hiatus from politics after his defeat as the Democratic vice presidential nominee. While he would not run for public office again until his 1928 campaign for governor of New York, at Howe's urging he began to familiarize himself with radio's potential as a political technology. Radio provided Howe and Roosevelt with a new medium through which they would apply at a national level the mass-mediated techniques of persuasion they had pioneered in their first campaign together.

Roosevelt's diligent study of the nascent craft of radio illustrates the degree to which hegemony requires hard work. Already a student of rhetoric and oratory, Roosevelt meticulously trained his voice, honed his delivery, and perfected his timing to exploit the new medium. Eradicating any traces of a regional accent and speaking at a slower rate than the typical radio orator, the modulation and pitch of his voice was so smooth that engineers never had to adjust their controls. His vocal mastery was such that he "seldom faltered on a word, rarely cleared his throat on the air, and never gave the impression that he was reading a prepared text." Exploiting radio's capacity to reach a socially and economically heterogeneous audience—especially those not served or represented by the print media—a contemporary study found that "between 70 and 80 percent of [Roosevelt's] vocabulary in his fireside chats consisted of the 1000 most common words in the English language." His efforts did not go unnoticed by the broadcasting industry. Industry professionals commented on his grasp of the technical requirements of the medium (the different vocal effects he produced by altering the angle of the microphone or the proximity of the microphone to his mouth) while station owners and network executives appreciated his ability to precisely time his broadcasts to fit within the time allotted by their programming schedule.[19]

Roosevelt's use of radio resulted in what *Broadcasting* magazine described as "a one man revolution of modern oratory."[20] In contrast to the nineteenth-century model of bombastic rhetoric and the grandiloquent platform oratory of Chautauqua speakers such as William Jennings Bryan, whose voice was said to carry over half a mile, the words most often used to describe FDR's radio voice were intimate, conversational, and informal. Unlike many of his political contemporaries, FDR understood that while he was speaking to a mass audience his interlocutors were listening alone or in small groups in close proximity to their radios and could control the volume of his voice themselves. The tone of his fireside chats was not pitched to rally the masses but to comfort isolated individuals who felt detached from each other, alienated from any sense of common purpose, and vulnerable to financial ruin.

The Roosevelt administration was also the first to systematically coordinate the dissemination of its message through the radio. Attuned to the political impact of advertising and public relations, FDR became the first politician to carefully monitor public opinion polls, the telegrams of listeners, and industry ratings in order to gauge the public response to his broadcasts. As president he devoted a portion of each day to reviewing "Howe's Daily Bugle"; Howe's summary of the press coverage and editorials about his administration from around the country. Beginning in his second term, FDR had the Radio and Film Methods Corporation make recordings of his speeches, which he would study to improve his delivery.

As radio became Roosevelt's primary medium of public communication, his "radio entourage" of presidential announcers and engineers established broadcasting facilities in the Oval Office and traveled with him to the executive retreats at Hyde Park, New York, and Warm Springs, Georgia.

If FDR's political success depended on the growth of radio, radio's rapid expansion owed just as much to his popularity and goodwill. Ownership of and access to the airwaves depended on a positive relationship with the administration. Unlike the newspaper industry, which enjoyed First Amendment protection from government control, radio was a new and malleable medium closely regulated by the government through the Radio Act of 1927, which affirmed public ownership of the airwaves, and subsequently under the auspices of the Federal Communications Commission (FCC) established by the Communications Act of 1934. Roosevelt's successful opposition to attempts to establish ownership positions in radio by political opponents such as newspaper magnate William Randolph Hearst sent a clear message to the broadcasting industry. Reliant on Roosevelt's goodwill for their operating licenses and because his broadcasts drew huge audiences and promoted radio listening as a social habit, broadcasting companies and networks were more than happy to provide him with the opportunity to directly address the American public without the journalistic filtering of print reporters, editors, and publishers.[21]

Radio also gave Roosevelt an advantage over members of Congress, who were only granted access to the airwaves on special occasions and thus were not able to establish the same bonds with the American public as FDR enjoyed. It also helped that close personal relationships existed between the White House and the two largest broadcast networks. "The close contact between you and the broadcasters," Henry Bellows, head of the Washington Bureau of the Columbia Broadcasting System (CBS) and Roosevelt's classmate at Harvard, told Press Secretary Steven Early, "has tremendous possibilities of value to the administration, and as a life-long Democrat, I want to pledge my best efforts in making this cooperation successful."[22] The enthusiastic cooperation of influential radio executives such as Bellows and journalists such as George Holmes, the chief Washington correspondent for NBC and Early's brother-in-law, was indispensable in helping the administration sell its policies over the air.

Labeled the first "rhetorical president," Roosevelt assembled a remarkable cast of literary figures, public intellectuals, and policy wonks to assist him in composing his talks, but as speechwriter Samuel I. Rosenman commented, "[T]he speeches as finally delivered were his—and his alone—no matter who the collaborators were . . . they expressed the personality, the convictions, the spirit, the mood of Roosevelt. No matter who worked with him in the preparation, the finished product was always the same— it was Roosevelt himself."[23] As Rosenman notes, the self-evidence of Roosevelt's performances stemmed in part from his involvement in their crafting. But FDR's expressed belief that he couldn't deliver a speech that he had not worked on himself reveals the sensibility of a performer who needed to translate his speechwriter's words into his own voice in order to deliver them to an audience convincingly. "Roosevelt himself" was, in the final analysis, less a product of his memorable rhetoric than of his signature oratory, a vocal performance that, like the eighteenth-century model of elocution, relied at least as much on conveying the sensibility of the performer as it did on the sense of the words he spoke.

Combining acting and broadcasting techniques with a voice ably suited for the exercise of power, FDR was generally acknowledged as the finest public speaker in the nation. The "mechanical excellence" of his instrument inspired the author of *The Way to Good Speaking and Singing* to recommend his voice as "an ideal pattern from which students may . . . build their own vocal method." If William Jennings Bryan and Daniel Webster were the "speech-making heroes of the nineteenth century," declared *Broadcasting*, then "FDR is the oratorical model of the twentieth."[24] Summarizing the effect of FDR's oratorical prowess in its advice to Wendell Wilkie during the 1940 presidential campaign, the journal commented, "When it comes to vote-getting in this day of radio and audiences by the millions, teamwork among the organs of speech is vital. How the vocal cords mesh may be more important than how the Hatch Act performs. An Adam's apple may win the election and determine the destiny of nations. We don't think how a thing is said should be equally as important as how it is thought, but in campaigning it is. Mr. Wilkie should take heed of this problem and realize that he is up against the greatest epiglottis in the known world."[25] Roosevelt may have been the first president to systematically study broadcasting techniques and the impact of radio as a public relations medium, but vocal training and market research merely revealed the best way to position an already formidable product: the "greatest epiglottis in the known world."

FDR's overwhelming popularity among working- and lower-class Americans, the unshakably loyal base of his support, was directly attributable to his radio addresses. As radio technology became more accessible, broadcast programming increased its offerings, and the cost of a radio receiver declined, it was the people hardest hit by the Depression who came to rely most heavily on radio. Public opinion polls confirmed radio's increasing influence as a primary source of news, finding that "dependence on radio became more prevalent as the income level of those interviewed fell," as well as "the popular belief, especially among the lower income groups, that radio was more accurate and unbiased" than newspapers.[26] The compelling narratives of Roosevelt's "chats" delivered in a plain English that eschewed facts and figures in favor of anecdotes and analogies—generated a political coalition deeply suspicious of the same faction of the print media and big business that resisted the New Deal.

Roosevelt took office at a time when the Great Depression threatened to destroy any sense of national unity or purpose by fraying the symbolic threads and economic ties that had bound the nation together through the postwar economic expansion of the 1920s. As "a means of communication that reached millions of people simultaneously," Roosevelt recognized radio's potential to unify a nation threatening to splinter into hostile camps under the weight of economic deprivation. For him, radio was an instrument capable of mounting "as powerful an assault upon sectional and parochial mentalities as any other single force in American history."[27] Faced with the determined resistance of powerful social and political constituencies, the successful implementation of New Deal policies would have been impossible without his unprecedented ability to articulate and disseminate his vision through the ether. "All that man has to do is speak on the radio," remarked a former Republican, "and the sound of his voice, his sincerity, the manner of his delivery, just melts me and I change my mind."[28] When Roosevelt's vigorous, enthralling, and reassuring baritone harnessed radio's occult and fetish power to ease Americans' anxiety over the debilitating diseases that wracked the presidential and national bodies, it produced the first national voice of the electronic age.

To assure a radio audience in the midst of the worst economic condi-

tions in the nation's history that the only thing it had to fear was fear itself reflects an abiding faith in both the grain of the voice and the fiat of
electricity. To engender that faith in others, despite overwhelming evidence to the contrary, was the prerequisite for FDR to constitute a society
of common feeling. Through the fireside chats that made him the most
recognizable voice in America, he utilized the reproducible voice as a
medium for healing an ailing nation through an aural politics of affect.
The fear Roosevelt urged Americans to resist was the "nameless, un-
justified terror which paralyzes needed efforts to convert retreat into advance."[29] Roosevelt's authority for convincing Americans that they could
overcome the crippling fear that gripped the country during the Depression was his own struggle with polio. Every time Americans heard him on
the radio they were reminded that their president had learned to overcome his paralysis, and they came to believe that he could help them
learn to overcome theirs.

In radio Roosevelt found the perfect medium through which to heal
the national body with the fertile grain of his voice. By rendering his
damaged body invisible, radio substituted his voice for his body, joining
his body natural to the body politic through an ethereal body, its mobility unhampered by physical limitations, its circulation unimpeded by material constraints. As an affective entity, Roosevelt's voice generated phantom limbs for a surrogate body—a body electric—and modeled the
process by which the body politic could overcome its own crippling affliction. Just as Reagan's audience knew he was not at Wrigley Field yet were
able to "see" the game through his voice, Roosevelt's audience knew both
he and the country were ill yet were able to envision a healthy president
and nation through radio's occult and magical power to make the invisible audible.

Because radio concealed Roosevelt's physical handicap he was able to
construct his public image aurally through what numerous commentators describe as the "authority" of his voice. On the radio, Roosevelt was
his voice. As his voice traveled through the ether, its authority and sincerity commingled to create the seductive and oft-noted intimacy between FDR and his audience. When he spoke, his listeners believed he was
talking directly to them. Millions of Americans sat by their radios and
agreed that they could practically feel him in the room. One might be

tempted to dismiss this sentiment as hopelessly subjective or merely metaphorical, or at the very least empirically unverifiable, were it not for the fact that it was reiterated incessantly in almost identical language by the people who heard him speak on the radio. So powerfully did Roosevelt's audience connect to him and connect him to the radio that many of them kept a photograph of him by the receiver.

"I have sat in those parlors and on those porches myself," FDR's labor secretary, Frances Perkins, recalled, "and I have seen men and women gathered around the radio, even those who didn't like him or were opposed to him politically, listening with a pleasant, happy feeling of association and friendship. The exchange between them and him through the medium of radio was very real. I have seen tears come to their eyes as he told them of some tragic episode . . . and they were tears of sincerity and recognition and sympathy."[30] The "exchange" between FDR and his radio audience epitomizes the powerful affective investments generated by the intercourse of stagecraft and statecraft in the age of mechanical reproduction. Just as Benjamin's "people whom nothing moves or touches any longer are taught to cry again by films," so, too, the tears of sincerity and recognition and sympathy shed by Roosevelt's listeners welled up in their eyes in response to a medium by which "[s]entimentality is restored to health and liberated in American style."[31] Roosevelt's restoration and liberation of sentimentality American style formed the basis of a society of common feeling, the utopian imagi-nation that promised relief from the national depression.

In his autobiography, no less an authority on the politics of affect than Ronald Reagan recalls the impact of Roosevelt's "strong, gentle, confident voice," which "resonated across a nation with an eloquence that brought comfort and resilience to a nation caught up in a storm and reassured us that we could lick any problem."[32] The communal comfort, resilience, and reassurance Reagan identifies FDR as producing through his radio voice bear a striking resemblance to what Benedict Anderson describes as "that remarkable confidence of community in anonymity" generated by the "mass ceremony" of "the almost precisely simultaneous consumption ('imagining') of the newspaper-as-fiction."[33] According to Anderson, print capitalism generally and the newspaper in particular played a critical role in constituting the newly imagined selves and social relations necessary for developing the imagined communities of the burgeoning nation-states of the nineteenth century. These animating fictions of nineteenth-century nationalisms generated by industrial revolutions in the technologies of transportation and communication, however, were less compelling in the wake of the economic devastation that followed the stock market crash. New mass ceremonies, and adepts trained in the controllable and transferable skills required to conduct them, were needed to address the resulting crisis of national representation. In response, media capitalism—radio, film, and finally television—came to serve a similar function for the imagined communities of twentieth-century nationalisms.[34]

Roosevelt shared Benjamin's optimistic view that the new media of mechanical reproduction promised to counteract the alienating and atomizing effects of modernity. Unlike Benjamin, FDR saw in radio the potential to democratize politics as well as culture. "Amid many developments of civilization which lead away from direct government by the people," Roosevelt asserted, "radio is one which tends on the other hand to restore contact between the masses and their chosen leaders."[35] The language Roosevelt employs to express his belief in radio's capacity to reanimate American democracy links his use of radio as a political medium for healing a national body to Reagan's story of how radio enabled him to connect two entities (the audience and the game) that were at a great distance from each other and from the voice that linked them. The encounter of a language and a voice, and its dissemination through the radio network, revivifies the dead wire, restoring contact between the leader and his body politic, the celebrity and his audience.

Roosevelt's fireside chats were broadcast from a small diplomatic reception room in the White House. A reporter for *Broadcast* magazine described the scene.

> Standing on either side of the President's desk were Carleton Smith, NBC announcer, and Bob Trout of CBS, each having a microphone on a platform in front of them. Aimed at FDR were four huge motion picture cameras heavily blanketed to suppress the noise. . . . Also pointed in the President's direction were about five cameras for still pictures. The room was cluttered with all sorts of portable electrical apparatuses and the floor was

strewn with cable leading to the President's desk. Lining the room facing the President, and watching his every move, were about twenty to twenty-five radio engineers, and sound and still photographers.[36]

Here, surrounded by the tools and technicians of mechanical reproduction, Roosevelt prepared to address the nation by visualizing his audience. Perkins describes how FDR would

> [p]icture in his mind the audience he was addressing. . . . He did not and could not know them all individually, but he thought of them individually. He thought of them in family groups. He thought of them sitting around on a suburban porch after supper of a summer evening. He thought of them gathered around a dinner table at a family meal.

When Roosevelt finally spoke, his voice conjured the informal and intimate setting he visualized in the form of a chat, a conversation among friends and not a formal political address.

> When he talked on the radio, he saw them gathered in the little parlor, listening with their neighbors. He was conscious of their faces and hands, their clothes and homes.
>
> His voice and facial expression as he spoke were those of an intimate friend. After he became President, I often was at the White House when he broadcast, and I realized how unconscious he was of the twenty or thirty of us in that room and how clearly his mind was focused on the people listening at the other end. As he talked his head would nod and his hands would move in simple, natural, comfortable gestures. His face would smile and light up as though he were actually sitting on the front porch or in the parlor with them. People felt this, and it bound them to him with affection.[37]

The bonds of affection Perkins describes FDR as generating are the genealogical descendants of the "higher bonds" that Thomas Paine believed to be the connective tissue for the collective American body politic fashioned in response to British demands for colonial fealty. In contrast to both the filial bonds linking Americans to Britain and the juridical bonds of contract and consent that Lincoln cited, and set aside, in his first inaugural, Paine invoked a "society of common feeling"; a people joined by the affective cords and chords of a bond that identified them as members of a distinct and exceptional tribe.[38] Following Paine's lead, FDR evoked the higher bond of a shared national sensibility that transcended ideological conflicts, and through the radio initiated isolated individuals into a society of common feeling through the grain of his voice. So completely were Roosevelt and the nation connected through his radio voice that the first FDR memorial, unveiled in Washington, DC, in 1997, featured a sculpture of a family gathered around a radio, transfixed by one of his fireside chats.[39]

Like his idol, the young radio announcer, too, would visualize his audience. Dutch and his friends all went to the same barber in Des Moines, and while he was on the air he would "picture" them at the barbershop, trying "to imagine how my words sounded to them and how they were reacting." When he spoke he did so "as if I was speaking personally to them. There was a specific audience I could see in my mind, and I sort of aimed my words at them."[40] A half century later Hugh Sidey, the presidential correspondent for *Time* magazine during Reagan's presidency, could still recall listening to his sportscasts as a child. "Life was hard for us, and the Depression seemed endless," he wrote, "but he managed to give us the feeling that things wouldn't always be that way, that they would get better."[41] Whether it represented a baseball game, a president, or a nation, the radio voice—an excellent substitute for the thing itself—continued to act on its audience long after contact had been severed.

Radio was the medium of mechanical reproduction through which FDR deployed the grain of his voice to convince Americans that they could overcome their economic and psychological depression by investing in the New Deal. Reagan's medium for stimulating affective investments in his imagi-nation was television. From the beginning of his tenure as governor of California, Reagan, like Roosevelt, faced opposition from the majority of newspapers in the state. To combat their attacks on his reduction in state programs, he "modernized the fireside chat," producing two- and fifteen-minute films that were distributed to television stations throughout the state.[42] He modeled his televisual strategies for achieving popular support on Roosevelt's use of radio as a means of connecting with his audience and connecting them to each other through a society of common feeling. The television spots were more moderate versions of the stinging criticism of the welfare state that had characterized Reagan's speeches since his days as a spokesman for General Electric. They also reflected the lesson he had learned from FDR, that the decisive component of political leadership was the ability to generate not ideological consensus but affective consent.

Rather than a point-by-point refutation of his critics' claims of the negative effects of cutting social services, Reagan utilized television to convey the utopian vision he had begun to articulate during his campaign for governor. The Creative Society was Reagan's New Deal, a "practical dream" that would "return to the people the privilege of self-government." It was a dream in which "government [would] no longer substitute for the people" but would "coordinate the creative energies of the people for the good of the whole."[43] For the rest of his political career, Reagan would employ the techniques pioneered by FDR's politics of affect to promote this new political theology designed to sever the bonds of affection that had connected Americans to the New Deal.

But if government would no longer "substitute" for the people what was the entity that would? Reagan's answer was the body electric. Exploiting technical and technological innovations in communications media to transform the practice of politics was as much a hallmark of the Creative Society as it had been of the New Deal. Louis Howe's use of personalized mailings prefigured the New Right's "direct mail" campaigns of the 1970s, which transformed political fund-raising and coalition building into precisely targeted and segmented practices with formal and strategic similarities to television's shift in programming strategy from mass market broadcasting to niche market narrowcasting. The influence of Howe's ready-to-print boilerplate articles on politics in the age of television was reflected in Michael Deaver's production of issue-specific video clips for strategic dissemination to targeted television markets. Howe's credo for the strategic management of the news—"if you say a thing is so often enough it stands a good chance of becoming a fact"—finds its echo in the Reagan administration's press strategy of "manipulation by inundation."[44] By the Reagan era, the capacities of technologies of mechanical reproduction and the sophistication of public relations techniques gave Press Secretary Larry Speakes sufficient confidence to declare, "If you tell the same story five times, it's true."[45] What for Howe "stood a good chance of becoming a fact" through the use of state-of-the-art technology and public relations at the turn of the century had become, through the fiat of electricity, indistinguishable from the truth.

During Reagan's presidency, the technology of television and the viewer's relationship with it were transformed as dramatically as radio was during FDR's administration. Between 1978 and 1989, the percentage of U.S. households that possessed a videocassette recorder rose from 4 to 60 percent while cable penetration increased from 17.1 to 57.1 percent. Pay-per-view—nonexistent in 1978—reached about one-fifth of all wired households by 1989.[46] The transformation in the way Americans watch television was the most influential of a range of technological innovations—including the electronic remote control, videodisc, camcorder, video game, people meter, and personal computer—that dramatically altered the way images fixed gazes during the Reagan years.

The strategic deregulation of the television industry also contributed to the development of a new mimetic regime. Under its Reagan-appointed chairman, Mark Fowler, the Federal Communications Commission set about eliminating any regulation that treated television differently from other businesses or impeded its potential for profitability. Acting on his belief that television was just another appliance ("a toaster with pictures"), Fowler eliminated FCC oversight of the system of public licensing of the airwaves established by FDR in 1934, abolished regulations requiring that a minimum number of broadcasting hours be devoted to news and public service programming, and increased the amount of advertising a station could run per broadcast hour. The networks took advantage of the FCC's relaxation of content requirements to produce news programming that was advertiser friendly, including the blend of information and entertainment commonly referred to as "infotainment," a revealing neologism coined in the 1980s.[47] The Reagan administration's exploitation and command of the new theatricality of television news was unparalleled. In terms of the production of television news as infotainment, the Reagan team had it all: a facility with dramatic structure; the ability to produce compelling story lines, narratives, and images; a skillful and performative use of repetition, serialization, and genre; and a president who had been training to play the role for a lifetime.

The Nation and Its Double

> The second day I was introduced to the rushes. . . . What a shock it was! It has taken me many years to get used to seeing myself as others see me, and also seeing myself instead of the mental picture of the character I'm playing. . . . [V]ery few of us ever see ourselves except as we look directly at ourselves in a mirror. Thus we don't know how we look from behind, from the side, walking, standing, moving normally through a room. It's quite a jolt.
>
> —Ronald Reagan, *Where's the Rest of Me?*

The ability of Roosevelt's and Reagan's radio voices to interpellate new forms of national belonging and identification is directly attributable to radio's capacity to constitute the body politic through the body electric. Reagan's account of watching himself on film for the first time illustrates how mechanical reproduction also reconstitutes the body of the performer with the controllable and transferable skills that charge the body electric. It is, however, as characteristic of the seasoned film actor as it is of the successful politician that the "jolt" of viewing oneself as others do (from a distance, through a screen, as an object among other objects, a commodity among other commodities) eventually dissipates and is forgotten. Over time the jolt is cushioned by the habitual self-scrutiny required by the task and the incessant need to reinvent oneself in front of the camera. For those, like actors and politicians, whose professional success depends on it, the "shock" of watching the image of the self as other eventually subsides, replaced by the desire to study and manipulate one's image on the screen. The information gleaned from repeated observation and rehearsal, experimentation and improvisation, is then transformed back into behavior ("walking, standing, moving normally through a room") as an embodied knowledge. The body stores this knowledge as *hexis*—Pierre Bourdieu's term for "political mythology realized, *embodied,* turned into a permanent disposition, a durable manner of standing, speaking, and thereby of *feeling and thinking.*"[48] The techne acquired by the film actor for a performance enacted before the camera rather than in

front of a live audience incorporates the pedagogy of mechanical reproduction into an embodied knowledge.

Severed from the constraints of both cultural heritage and historical
determinism, the performance of the film actor, unlike that of the stage
actor, is disengaged as well from the "character" he or she depicts. In Benjamin's formulation, the stage actor represents "someone else" (a character) while the film actor "represents himself to the public before the camera"[49] Film intensifies the modernist ontology of the self-conscious self
and the self as perpetual performer, the protean subjectivities enabled by
mechanical reproduction. What Benjamin identified as the shared skills
of the actor and the politician transform Thomas Hobbes's political and
theatrical relationship between the person and the sovereign as representatives of the self. In the age of mechanical reproduction, through the
technologies of electronic media, actors and politicians alike no longer
represent an autonomous self but a repertoire of images of imaginatively
available subjectivities.

What Benjamin could not imagine writing in Germany in the 1930s,
his insights influenced by the rising specter of National Socialism, was
that in the American context the "tasks" of actor and politician would co-
incide in a society governed by mass-mediated performance. As Reagan's
education demonstrates, in a society saturated with the electronic media
to a degree Benjamin could never have envisioned, the actor and the
politician would share the limelight in what Guy Debord termed "the society of the spectacle." In the "new selection," the "selection before the
equipment," the task of the political and cultural performer would be the
same: the mediation of social relations through images. It is as images of
the actual and imaginable dimensions of the body politic that performers
and politicians enact their shared task as mediators of social life in the
imagi-nation.

Ironically, it was a film about the shared role of performers and presidents in constructing the American imagi-nation that helped derail
Ronald Reagan's bid for film stardom and pushed him toward politics.
King's Row (1942) was Reagan's last and best shot at becoming a movie
star. As a reward for his performance as George Gipp in *Knute Rockne—All
American*, Reagan was cast for the first time as a first lead in a major studio
production. Warner Brothers spent the princely sum of thirty-five thou-

sand dollars to acquire the rights to Henry Bellaman's best-selling novel and assigned some of its top talent to convert it to the screen. Based on the audience response to Reagan in sneak previews, the studio offered him a seven-year contract that would make him the tenth highest paid actor in Hollywood by 1946. Reagan, who some had taken to referring to as the Errol Flynn of B movies, had made the A-list, ranking just behind Flynn at number nine and well ahead of Rita Hayworth at number eleven.[50] While *King's Row* was not a box office success, it received three Academy Award nominations, including one for best picture, and according to Reagan it was also "the only picture I was in for which there was ever any talk of getting an Academy Award."[51]

King's Row supplied the title and animating metaphor of Reagan's book *Where's the Rest of Me?* The memoir's rejection of the limited ontic status of the actor for the wholeness of the political performer paradoxi-

---

Photo: Broadway showman, writer, and producer George Michael Cohan plays the role of Franklin Delano Roosevelt in *I'd Rather Be Right than Be President,* ca. 1935–42. Photo © Bettman/Corbis.

cally affirms the performance-based ideology of American identity exemplified by another Warner Brothers film nominated for an Academy Award that year. The star of *Yankee Doodle Dandy* (1942) was Jimmy Cagney, the actor Warner Brothers promoted for the Oscar instead of Reagan. The "Yankee Doodle Boy" played by Cagney was George M. Cohan, the most prominent figure in American musical theater in the early twentieth century. Described by one critic as "nothing short of a brilliant tour-de-force of make believe,"[52] *Dandy* tells the story of a boy born into a family of itinerant troupers on the Fourth of July at "the beginning of the Horatio Alger Age," a vagabond hoofer who through hard work, cockiness, and "songs that express America" becomes the toast of Broadway. Like Reagan's autobiography, *Dandy* is a cultural artifact that demonstrates how the representational techne of Hollywood's golden age made America and Americans through a process Michael Rogin has termed "self-making through role-playing."[53]

Beginning with his performance as Tom Powers in *Public Enemy* (1931), the characters Cagney played for Warner Brothers in the 1930s defined the studio's trademark urban crime dramas. By the time he made *Dandy,* Cagney was the studio's top box office attraction. Cagney's roots, however, were in the musical theater. He often described himself as a song and dance man at heart "who was led down the wayward path of gangsterism by the movies."[54] Cagney began his career as a performer on the vaudeville circuit and Broadway prior to appearing in "legitimate" plays and moving to Hollywood. When his career as a Broadway dancer stalled, he formed the Cagné School of Dance to train aspiring Broadway hoofers. While he had never worked with Cohan, he was an extremely skilled dancer who knew Cohan's work and had danced on Broadway with performers who had appeared in Cohan's productions.

In addition to a desire to return to his roots, Cagney had political motives for playing Cohan. His leftist-liberal politics had left him vulnerable to highly publicized accusations that he was a member of the Communist Party.[55] To counter his image problems, Cagney's brother William proposed to Jack Warner that they "make a movie with Jim playing the damnedest patriotic man in the country."[56] Cagney was in the last year of his contract with Warner Brothers and the studio was eager to please its often disgruntled star. Cohan's approval was sought and received,

Warner's top producer, Hal Wallis, was assigned to the project, William Cagney was brought on as associate producer, and Robert Buckner—who also wrote the screenplay for *King's Row*—was selected to write the script. Production on the film began the day after the attack on Pearl Harbor, an auspicious coincidence for a film whose patriotic zeal reflected the national mood in the early days of World War II.

That the "biopic" would embellish the facts of Cohan's life with a liberal dose of fancy was an assumption shared by all involved. The nature of the treatment of Cohan's life envisioned by the production team was spelled out in his contract with Warners, in which he agreed to provide three new additional songs, music and piano arrangements, and material for the script, "which may be wholly or partly fictional." Speaking of his screenplay for *Santa Fe Trail* (in which Reagan played Gen. George Custer), Buckner confided to Wallis, "I don't give . . . a damn about strict historical accuracy if it hamstrings a story."[57] Michael Curtiz, *Dandy's* Hungarian-born director and a legendary mangler of English, confessed to Jack Warner, "Vell Jock, the scenario isn't the exact truth but ve haff the facts to prove it."[58] The response of Cohan's daughter Georgette would surely have pleased everyone involved in making the film. "That's the kind of life," she remarked approvingly, "daddy would like to have lived."[59]

In the opening scene of the film the aging song and dance man is apprehensive. It is opening night, and he has made a triumphant return to Broadway after a long absence. The show is a hit, but he is worried. He is impersonating Franklin Roosevelt in a satirical revue entitled *I'd Rather Be Right,* and he has just been summoned to the White House for an interview with the "real" president. When he enters the foyer of the White House he is greeted by a "colored butler," who, much to Cohan's surprise, proves to be a big fan. As he escorts Cohan upstairs, the butler enthusiastically reminisces about seeing his youthful performance as George Washington, "singing and dancing about the grand old flag." When Cohan enters the Oval Office the camera frames him standing, facing the camera. In the foreground is the president, seated, his back to the camera. As with Reagan's image on the screen above the stage, all we see is the head of the performer. Here, however, the body the performer's head sits atop is that of the president of the United States.

"Well, hello there," says FDR, "how's my double?" Cut to Cohan, who fills the screen.

Emboldened by FDR's positive response to his satirical portrayal, Cohan proceeds to tell the president the story of his life. In a series of flashbacks the film shows us how, in the words of an enthusiastic theater manager, he "invented the American success story." When we reach the final curtain of the opening night of *I'd Rather Be Right*—the scene with which the film began—the president reveals the reason he has sent for Cohan. In a theatrical presentation that evokes the Academy Awards, the president hands him a medallion (could it be an "Oscar"?) and reads the inscription, awarding him the Congressional Medal of Honor "for his Contributions to the American Spirit." The honor renders Cohan "speechless" (not literally, of course, for he still needs to provide the cue for the president's speech, which defines the entertainer's role in the republic). "But this medal is for people who have given their lives to their country or done something big," he modestly protests. "I'm just a song and dance man, everybody knows that." The president's reply, like the medal he bestows on Cohan, acknowledges the role of the performer and vocal culture in the construction of American identity.

> A man may give his life to his country in many different ways. . . . Your songs were a symbol of the American Spirit. "Over There" was just as powerful a weapon as any cannon, as any battleship we had in the First World War. We're all soldiers. We're all on the front. We need more songs to express America. I know you and your comrades will give them to us.

As Cohan takes his leave he tells the president not to worry about the war that has just begun. "We've got this thing licked," he says. "Where else in the world today could a plain guy like me talk things over with the head man?" This populist expression of American Exceptionalism receives the president's endorsement: "Well, that's as good a definition of America as any I've ever heard."

In *Yankee Doodle Dandy*, the life of the song and dance man both embodies and mediates national history. Like Thomas Betterton's burial in Westminster Abbey (the first time an actor had been accorded the honor),

Cohan's award was the first time an actor had received the Congressional Medal of Honor.[60] Both the film and the award signify a transformation in the relationship between "the Imaginary and Real Monarch" in a society of "Free-Born people."[61] Cohan—like the republic for which he stands and stands in for—was born on the Fourth of July and traced his lineage from the theater, described by John Adams, in which the self-evident because self-made man was to make his true figure.

The exchange between Roosevelt and Cohan also marks an epitomizing event. Although it is awarded by Congress, the Medal of Honor is presented by the president, and in the transfer a symbolic debt is paid and a new era ushered in. As the "colored butler" attests, Cohan's years of impersonating American icons from George Washington to Uncle Sam had earned him the honorary title of "prince of the American theater."[62] But as Thomas Paine asserted, in a society of common feeling there is a higher pedigree than royalty. The Medal of Honor acknowledges a more startling transformation for Cohan than that of ordinary guy to prince, an identity whose genealogy Cohan himself announces in the lyrics of the film's title song, "Yankee Doodle Dandy."

> *I'm a Yankee Doodle Dandy*
> *A Yankee Doodle Do or Die*
> *A real live nephew of my Uncle Sam*
> *Born on the Fourth of July*

The song joins the performer to the nation through a common lineage, mythic narrative, and birth date. As the film makes clear, they are also connected by their shared role in the creation of the society of common feeling through a culture of performance.

Like Reagan's description of his own birth scene in *Where's the Rest of Me?* Cohan's arrival is equated with the birth of a nation sired by performers. It is the Fourth of July, 1878, and, as his mother prepares to give birth, his father, who has been performing across town, desperately tries to cross a street blocked by a parade. When Jerry Cohan (Walter Huston) finally arrives at his wife's bedside, waving a flag, the doctor suggests naming the baby George Washington in honor of the day. Nellie Cohan (Rosemary DeCamp) deems the name "too long to fit on a billboard." The line is played for comedy but rings true nonetheless. To become a Cohan required a name that fit on a marquee. To warrant a movie about his life, however, Cohan had to make a name for himself—acknowledged by the Medal of Honor and emblazoned in the title of the film—a name whose genealogy signifies the connection between the song and dance man and the nation he represents.

The original "Yankee Doodle" became famous as a Patriotic anthem during the Revolutionary War. It first emerged in the United States during the French and Indian War, when a British officer, scornful of the colonial militiamen's lack of polish and discipline, wrote "Yankee Doodle" as a derogatory commentary on his bumpkin cousins. (Americans were called Jonathans by the British, and the word *Yankee* is most likely derived from the Dutch word *jankee* or "little John"). At the battle of Lexington, British troops played "Yankee Doodle" to mock the colonial army as it marched through the countryside. As the *Pennsylvania Gazette* reported, however, while "the Brigade under Lord Percy marched out, playing, by way of contempt, *Yankee Doodle*," after being defeated "they had been made to dance to it."[63] The British again played the song to deride the colonists at Bunker Hill, but by this time the Jonathans had claimed the tune as their own and defiantly sang its lyrics as the British retreated. By the end of the war, "Yankee Doodle" provided both the tune and the lyrics to which America marched. In a reversal of the song's original intent, the Marquis de Lafayette described Britain's General Cornwallis marching toward the American lines to surrender to George Washington's army at Yorktown while the French army played "Yankee Doodle" to "discomfort" the British.[64]

The defiant appropriation of "Yankee Doodle" as a march of independence was refashioned in Cohan's employ. He wrote "Yankee Doodle Dandy" for the Broadway musical *Little Johnny Jones,* in which the title character, an American jockey, declares his intention to ride the pony Yankee Doodle to "give America / the English derby cup." Cohan restages Paul Revere's ride—an event that inaugurates Yankee Doodle's transformation from national joke to national hero—as a sporting competition whose stakes were national pride. Because of his unparalleled equestrian skills, the British "[h]ave offered Johnny anything" to stay and ride in Britain. With political independence from Britain long ago established, what is at stake here is cultural hegemony. Horse racing is merely the occasion for engaging an older contest between Britain and America over the rights to cultural property and national representation.

While Little Johnny Jones has no recognizable historical referent, his name and story point to an identifiable theatrical predecessor. The character of Yankee Johnathan was the first postrevolutionary addition to American acting's "lines of business," the conventional categories of stock types and roles. Yankee Johnathan was a wholly American contribution to the "eccentric" business line, which—reflecting the proliferation of ethnic, racial, religious, and linguistic difference in America—would expand to include characters such as the stage Indian, the immigrant Irishman, and the "Sambo" darkie. "Adepts of this line," observes Joseph Roach, "learned how to emphasize the eccentricities of the characters through mimicry of their speech." Articulating "the rhythms and inflections of spoken dialect," eccentric characters vocally materialized their lines of business as a mimic embodiment of the drawing of social lines between assimilation and exclusion.[65] Nineteenth-century American actors created a range of distinctively American lines of business through a vocal practice that, like Revolutionary War era elocutionists, generated culturally coded symbolic bodies. Embodied by American actors, these new theatrical characters both reproduced and mediated socially constructed lines of ethnicity, class, and race.

Mimicry, however, always produces an overabundance of signification, calling forth more or different bodies than it intends. "[T]he discourse of mimicry," comments Homi K. Bhabha, "is constructed around an *ambivalence;* in order to be effective, mimicry must continually produce its slippage, its excess, its difference."[66] While both the ideology of *Yankee Doodle Dandy* and the lyrics of "Yankee Doodle Dandy" proclaim the "name and fame and boodle" to be acquired in a society in which a "plain guy" is free to pursue whatever line of business he desires, the body of the performer often tells a different story. In *The Phantom President,* his first talking picture and only musical performance in a movie, Cohan played a traveling medicine show man who is a dead ringer for a dull presidential candidate. A scene in which Cohan, in blackface, sings a song entitled "Maybe Someone Ought to Wave the Flag" is followed by a tap dance copied almost step for step by Cagney playing Cohan playing Little

Johnny Jones performing the "Yankee Doodle Dandy" number in *Dandy*.[67] While Cagney's voice and Cohan's lyrics express the jingoistic sentiments of Little Johnny Jones, Cagney's dancing and Cohan's choreography materialize a body animated by the productive union of patriotism and racial cross-dressing.

In the lyrics of "Yankee Doodle Dandy," the equestrian Little Johnny Jones claims his inheritance as "a real live nephew of my Uncle Sam," but his dancing speaks to the legacy of miscegenation and his kinship with the lawn jockey. "I love to listen to the Dixie strain," Johnny sings, reminding us that Paul Revere's most notable night-riding descendants wore white hoods and robes. "Yankee Doodle Dandy" rationalizes the problematic ancestry of both Johnny and Cohan—two minstrel men "born on the Fourth of July"—by a performance strategy Michael Rogin describes as characteristic of the blackface musical film: "In defining Americanness as entertainment . . . blackface musicals . . . [present] American identity in terms of performance and self-making. . . . They make themselves as performances, and not the world they represent, the basis for American patriotism."[68] *Yankee Doodle Dandy,* like the Reagan presidency, both draws on and adds to the cultural archive of performance techne capable of stimulating the imagination as a social process and producing the spectacle of social relations mediated by images.

When Johnny loses he is accused of throwing the race and is forced to stay in England. As the ship carrying his American fans is about to depart London, a character credited only as "Actor"—played by Cohan's father Jerry (Walter Huston)—tells Johnny to watch the ship for a signal that he has obtained evidence to exonerate him. The ship sets sail for New York, and Johnny sings "Give My Regards to Broadway" to the departing passengers. Broadway and Dixie stand in for America in the nostalgic song and dance of Johnny's exilic longing. His mournful soft-shoe routine is interrupted by what the screenplay describes as "a rocket," which "arches gracefully up into the top of the stage, and explodes like a brilliant scattering of stars."[69] A stage effect—"the most daring and exciting trick that had ever been pulled on the New York Stage"—initiated by "Actor" signals the recovery of Johnny's lost innocence as surely as the glare of the rockets and the bursting of bombs gave Francis Scott Key all the proof he needed at Fort Henry.[70] While Cohan's and Johnny's claim to be the

nephew of a cultural icon is genetically suspect, their "singing and dancing about the grand old flag" declares the genealogy of a performance that
borrows its sound and imagery from the American Revolution and its
choreography and kinetic memory from blackface minstrelsy. Their declaration of independence electrifies the performance techne that shaped
the nation in order to generate a national voice and symbolic body capable of evoking a society of common feeling.

"The Grand Old Flag" is the number that follows Johnny's exonera-
tion in the film, and it is cited on the Medal of Honor as one of Cohan's
"contributions to the American Spirit." The imagery and music are a patriotic montage and medley of the greatest hits of the Revolutionary War.
The choreography, however, is pure minstrelsy. The number is choreographed and shot with a verve and energy that is, thankfully, unparalleled
in the history of the American musical. The cumulative effect—a sensory
and semiotic overload—induces a sort of ideological vertigo not uncommon in the Age of Reagan. When images of the nation's mythic history
are so thoroughly processed through and mingled with the images of
American popular culture they make themselves as performances, and
not the past they represent, the basis for American patriotism.

Cohan expresses the putative ideology of *Dandy* in the scene that follows the opening of *George Washington Jr.*, the play that the White House
butler refers to at the beginning of the film. When he is asked by a newspaper reporter to share the secret of his success, Cohan replies, "I'm an ordinary guy who knows what ordinary guys want to see." Really? Like Reagan's contention that he owed his political success not to his acting
training but to "[making] sense to the guy on the street," Cohan's claim is
undermined by the education he received.[71] As the film shows but does
not tell, Cohan's popularity stems from a childhood devoted to learning
the craft of the song and dance man, an adolescence spent honing those
skills in the provinces, and an adulthood devoted to cultivating a theatrical empire as an actor, writer, composer, arranger, choreographer, dancer,
theater owner, manager, producer, and promoter. What the Roosevelt
character calls the "powerful weaponry" of Cohan's songs was the result
of a lifetime spent acquiring the musical and theatrical chops to create the
skillfully scored and choreographed patriotism that naturalized the national body of his era.

The repressed message of the film is that embodying the voice of a nation, like hegemony, is hard work. That it is the president's and the performer's shared duty to undertake this task is underscored in the film by establishing their voices as the primary characteristic for identifying them both individually and as doubles. At the beginning of the film, as the title appears on screen, the orchestra swells, the credits roll, and we are tempted to sing along ("I'm a Yankee Doodle Dandy, a Yankee Doodle do or die"). The film shrewdly recognizes that no vocals are necessary. We may not hear Cohan's voice (and might not recognize if it we did), but we know the voice he has given us through his songs ("I am that Yankee Doodle boy"). In the film's final flashback, directly before Roosevelt presents the Medal of Honor, Cohan performs the "Off the Record" number from *I'd Rather Be Right*. Again, it is not Cohan's voice we hear but FDR's, or rather Cagney's voice mimicking Cohan impersonating Roosevelt. This palimpsest of voices is the national voice articulated by the performer, singing in the voice of the president, in a performance that, as Michael Taussig writes of sympathetic magic, "affect[s] the original to such a degree that the representation shares in or acquires the properties of the represented."[72]

Like "natural theatricality," mimicry naturalizes its effects through the theatricalization of its difference from what it mimics. In *Dandy*, the similarity between the president and the performer is naturalized through the theatrical doubling of their bodies. Roosevelt's face and body are never revealed to the camera, which (with the exception of one dramatic shot at the end of the film) always frames him in the foreground, from the shoulders up, back to the camera, with Cohan in the background facing FDR and the camera. By the end of the film, having repeatedly framed each flashback with this image, Cohan's face fills out the back of Roosevelt's head just as in the flashbacks the performer's dancing legs literally stand in for the wheelchair-bound president. They are two sides of the same coin (heads the actor playing the actor, tails the actor playing the president), an overdetermined doubling in which all that is required to portray the president of the United States is a faceless voice-over. Even though the voice-over exaggerates FDR's vocal characteristics (or perhaps because of it), the voice is unmistakably Roosevelt's. We know it is him for the same reason Noonan was drawn to him, because even fifty-odd years later, through the technologies of mechanical reproduction, we still hear his voice. To bring the argument full circle, what the actor vocalizes is the grain of a voice that materializes a symbolic body, a hybrid of the president and the performer joined by their shared ability to embody a performative language of American identity. The grafting of the performer's face and legs onto the president's body is naturalized by their complimentary capacities to sing and speak for *the nation as theater,* and by the kinetic performance of their hyphenated body.

It is worth noting that the process by which the crippled president's body is made whole by the kinetic and vocal capacities of the performer is inverted in Reagan's autobiography, in which he describes how his greatest acting triumph revealed that as an actor he was "only half a man."[73] For Reagan, it is only as president, his role of a lifetime, that the performer will fill out the missing parts of his body. In rejecting the limited ontic status of the actor, however, Reagan reaffirms the performance-based ideology of American identity that makes patriots of colonial subjects and presidents of performers. *Where's the Rest of Me?* reinforces the repressed message of *Yankee Doodle Dandy,* testifying to the prodigious amount of training, rehearsal, and self-promotion that goes into effortlessly expressing the voice of the people. It is Hollywood's ideology of self-making through role-playing—shared by the Cagney film and the Reagan book and presidency—that nominates the performance as the surrogate president.

Peggy Noonan suspected that Ronald Reagan had a special reverence for the Roosevelt character in *Yankee Doodle Dandy.* She had "an intuition" that Reagan's "idea of the presidency and how to be president" was somehow connected to the film. Preparing to draft Reagan's farewell speech to the nation, she finally summoned the courage to find out if she was right. When she recalled the movie for him—Cagney, Cohan, the Academy Award—his eyes grew "warm with interest." She pursued her opening.

> "And in this movie at the very end you may remember a lovely scene in which Cagney-as-Cohan is called into the White House to receive their

version of the Medal of Freedom. And it's a beautifully played scene, re-member? The actor who played FDR is warm, and so complimentary, and Cagney is so moved, and he says, 'My mother thanks you, my Father thanks you,' and they shake hands and Cagney leaves—"

He nods, remembering. His eyes shine.

"—Cagney leaves FDR's office and gets to the big marble stairs over there

Photo: Jimmy Cagney dances in the 1930s. Photo © Getty Images.

in the residence, and he starts to dance down the stairs. Just out of joy he dances all the way down and goes out to Pennsylvania Avenue, where he joins some soldiers who are marching, singing, 'Over There.'"

"Oh yes, I remember."

"Mr. President, I have always had a hunch that movie had a special resonance for you, that the fellow playing FDR had something to do with how you conducted yourself in the presidency—that people came in here and you put them at their ease and thank them for their accomplishments. And I've seen it, by the time you were done with them they wanted to dance down the stairs."

"Oh, well." He is modest and pleased.

"You were moved by the movie."

"Oh, yes."

"And it made an impression, and—was it for you unforgettable?"

"Yes." He is eager.

I leaned in.

"Why, Mr. President?"

"Because no one knew Jimmy Cagney could dance."[74]

Noonan was searching for a transcendent image of the Reagan presidency. What she found was the incandescent memory of the performer's dancing body.

CHAPTER FOUR

Moving Pictures

You talkin' to me? You talkin' to me? You talkin' to *me*? Then who the hell else are you talkin' to? You talkin' to me? Well I'm the only one here. Who the fuck do you think you're talking to?

—Travis Bickle, *Taxi Driver*

On 30 March 1981, John Hinckley Jr. fired six "Devastator" bullets from a .22 caliber pistol at the president of the United States. Unlike John Wilkes Booth, who after shooting Abraham Lincoln, leaped to the stage of Ford's Theater crying "Sic semper tyrannis" (Thus always to tyrants), no dramatic political declaration accompanied Hinckley's act. According to Hinckley, he did it for love . . . and for the movies. He did not shoot

---

Photo: John Hinckley Jr. sits on fence wall in front of the White House. The picture is undated but believed to have been taken less than a year prior to his attempt to assassinate Ronald Reagan in 1981. Photo © Bettman/Corbis.

Ronald Reagan because he was the president, but because he was acting out the plot of a movie, *Taxi Driver,* in which Travis Bickle (Robert DeNiro) bids to win the heart of Iris (Jodie Foster), a twelve-year-old prostitute, by attempting to assassinate a political candidate. In a letter to the *New York Times,* Hinckley clarified his homage: "The shooting outside the Washington Hilton Hotel was the greatest love offering in the history of the world. I sacrificed myself and committed the ultimate crime in hopes of winning the heart of a girl."[1] Hinckley took his cue for action and romance from the movies. The rest of us entered the frame by watching the footage of the shooting repeatedly on television and parsing its effects on radio talk shows. As with most of the events that touch our lives, we, like Hinckley, sought understanding through the media that constitute the circuit of electronically relayed stories and images by which we come to know our world and take action in it.

When Hinckley told a reporter from *Newsweek* that assassination attempts are rarely politically motivated, he appeared to confirm the consensus view that his actions stemmed from ulterior motives. But the reason Hinckley's act was difficult to explain in political terms is because the practice of politics in the Age of Reagan bears only a glancing resemblance to any historically recognizable theory of political engagement. Both Reagan and his would-be assassin were products of an electronically massmediated public sphere that has redefined the basis of political representation in the United States. The right to representation, "once a revolutionary insistence in the articulation of an American self," observed cultural critic Paige Baty, "has been translated under conditions of normative mass mediation into the 'right to be *as* representation.'"[2] To *be* in a society saturated with representation is to circulate through the virtual public sphere that forms the crucible of representation for the personal and political subject alike. From this perspective Hinckley's seemingly apolitical motive for assassination exemplifies the dominant mode of political engagement at a time when the media that produced both Hinckley's fantasy and Reagan's presidency transformed the way Americans imagine, think about, and practice politics.

When Hinckley dropped out of college in 1976 and moved to Los Angeles to become a songwriter he entered the fraternity Ronald Reagan had joined forty years earlier. Exiles from the quotidian world of middle America, these modern-day Pilgrims were chasing a new American dream as far removed from Plymouth Rock as they could travel and still remain within the promised land. Here, in a barren desert crafted into a lush oasis, they each received a new education befitting their artificial paradise. While in Hollywood, Hinckley saw *Taxi Driver* at least fifteen times. His strategy for wooing Jodie Foster was not, however, simply a slavish imitation of Travis Bickle's. It was, as Richard Schechner has written of all performance, "repetition with revision."[3] Before Iris, Travis Bickle is drawn to Betsy (Cybill Shepherd), a political campaign worker who rejects him after he takes her to see a pornographic film. To make amends for the film's graphic depiction of his desire for Betsy, Bickle decides to assassinate the candidate she works for. Recombining the plot elements of *Taxi Driver,* and the real and reel lives of its actors, Hinckley's cinematic fantasy demonstrates the way we all integrate and personalize the education we receive as participants in what Raymond Williams called "the dramatized society."

Hinckley's desire to make history was nothing new. However, the widespread belief Hinckley shared—that anyone may do so—is directly attributable to the education of the imagination supplied by radio, film, and television. The unparalleled increase in the representations of possible lives and worlds circulated by electronic media, argues Arjun Appadurai, "means that ordinary lives today are more often powered not by the givenness of things but by the possibilities that the media (either directly or indirectly) suggest are available." This is not to say that the possibilities Appadurai refers to are equally or actually available to be realized by everyone. But when these possibilities are globally disseminated they engage us all in the play of imagination. Even those with seemingly the least freedom to define their fate, Appadurai suggestively concludes, "no longer see their lives as mere outcomes of the givenness of things, but often as the ironic compromise between what they could imagine and what social life will permit."[4] From this perspective the political implications of Hinckley's motive begin to be discernible. Viewed within the cultural context of a disturbingly large number of violent attacks on visible media celebrities in the United States since the 1960s, Hinckley's act connects John Lennon and Andy Warhol to Martin Luther King and the Kennedys as *political* martyrs. In each instance the assassin's refusal of Appadurai's "ironic compromise," the unwillingness to settle for "what social life will permit," articulates a widespread sense of inadequacy and frustration shared by large segments of a generation raised on movies and television. Unable to reconcile their electronically generated dreams and aspirations with the material reality of their lives these underrepresented revolutionaries train their resentment on those they perceive to have attained the media exposure they have been denied.

Paul Schrader's screenplay for *Taxi Driver* was inspired by Arthur Bremer, who attempted to assassinate Alabama governor and presidential candidate George Wallace in 1972. In his memoirs—published with the media-savvy title *An Assassin's Diary*—Bremer envisions killing a powerful politician as his ticket to celebrity and dwells obsessively on the staging of the act in such a way as to command maximum media attention. Bremer's diary entries exhibit little malice toward his intended victim. Instead, they reflect in great detail on the scenario of a triumphant revenge against the forces that have rendered him invisible and impotent by refusing to represent him. The diary chronicles a childhood spent seeking refuge from abusive, alcoholic parents by pretending that he "was living with a television family."[5] Frustrated at his inability to get close enough to his initial target, President Richard Nixon, Bremer angrily and conflictedly fantasizes about destroying his writings: "Burn all these papers . . . & no one would ever know ½ of it. But I want em [*sic*] all to know. I want a big shot & not a little fat noise." Pushed aside by a news photographer shooting protesters at a Nixon rally, Bremer laments his lack of audibility and visibility and the media's unwillingness to give him *his* shot: "Those noise makers were all on news film! He should of [*sic*] photographed the quiet ones. He never pointed his camera at me."[6] Resolving to assassinate Wallace instead of Nixon, Bremer worries that he has set his sights too low: "I won't even rate a T.V. enteroption [*sic*] in Russia or Europe when the news breaks—they never heard of Wallace. . . . He won't get more than 3 minutes on network TV news."[7]

"On every street in every city," proclaimed *Taxi Driver*'s tag line, "there is a nobody who dreams of being a somebody." Bremer's rage at his inability to attract the media coverage he believes he is owed is eerily etched in celluloid by DeNiro's performance as Travis Bickle, pacing his apartment, armed to the teeth, rehearsing the performance of vengeance and the delivery of his defining phrase: "You talkin' to me?" The actions of

Bickle, Bremer, and Hinckley all derive from the unbearable realization that—in a life no longer measured by the anomie of Prufrock's coffee spoons but by the adrenaline rush of sound bites and photo ops—nobody is interested in talking to them. Assassination is their shot at representation. What other form of representation (or revenge) could they conceive of in a media-saturated society that had denied them their fair share of love and airtime?

While the actions taken by these would-be assassins were extreme, the combination of desire and resentment they expressed toward the media in rationalizing their actions are extremely common. The trial testimony of Dr. Park Dietz, the leader of Hinckley's government-appointed team of psychiatrists, characterized him as an overprivileged, self-absorbed loner who, beginning with a fascination with the Beatles, "became exceedingly interested in fame, in the notion of success, in fame in a way that would not require a great deal of effort." Hinckley's pathology, Dietz testified, stemmed from a "long-standing interest in fame and assassination" and an unhealthy fascination with "the publicity associated with various crimes." The psychiatric report submitted at trial by Dietz, however, paints a more detailed and recognizable diagnosis, "an identity disturbance manifested by uncertainty about several issues relating to identity, namely self-image and career choice; and chronic feelings of emptiness or boredom; features of passive-aggressive personality disorder include *resistance to parental demands for adequate performance for occupational and social functioning.*" Dietz's diagnosis is as remarkable for its succinct summary of a widespread social phenomenon as it is for his myopic attribution of these traits to a single disturbed individual. The etiology he described so clearly characterized an entire generation disillusioned with the distance between the seemingly effortless fame and affluence promised by the media and the harsh economic and social realities of postindustrial capitalism that reporters at the trial dubbed these personality traits symptomatic of "dementia suburbia."[8]

Confining this media-influenced dementia to the suburbs, however, continues to underestimate the ubiquity of its effects. Variations of the symptoms that Dietz ascribes to Hinckley appear throughout the psychological and sociological literature of the Reagan years to describe a wide range of American cultural activity, predominantly youth based, from urban gangbangers to rural cultists, and social phenomena as varied as "wilding" and the militia movement. Both Dietz's diagnosis and the reporters' playful neologism undervalue the affective force of electronically mass-mediated popular culture in generating aspirations and expectations for something more than "adequate performance for occupational and social functioning." For Hinckley, Bremer, and Bickle, political assassination was a means to an end, the representation by dramatization that would accrue from their performances and the media coverage they would command: Butch or Sundance, guns blazing, racing toward their own demise . . . and right at the camera.

While neither Hinckley nor Bremer ascribed any political motivation to his shooting spree, they both cited the influence of the most infamous presidential assassin in American history; the one who prior to Ronald Reagan had also been the most famous actor in American politics. Hinckley, on one of his scouting trips to Washington, anticipated the immortality he sought by having himself photographed in front of both the White House and the theater in which John Wilkes Booth shot Abraham Lincoln. "Got to think up something cute to shout after I kill [Nixon]," Bremer wrote in his diary, "like Booth did."[9] Booth's melodramatic staging of Lincoln's assassination from the balcony of Ford's Theater situates him within a long tradition in the United States that links performance forms and players to political movements and audiences. The actor's choice of venue to avenge the South and reclaim the United States as an Anglo-Saxon republic is emblematic of a widespread belief—shared by Lincoln and other avid theatergoers of the nineteenth century—that the stage was an important forum for mediating the identity of America and Americans.

"Sic semper tyrannis" are the words Brutus is reputed to have spoken when he slew Julius Caesar. In a republic established in opposition to the tyranny of George III, and across the Potomac from Ford's Theater, the Commonwealth of Virginia had previously acknowledged the political efficacy of Brutus's declaration by adopting his words as its state motto. While the Bard did not utilize Brutus's admonition in *Julius Caesar*, it was Shakespeare who fortified Booth's political imagination and his resolve to perform tyrannicide. As the leading family of the nineteenth-century

American stage, the Booths were the most influential interpreters of Shakespeare's plays as scripts for theatrical and political action. Like his father, Junius, and his brothers, Edwin and Junius Jr., John Wilkes was renowned for his performances as Hamlet and Richard III, two of Shakespeare's bloodiest political actors and the roles by which nineteenth-century stage tragedians in the United States were measured. That *Julius Caesar* would provide the script and scenario for Booth's most infamous performance seems in retrospect to have been predetermined by the middle name of both his father and his younger brother: Brutus.

As Bremer noted often in his diary, "the ironies abound." George Wallace, the tyrannical target he finally settled on, was the contemporary politician who came closest to realizing Booth's vision of a racially pure republic. Hinckley's choice was the political performer who would restore to its former glory the relationship between statecraft and stagecraft so badly stained by Booth. In both cases the quest for immortality, for the media memory that promised life after death, was foiled by a flawed performance. In the confusion that ensued after he took his errant shot, Bremer forgot to utter the "cute phrase" he had devised to seal his legend ("A penny for your thoughts"). Hinckley's only enduring legacies were a reevaluation of the insanity defense and an increase in the security details for democracy's doppelgängers—celebrities and politicians.

The only performer to realize his media dreams from this cycle of carnal, bloody, and unnatural acts was also the only politician to ever share both Lincoln's office and Booth's profession. As any aficionado of the stage would surely have recognized in advance, it was Reagan who had garnered the most memorable role. As Reagan himself wrote of dying onstage in the Eureka College production of *Aria da Capo*, "[N]o actor can ask for more. Dying is the way to live in the theater." According to him, it was his performance in *Aria Da Capo* at the Eva La Galliene one-act play competition at Northwestern University in 1932 that prompted the head of Northwestern's Drama Department to suggest he consider becoming an actor. As a college senior assessing his prospects during the Great Depression, Reagan claims he had never seriously considered pursuing acting as a career until that moment.[10] Just as Reagan's stage death marked the birth of the actor, so his near death on the political stage marked his rebirth as president. "How the attempted assassination has tipped the program of the Congress, I don't know," lamented House majority leader Tip O'Neill, "but it has done that."[11] For budget director David Stockman, Reagan's recovery allowed the administration to frame the budget debate as a referendum on Reaganomics in "far more politically compelling and dramatic terms: Are you *with* Ronald Reagan or against him?" What was surely the most theatrically astute response to Reagan's post-assassination performance came from communications director David Gergen: "The March shooting transformed the whole thing. We had new capital. [It] gave us a second life."[12] By taking the bullet, Reagan was born again, baptized in the river of cultural memory and invested with its capital. Two months into his presidency, initiated into the pantheon of American political martyrs, he was handed a career-making role.

Hinckley was not the first to have turned to the memory of Booth as a means of removing Ronald Reagan from the political stage. "You know I'm running against an actor," incumbent California governor Pat Brown announced to a group of elementary school girls during Reagan's inaugural political campaign, and "you know who shot Abraham Lincoln, don't you?"[13] Invoking the historical mistrust of the moral character of the actor and blurring the boundaries between statecraft and statecraft, however, proved to be Brown's undoing. The overwhelmingly negative response to Brown's slur (captured in a television documentary sponsored by his campaign) was the final nail in his political coffin. His off-the-cuff remark, like his campaign's repeated attacks on Reagan as a mere actor, reflected his crucial misunderstanding of the historical relationship in politics between the performer and the statesman as costars in the production of American memory.

What Lincoln, Booth, and Reagan all possessed (and Brown most decisively lacked) was an appreciation for the acting profession and its efficacy in evoking the foundational declarations of independence from which all subsequent American political movements have derived their affective appeal and claimed their rights of memory. Most significant of all, Brown's clumsy joke misconstrued the threat posed by the actor within the American political tradition: Ronald Reagan sought not to bury Abraham Lincoln but to embody him. As a political performer, Reagan masterfully played what Lincoln in his first inaugural address called "the mystic chords of memory"—the actor's stock-in-trade—to invoke

America's mythic past and "swell the chorus of the Union."[14] Lincoln, Booth, and Reagan were all prone to invoking the memory of the martyred patriots of the American Revolution to justify their own bloody causes, be it civil war, tyrannicide, or the dismantling of the welfare state. Ironically, it was perhaps Booth who best summarized the contradictory claims of nostalgia and progress that have always connected the politician to the actor as co-mediators of the transmission and transformation of tradition. "The country," Booth lamented while plotting to mute the voice that would swell the national chorus, "is not what it was."[15] In his appeal to a mythic golden age as the basis for reanimating an endangered political theology (white supremacy in an Anglo-Saxon nation), he calls on the memorial authority of the dead and the cultural and political performers who represent them.

In failing to acknowledge the significance of Californians' election of another actor and former Screen Actors Guild president, George Murphy, as their junior senator the previous year, Brown also failed to recognize the new role for the professional actor as a body electric in a political environment in which electronic media were fast becoming the primary mise-en-scène for enacting the rites of memory. In the Age of Reagan—as charging the bodies became increasingly dependent on a mastery of media—the skills of the actor assumed a singular importance in the domain of political representation. Electronic media transformed the alchemical relationship between cultural and political performers. What distinguished this new relationship from its previous incarnations in American politics was that conventional appeals to history as a means of establishing political legitimacy were increasingly superseded by claims staked on the fertile ground of cultural performance forms and traditions. This performative turn in American politics—signaled by the ascension of radio, film, and television as political technologies—entered a new dimension with the election of the nation's first president fully schooled in the art and craft of mass-mediated performance.

The impetus for Hinckley's act and its timing—the day of the Academy Awards ceremony—typifies an understanding of the role of electronic media in the twentieth century as similar to that of the stage in the nineteenth. The celluloid immortality Reagan possessed and Hinckley sought was articulated by the theme of that year's awards: "Movies are forever." On the evening he was shot, Reagan was scheduled to address the academy from the White House. "Film is forever," were the words the president was to speak: "It is the motion picture that shows all of us not only how we look and sound but—more important—how we feel."[16] In the Age of Reagan, television and motion pictures became our primary resource for learning how to look, sound, and—most important—feel. In the church of electronic media, in the land where mass mediation has become a national religion, we are compelled by shafts of light emitted from a screen and we cleave to the glowing rock. During the Reagan presidency how we felt was determined by how we responded to what we witnessed on the screens that fixed our gaze, and whether we believed these visions reflected our authentic feelings or produced them for us.

An Actor Prepares

> In a town like Dixon during the early 1920s, the silent movie was still a novelty, "talkies" hadn't been invented yet, visits by vaudeville troupes were still rare, and television was something you read about in science fiction stories. People had to rely on themselves for entertainment.
>
> —Ronald Reagan, *An American Life*

Like most of Ronald Reagan's memories of childhood close inspection reveals a more complex reality. Silent movies may have been a novelty, but they provided the young Reagan with a form of entertainment that, along with radio and Chautauqua, helped shape his education and aspirations. While living in Tampico prior to moving to Dixon, Reagan carried coal to Burden's Opera House (the same venue where the Reagans performed as the first family of Tampico theater) in return for free admission to the silent westerns that showed on Monday or Tuesday evenings. In the summer, when it was too hot to be indoors, the manager of the Electric Theater roped off Main Street and screened silent movies outdoors with a soundtrack provided by the school band.[17] In Dixon, Reagan regularly attended the movies, and it was there—with "eyes turned misty by the cinematic perils that befell Mary Pickford and Pearl White" or imagining "galloping over the prairie" like the western heroes played by William S. Hart and Tom Mix—that he first "fell in love with the movies."[18]

The first of the cinematically described events Reagan credits with spurring his imagination to dream of Hollywood occurred during the Thanksgiving vacation of his freshmen year at Eureka College. Watching a touring theatrical production of R. C. Sherriff's *Journeys End,* Reagan describes being "drawn to the stage that night as if it were a magnet, astonished by the magic of an ordinary man convincing an audience that he was someone else." That Reagan would place so much weight on this particular production is curious. The play itself—"a tragedy set in World War I that focused on the emotions of a weary, emotionally bruised military officer, Captain Stanhope"—was most notable for providing the West End debuts of the director James Whale and the twenty-one-year-old Laurence Olivier.[19] Its Broadway run was successful enough to generate several touring companies, including the one Reagan saw. Throughout his childhood, however, he had attended and performed in numerous plays, and it is hard to believe this was the first time he had experienced the "magic" that attracted him like "a magnet" to the stage.

It is more likely that the production was memorable for Reagan only in retrospect, as a sign of his destiny. Just prior to his enrollment at Eureka, Ellen Marie Johnson was hired by the college's English Department and assumed the role of faculty adviser for the extracurricular theater activities on campus. Johnson invigorated and expanded the theater program by organizing a drama society and increasing the number of student productions. When, shortly after Reagan saw *Journey's End,* Johnson cast him as Captain Stanhope in the Eureka College production it was "as if God was carrying out His plan with my name on it." It was Johnson who also arranged for tiny Eureka College to compete with hundreds of bigger schools at Northwestern University's one-act play competition, a contest for college actors that Reagan called "comparable to the Super Bowl."[20]

Shortly after returning to Eureka from that fateful Thanksgiving break, Reagan would have another epiphany involving an audience. On 28 November 1928, a midnight meeting was called to gain student support for a strike to force the resignation of Eureka's president.[21] Reagan was the only freshman asked to speak at the rally.

> I'd been told that I should sell the idea so there'd be no doubt of the outcome. I reviewed the history of our patient negotiations with due empha-

sis on the devious manner in which the trustees had sought to take advantage of us. *I discovered that night that an audience has a feel to it and, in the parlance of the theater, that the audience and I were together.* When I came to actually presenting the motion there was no need for parliamentary procedure: they came to their feet with a roar—even the faculty members present voted by acclamation. It was heady wine. Hell, with two more lines I could have had them riding through "every Middlesex village and farm"—without horses yet.[22]

Listening through the hoofbeats of Paul Revere's ride one can discern a carnal desire stimulated by the "feel" of an audience, an urgent desire to get "together" with it, to contact and move the collective by convincing it that he was somebody else. This desire magnetizes the heart of the performer. Lou Cannon, the political reporter who began covering Reagan in the mid-1960s, observed that he "loved the roar of the crowd" and "shrank from confrontations unless he was on stage." When kept too long from an audience, Cannon observed, "he could become distracted and listless."[23] Reagan's relationship with an audience animated him, and it was the lengthiest and most intimate relationship of his life.

Reagan's affair with the audience and the effect it had on him did not sit well with Mugs Cleaver. Two years into his radio career Dutch opened a letter and the fraternity pin and engagement ring he had given her tumbled out. Although Reagan was still struggling to establish himself as a radio broadcaster, Mugs saw the writing on the wall. "I didn't want to bring up my children in Hollywood," she explained to Edmund Morris. And besides, Reagan "had an inability to distinguish between fact and fancy."[24] How could he not? According to him, Nelle's favorite maxim was "Judge everyone by how they act, not what they are." Reagan cites his mother's words as an admonishment to assess people's worth by the content of their character and not by the color of their skin.[25] "By their deeds ye shall know them" would be the biblical equivalent. But the words chosen and the sentiment expressed are at odds. The words enunciate—in terms similar to those of Mugs's graduation address—the paradox of natural theatricality, a prominent feature of Reagan's education that would be entirely naturalized when he moved to Hollywood.

In 1936, when Reagan covered the Chicago Cubs' spring-training season on Catalina Island in California, Mugs's worst fears would be realized. Through Joy Hodges, a singer who had worked at WHO before moving to Los Angeles to try her luck in the movies, Reagan was introduced to a talent agent, Bill Meiklejohn. Meiklejohn arranged a screen test for Reagan at Warner Brothers by telling the casting director, Max Arnow, that he had "another Robert Taylor sitting in my office." During his audition (which consisted of reading a scene from *Holiday* by the playwright Phillip Barry, in whose *You and I* Reagan had costarred with Mugs in high school), Reagan's voice reminded Arnow of "a promising young actor, Ross Alexander, who—on the verge of stardom at Warner Brothers—was a tragic suicide." When Reagan arrived at the studio to begin work, he was told by Arnow he would be playing a radio announcer in *Love Is on the Air*, based on the Broadway play *Hi, Nellie*, a scenario the director, Brynie Foy, had made "about six times" but never with a radio setting. If distinguishing between fact and fancy was difficult for Reagan before he arrived in Hollywood, he didn't stand a chance once he got there. Few did in a world where opportunity knocked because of a physical resemblance to one actor, the door opened because of a vocal similarity to a second actor, admission was granted on the basis of the ability to impersonate a fictional character, and the job itself entailed taking on a role Reagan had been playing professionally for the past four years, in a screenplay based on a stage play, the plot of which the studio continuously recycled on celluloid.[26] How could anyone in this world judge another by "who they are"? How else would it be possible to evaluate someone except by how they acted?

In Hollywood, Reagan quickly discovered that acting in films was only part of his job and no more governed by fantasy than the rest of it. Prior to beginning production for *Love Is on the Air*, he described his first Hollywood role as a bewildered participant "in an off screen drama that might have been called *The Remaking of Dutch Reagan*." Arnow told him his hair had to be changed and sent him to the House of Westmore, where his "Harold Teen haircut—short and parted down the middle"—was transformed into a large pompadour and his part was moved from the middle of his head to the right side.[27] A year later the studio, feeling "that his dark hair looked too Latin or Mediterranean on black and white film . . . lightened it to an auburn color to reinforce his all-American look."[28] His eyeglasses were replaced with contact lenses. He was given darker makeup, deeper laugh lines, and imitation dimples to hide the deep crevice that years of wearing heavy glasses had dug into the bridge of his nose. He was sent to a dialogue coach to break his radio announcer's habit of "talking chin-up and stiff-necked." When cameramen complained that his neck was too short for his shoulders and his head was too small, he was sent to Wardrobe, which pointed him to fellow Warner Brothers actor James Cagney's shirt maker, who had designed a deep-V collar to solve Cagney's similar problem.[29] As president, Reagan wore contact lenses, the same slicked-back pompadour parted on the right, and the deep-V collar on all his shirts. Except when angry, he always spoke with his chin down and neck relaxed.

It was also Arnow, along with a team of publicists, who proposed the biggest change. They deemed "Dutch," the nickname Reagan had been known by all his life, an inappropriate name for the image they were constructing. Reagan, however, was not as much of a rube as they assumed. Through the influence of B. J. Palmer, he had already developed a familiarity with the somnipractic arts. "May I point out," he responded, "that I have a lot of name recognition in a large part of the country, particularly in the Middle West, where I've been broadcasting sports. I think a lot of people would recognize my name on theater marquees."[30] He was probably correct. The previous year a *Sporting News* poll had ranked him as the fourth most popular baseball announcer not working in a major league town.[31] The broaching of marquees, however, appears to have sealed his fate. "One of them said, 'Dutch Reagan? You can't put Dutch Reagan on a marquee.'" It was at that moment that Reagan named his own image by reclaiming his given name:

> I had never liked my first name and in school and on the radio, I'd always used my nickname. But I made a spot decision that I'd be happier using my real name than some moniker dreamed up by a press agent, and so I ventured inquiringly:
>
> "How about Ronald? . . . Ronald Reagan?"
>
> They looked at each other and began repeating it to one another, "Ronald Reagan . . . Ronald Reagan . . . "
>
> "Hey, that's not bad," one said.
>
> Pretty soon you would have thought *they* had thought it up.[32]

And "Ronald Reagan" was born again as a celluloid celebrity.

A Star Is Born

The celebrity was one of the most effective products of the twentieth century for defining subjectivities and the style and habits of behavior that correspond to them. The function of celebrity in conflating the realms of production of mass culture and politics is critical to an understanding of Reagan as a political performer. Reagan was an actor president but he was also a celebrity president, a valuable commodity in a political arena that increasingly borrowed its techniques and strategies for generating affective investments from the industries of popular culture. Reagan was not the first celebrity president. One could argue that FDR, as he did in so many other areas, pioneered the form. And it is indisputable that John Kennedy, thanks to his father's connections in Hollywood and his own proclivities and charisma, fit the bill. But it was not until the presidency of Ronald Reagan that the processes of celebrification were systematically applied to the making of a president. It is not until the Age of Reagan that the realms of politics and popular culture became virtually indistinguishable, and it was through the techne of electronically mediated celebrity that these two realms were most fully conflated.

Since the late nineteenth century the American celebrity has been a lightning rod for channeling and conducting the diffuse power of the body politic. P. David Marshall traces the rise of modern celebrity as a response to the same anxiety that gripped Henry Adams as he stared down Broadway, anxiously acknowledging the emergence of the crowd and the mass as powerful symbolic forces. According to Marshall, the celebrity represents a site for hegemonic processes focused on both rationalizing the threatening irrationality of the crowd and for constructing ideological support for the maintenance of control and order. This double function leads Marshall to posit a dialectic at work in the construction of celebrity such that the celebrity "can be positioned somewhere between the dominant culture's rationalization of what it sees as irrational and the popular audience's use, identification, and expression of the affective power that the celebrity as a system of rationalization has been positioned to reflect."[33] Reflecting the constant jockeying among conflicting social forces for semiotic control, the modern celebrity is coterminous with the development of the political and affective economies of mass culture.

But while Marshall reads the celebrity sign as a *text* inscribed with the discursive representations of identity formation, contemporary celebrity, as evidenced by Reagan, might be more accurately conceived as a *performance effect*, the staging of the body electric on the media screens that represent the public sphere. Paige Baty suggests that mass-mediated culture ("the images, stories, persons—in short, the host of productions—circulated through the mass media") operates through both a literal/material and figurative/imaginary process that "authorizes" public life by replacing the citizen into the body politic as the mediator of these "productions."[34] Electronic media provide the citizen with representation by initiating her "into the codes and orders of the greater political cultural economy through her relation to a common repository of memory."[35] Under the fiat of electricity the celebrity becomes an influential arbiter of cultural memory, endowed with the symbolic capital that makes it a productive and reproductive site of subject formation.

The evolution of celebrity in the twentieth century loosely parallels the trajectory sketched by Warren Sussman from a culture of character to a culture of personality and from a producer-driven economy to a consumer-stimulated one.[36] The culture of character conflated attributes of the celebrity with those of the hero. It assumed that if an individual possessed heroic qualities and character his celebrity (in this model women were rarely figured as celebrities) would become self-evident through his actions in the public sphere. Prior to the advent of the movie industry, celebrity was conceived in terms similar to the oratorical ideal of eighteenth-century elocutionists, as a publicly visible reflection of an authentic private self. The advent of motion pictures changed all that by codifying and publicizing the celebrity as a marketing device for its industry and product.

Lodged in the DNA of movie star celebrity are the commercial and suprascientific strains that flow through its bloodlines. Motion pictures emerged from the same nineteenth-century fascination with matter and motion that led Henry Adams to call for a new education capable of probing their mysteries. The men who invented motion picture technology, however, were not interested in mass entertainment. They sought to render visible what the human eye could not see. In 1872, at the behest of the railroad magnate Leland Stanford, on whose farm Stanford University would soon be built, the photographer Eadweard Muybridge conducted a series of time-motion studies to discover whether a moving horse ever lifted all four legs off the ground at once. By 1878, using twelve cameras arranged at intervals along a track, Muybridge was able to provide conclusive visual evidence of all four hooves suspended in the air. The following year, while searching for a way to animate his images for public display after the publication of his photographs in scientific journals around the world had made him a fixture on the lecture circuit, Muybridge invented the zoopraxiscope, a device capable of projecting his still images onto a screen in rapid succession to give the illusion of motion. Almost simultaneously, the French scientist Etienne-Jules Marey—seeking to develop a scientific method capable of proving Darwin's theory of evolution—invented a graphic instrument for recording movement as a means of demonstrating how alterations in organic functions over time resulted in changes in organic forms. Marey and Muybridge shared a common scientific lineage and a belief that if nature's methods could be understood they could be reproduced. Like Muybridge, Marey's subjects were animals in motion. In 1882, his aspirations were partially realized when he invented the first motion picture camera, "a kind of photographic gun" capable of photographing birds in flight at twelve exposures per second.[37]

The story of the development of modern celebrity begins with the first commercial application of motion picture technology. "I am experimenting upon an instrument that does for the eye what the phonograph does for the ear," Thomas Edison wrote in 1888, "which is the recording and reproduction of things in motion." Unlike Marey and Muybridge, Edison was not interested in the science of time-motion studies or evolution. While Adams lamented the erosion of unity and order in a world in which the only certainty was that "Matter was Motion—Motion was Matter—the thing moved," Edison seized on this same understanding, so unsettling to Adams, as an opportunity for a new synthesis of science, entertainment, and commerce. While he did little to advance the scientific development of motion picture technology, he was (as was so often the case) the first to take it to the market. His kinetoscope, the first commercial motion picture machine, debuted at the Chicago World's Columbian Exposition in 1893. The opening of the first kinetoscope parlor in New

York City the following year signaled the beginning of the end for the character-driven myth of celebrity, whose subjects Joshua Gamson describes as "the great and talented and virtuous and best-at" who "rise like cream to the top of the attended-to."[38] Kinetoscope parlors were quickly replaced with nickelodeons, and a technology produced by science and consumed for amusement became the first form of mass entertainment.

The transition from the scientific development of the technology of motion pictures to the entertainment industry of the movies reflects the changing social dynamic in the United States at the turn of the century. Movies were developed and dominated by men who did not share Adams's social, ethnic, or religious background. In contrast to Edison, who envisioned motion picture technology as a medium for the wealthy, these immigrant entrepreneurs recognized the commercial possibilities of attending to the "unattended-to." Unlike earlier forms of mass media (the newspaper and the magazine, for example, which initially catered to the Anglo-Protestant elite before targeting a popular audience as literacy and discretionary income became more widespread), the movies engaged a mass audience from the beginning. The nickel and visual literacy required to gain entrance to the nickelodeons were generally available to recent immigrants with little money and an imperfect knowledge of English. As Robert Sklar documents in *Movie-Made America,* while the initial curiosity about the kinetoscope transcended class boundaries, motion pictures came of age as a social and economic phenomenon by connecting with the needs and aspirations of a growing urban, immigrant, working class.[39]

With the arrival of the motion picture and the new possibilities it provided for the "organization, availability, and visibility" of "fame technologies," celebrity began to be both democratized and systematized.[40] And the idea of celebrity was inextricably bound up with the promise of stardom. As the new century began, D. W. Griffith introduced the close-up to the visual grammar of the motion picture. By isolating and magnifying the actor's face, the close-up established a heightened sense of intimacy between performer and audience. The close-up also isolated the individual from the crowd, identifying the face on which it trained the audience's gaze as distinctive and distinctively compelling. Béla Balàzs proposes that the primary innovation of the close-up was that it revealed the apparently "unmediated personality of the individual," instilling in an audience the essential response for the creation of a new relationship with the actor: the belief that it was witnessing the performer as a "unique person."[41] And the star was born.

In 1910, the year before Reagan was born, the first movie fan magazine, *Photoplay*, was founded, and was quickly followed by a host of others. Never slow to profit from a good idea, the Hollywood studios soon developed their own in-house publicity apparatus and began marketing their films through the strategic manufacturing of their actors as stars. The early phases of the motion picture industry's deployment of celebrity as the machinery of star making might be termed "the age of discovery." The early film stars rarely had a public history. It was their status as "unknowns" that allowed inventive publicists to create biographies that would resonate with their film roles and at the box office. In 1914, the year after the opening of the first American theater built specifically for motion pictures, Fox Studios released *A Fool There Was*, Theda Bara's film debut, which was preceded by a publicity tour to launch her as a Hollywood star. Prior to entering the movies Bara had been a bit player on Broadway, but Fox billed her as the Egyptian progeny of "a sheik and a princess, given in mystic marriage to the Sphinx, fought over by nomadic tribesman, clairvoyant and insatiably lustful."[42] This was a major makeover for a Jewish girl from Cincinnati. Her celebrity was predicated on the seamless relationship between her invented biography and her role in the film, which—well before *Dracula* was first converted to celluloid— introduced the term *vampire* into motion pictures. The term used to describe the predatory character Bara played and would play numerous times in her many "vampire" films, referred to the blood-sucking sexuality of her screen persona. In positioning Theda Bara as a star, Fox created a star persona that was both larger than life and an excellent substitute for it.

In the more sexually adventurous postwar climate of the 1920s, the dangerously desirable vampire became the desirably dangerous vamp, a term that came to define an entire genre of seductive starlets. The truncation of vampire to vamp signals a new genre of star and a shift in the terms of celebrity that was reflected in the emergence of a new set of ideals for the relationship between the star's private and public self. With increasing attention being paid to Hollywood, the veil of mystery that had shrouded the movie star's private life began to lift and the more fantastical elements of the celebrity narrative were discarded in favor of what Richard Schickel calls a larger than life "blown-up version of the typical." The addition of sound to movies in the late 1920s lifted the veil even farther, and as Schickel coyly remarks, "What seemed to be [the stars'] last significant secret, their tones of voice, was now revealed, or so it seemed."[43]

By the 1930s, many performers, like Reagan, were arriving in Hollywood with a body of stage or radio work that had already established them in the public eye and ear. In addition, Hollywood itself had become the third-largest source of news in the country and was covered by some three hundred correspondents. Even the Vatican posted a reporter, no doubt to keep an eye on the competition. By 1939, the golden year of Hollywood's golden age, the movies were the nation's fourteenth-largest business in terms of volume and eleventh in terms of assets. There were more movie theaters (15,115) in the United States than banks (14,952), and more than fifty million Americans attended those dream palaces in an average week.[44] Hollywood and its talent had become, in short, far too publicly visible to continue to promote mystic marriages to the Sphinx as part of an actors' star narrative. Or so it seemed.

The new "realism" occasioned by new sound and picture technologies and the relentless publicizing of the private lives of the stars demanded a new mimetic relationship between their real and reel lives, one that *seemed* to be transparent. The new mode of celebrity production would continue to encourage audiences to identify with an image of the star generated by the roles the star played in movies and shaped by studio publicity teams. But two dramatic changes would occur. First, the criterion for celebrity would shift to a supra-ordinariness in which the star's role was not to tower over his or her fans but to create an intimate connection with them. While there were notable exceptions to this formula, they *are* exceptions to a trend that began in this period to chisel celebrity down to a size that encouraged greater identification by consumers and allowed for a more finely targeted deployment of the star image. The second significant change in the production of celebrity was that the somnipractors' guild of star makers would dramatically swell in number.

By the time Reagan got to Hollywood, studio publicity, advertising, and "exploitation" crews with up to one hundred employees at the major studios constituted a star-making machinery on a par with the studios' technologies of movie making. "In those days," Reagan nostalgically recounts, "the great stars were built up over time and their names and faces became as familiar to people as their next of kin. The studio publicity machine saw to that." Writing about Bette Davis, Cathy Klaprat describes how stars were born at Warner Brothers.

> To begin, the department manufactured an authorized biography of the star's personal life based in large part on the successful narrative roles of the star's pictures. The department would disseminate this information by writing features for fan magazines, press releases, and items for gossip columns. A publicist would then be assigned to handle interviews and to supervise the correct choice of makeup and clothing for public appearances. Finally the department had glamour photographs taken that fixed the important physical and emotional traits of the star in the proper image.[45]

If the new objective of celebrification was to construct the physical and emotional traits of stars in such a way as to make them as familiar to their fans as possible, then Reagan's image was the quintessential expression of the star as next of kin. His celebrity image—which he described to a movie fan magazine as "Mr. Norm"—was built around his ordinariness. And if Reagan could play the role Hollywood could produce it. "Every performer had a publicity agent whose responsibility it was to see that you were in the trade papers, the gossip columns, and the movie magazines: It built an image of you. That's what sold the tickets."[46]

The studios constructed and projected the image, but they needed the complicity of the gossip columnists and fan magazines to disseminate it. In Louella Parsons, Reagan found a powerful ally for enhancing his image. Parsons, like Reagan, hailed from Dixon, Illinois, and she generated roles and publicity for him, introduced him to Jane Wyman, and promoted the "dream marriage" between "Mr. Norm" and "Button Nose" when they married. During World War II, Parsons arranged for their relationship to be chronicled in serialized form through publication of the letters they exchanged while Reagan was "away at war." The fact that he was stationed with a U.S. Air Force propaganda unit based at the Hal Roach Studios in Culver City, California, was of little concern to the air force or the studio, the movie magazines or their readers. That Reagan went home to his wife most nights during the war was of no interest to the image makers (because it didn't fit their story line) or to a public eager to believe in the heroic sacrifices Wyman and Reagan were making to support the war effort.

The notion that a normal guy like Reagan could become a Hollywood celebrity and still retain his commitment to his country was good for all parties concerned, especially Warner Brothers. The publicizing of Reagan's contribution to the war effort was characteristic of an industrywide effort that adapted John D. Rockefeller's credo that "what was good for Standard Oil was good for the country" to the movie business by promoting Hollywood's interests as synonymous with those of the nation. Harry Warner, in a characteristic industry pitch, stressed the importance of Hollywood's product to the American economy by proclaiming, "[O]ur films fairly shriek 'Buy American.'"[47]

What was good for Warner Brothers, however, had its cost. The price of stardom in the golden age of Hollywood was that your image was no longer your own. In 1935, Myrna Loy confided to her fans, "I daren't take any chances with Myrna Loy, for she isn't my property. . . . I couldn't even go [to the corner drugstore] without looking 'right' you see. Not because of personal vanity, but because the studio has spent millions of dollars on the personality known as Myrna Loy. *And I can't let the studio down by slipping off my expensive mask of glamour. I've got to be, on all public occasions, the personality they sell at the box office.*"[48] This lesson was well learned and spread rapidly to other areas of mass entertainment. It is particularly pervasive today among professional athletes, who when they reach a certain level of stardom begin to refer to themselves in the third person ("That is a decision that Allan Iverson is going to have to make for himself," I heard basketball player Allan Iverson say recently, as though the self that had uttered the words bore no relation to the celebrity entity "Allan Iverson.") The transition from celebrity as a personally revelatory private self to a relentlessly performing public self began in Hollywood at just about the time Ronald Reagan appeared on the scene.

Sympathetic Magic

> On the one hand, some try to explain Reagan's extraordinary success in politics by saying he gets by because he is "just an actor." On the other hand, we are told he was not even a good actor—which seems to make his political success more mysterious. Which is it to be? Is he just reading lines, following his script, using theatrical skills, as President? Or did a man lacking the depth for great roles in the theater somehow acquire a knack for filling the most responsible job in the world? . . . How did a man who could not master his chosen profession, after such prolonged endeavor, pick up new skills late in life? How explain the rise to the very top of politics, and heady triumphs there, after comparatively meager returns on a lifetime of trying as an actor?
>
> —Garry Wills, *Reagan's America*

Concern with the fit between the actor and the role in the performance of the presidency is not without precedent in American history. The nation's political and performance practices have been inextricably intertwined from the beginning. Wills's questions probe an arterial network that has propelled the performer and the politician together into the symbolic heart of the republic since its dawn's early light. Reagan's presidency conjured an enduring vision of America as a nation "designed by Providence," as John Adams phrased it, "for the Theatre, on which Man was to make his true figure."[49] As I argued in chapter 1, if in the process of fulfilling America's errand in the wilderness, as Adams envisioned it, the relationship between the theatrical and the historical he proposes is something more than metaphoric, then the question that has vexed Wills and countless others is, I believe, not a trivial one.

To trace Reagan's performance trajectory along the tangled lines of business of American culture, commerce, and politics, however, requires posing a question that precedes the one Wills proposes. Not "*can* he act?" but "*how* did he act?" is the critical question for evaluating Ronald Reagan as a work of art in the imagi-nation. This is not a simple question to answer given how little formal acting training Reagan received or sought. With the exception of high school and college drama productions Reagan had no stage career to speak of. While in Hollywood he never engaged an acting coach or took an acting class. Unlike many film actors of his day, who made a number of pictures with the same director and developed an acting method to fit that director's style, Reagan never developed that kind of relationship with any director.[50] Dialogue coaches were assigned to the sets of many of Reagan's movies to provide assistance with various aspects of speech, including enunciation, dialect training, and even line readings. As with the instruction he received as a novice radio broadcaster, Reagan's willingness to incorporate their suggestions for adapting his radio voice to film highlights his capacity for taking direction but provides little insight into his acting style or method.

Thomas Schatz argues that individual actors' styles and methods were largely irrelevant in the studio era, "no more than an inflection on an established studio style." What André Bazin termed "the genius of the system" was manifested in the production of films in which "star, genre, and technique coalesced into an ideal expression of studio style."[51] Studio producers and production methods, Schatz contends, not screenwriters or directors, were what defined an actor's persona and a film's style. It is true that Reagan had very little say in the films in which he was cast, the directors he worked with, or the roles he played. It is also true that he desired and lobbied to play western heroes throughout his time in Hollywood and that "Mr. Norm" is not the image he would have chosen for himself. However, even at Warner Brothers, where a factory-oriented approach to production and an emphasis on formulaic genre films resulted in "the most distinctive house style in Hollywood," Reagan's acting roles are not easily pigeonholed in a specific genre.[52] Unlike the Warner Brothers stars of the 1930s and 1940s, who defined the studio style in urban crime dramas (James Cagney and Edward G. Robinson), backstage musicals (Dick Powell and Ruby Keeler), epic swashbucklers (Errol Flynn and Olivia de Havilland), and the like, Reagan's acting persona, technique, and style were never identifiable with or defined by a single genre.

Reagan's screen appeal and offscreen image were largely the product of a seamlessness between his onscreen and offscreen personas, something most film actors of the day aspired to but rarely achieved. Watching his movies, one is inclined to agree with Nancy Reagan that "There are not two Ronald Reagans" and very little variation in his performances or between one image and the next. Nelle Reagan reinforced her daughter-in-law's assessment in her response to seeing her son in his first film. "That's my boy," she said. "That's my Dutch. That's the way he is at home. He's no Robert Taylor. He's just himself."[53] While this quality limited Reagan's range as an actor and his access to desirable film roles, it would serve him well in the cynical profession of politics, where, as Nancy observed, "you look in back of a statement for what it means." "It takes people a while to realize," she confided reassuringly, but "with Ronnie you don't have to look in back of anything."[54] It is the depthlessness of the images projected onto the screen that allows us, if we are looking for it, to glimpse our own reflection. "What is it, Governor, that people see in you?" Reagan was asked on the eve of his election as president. "Would you laugh," he replied, "if I told you that I think, maybe, that they see themselves and that I'm one of them?"[55]

Reagan's own discussions of his approach to acting tended toward the glib and superficial and were inevitably framed by another purpose. In *Where's the Rest of Me?* (published the year after his nationally televised speech in support of Barry Goldwater's campaign for president had established him as a viable political candidate), Reagan credits his high school English teacher, B. J. Fraser, with teaching him "almost all I know about acting today," without specifying what that knowledge entailed. Instead of expounding on the actor's craft, Reagan follows his comment with a parenthetical one-liner, "(and if the people back there will quit shouting, 'That's not much!' I'll be quite happy)."[56] The parentheses, like the title of his memoir, distance the gubernatorial candidate from his actor past, while the characteristically self-deprecating one-liner paradoxically displays the would-be politician's pride in his accomplishments as a performer. In an era in which actors running for political office were viewed with suspicion if not incredulity, Reagan was quick to emphasize that while he had learned many valuable lessons in Hollywood it was through his involvement in the political sphere that he would reclaim his missing parts.

In his post-presidential memoir *An American Life,* Reagan no longer feels the need to apologize for his careers prior to politics. Unconcerned with the anticipation of future political campaigns and eager to solidify his legacy as president, Reagan's narrative pitches his political tent on the fertile ground seeded by the performer. The difference is evident in the additional lines Reagan writes on the influence of B. J. Fraser. Here Reagan depicts Fraser as a prototype for the acting gurus of the American "method," who after World War II established teachers of acting as industry celebrities on a par with the stars they coached. Fraser arrived in Dixon shortly after the Reagans, and his impact on the high school theater program influenced Mugs's graduation address, as well as the decision to include theater facilities in the design of the new high school. "Prior to Fraser's arrival in Dixon," Reagan recounts, "our high school's dramatic productions had been a little like my mother's readings. Students acted out portions of classical plays or out-of-date melodramas." Fraser staged full productions of contemporary Broadway plays "and gave a lot of thought to what acting was all about."

> He wouldn't order you to memorize your lines and say: "Read it this way." . . . Instead, he'd teach us that it was important to analyze our characters and think like them in ways that helped us *be that person* while we were on stage.
>
> During a rehearsal, he'd sometimes interrupt gently and say: "What do you think your character means with that line? *Why* do you think he would say that?" Often, his questioning made you realize that you hadn't tried hard enough to get under the skin of your character so you would understand his motivations. After a while, whenever I read a new script, I'd automatically try first to understand what made that particular human being tick by trying to put myself in his place.[57]

Reagan self-consciously links B. J.'s training to his own partial understanding of method acting techniques for developing a character: "becoming" rather than impersonating the character, analyzing the character's psychological motivations or intentions, uncovering the character's interior life, and immersing oneself in the character's world.

What is curious is that there is almost no evidence in Reagan's accounts of his process as an actor to indicate that he was ever aware of or guided by these techniques in his own preparation to play a role. His memoirs are almost entirely devoid of any substantive discussion of his process as an actor. The one notable exception occurs at the beginning of *Where's the Rest of Me?* a title derived from a line in the film *King's Row* in which he played the role he considered the biggest and best of his career and "the one that brought me star status."[58] In *King's Row,* he portrays (in his own words) a "gay blade" named Drake McHugh "who cut a swathe among the ladies." Drake takes up with the daughter of a prominent surgeon who is not pleased with the match. When Drake is injured in a railroad accident the surgeon father unnecessarily amputates his legs while he is unconscious.

The scene in which Drake wakes up to discover that his legs are missing was, in Reagan's estimation, his greatest test as an actor. "Coming from unconsciousness to full realization of what had happened in a few seconds it presented me with the most challenging acting problem of my career." In a humble assessment of his resources as an actor, he recalled that he felt he had "neither the experience nor the talent to fake it." In order to rise to the challenge of the scene he could not rely on his insufficient acting technique alone. "I simply had to find out how it really felt, short of actual amputation," he wrote. He tried an ethnographic approach, interviewing doctors and amputees. But this method got him nowhere. "I was," he wrote, "stumped." In the end no technique or method proved sufficient. It is the missing limb, he implied, that enabled him to acknowledge his limitations and succeed, "in some weird way," by putting himself "as best [he] could, in the body of another fellow."[59] Here we can observe the performative practice of surrogation at work.

Just as his performance at Northwestern sparked his dream of becoming an actor, the experience of playing Drake McHugh, more than thirty years prior to launching his political career, emerges retrospectively as the primal scene of Reagan's transformation from actor to politician. In achieving the pinnacle of his success as an actor, he recounts, "I had become a semi-automaton," an acting amputee, who had been, in Brian Massumi and Kenneth Dean's characterization, "limping along through life repeating his lines." As an actor, Reagan became whole by appropriating "the body of another fellow." As president, the body he would have to perform to achieve wholeness would be "everybody," the body politic. He verges on saying outright that the political magic he would work is akin to national possession: "countless bodies unified by the same American spirit, one glorious body politic repeating in unison an old actor's favorite lines."[60] Although it is suggestive with regard to the body politics involved in the incarnation of a body politic, what is missing in Massumi and Dean's hyperbolic formulation is the triumph of fancy over fact in Reagan's parable of the scene that would ultimately transform him from an amputated actor into a presidential performer capable of embodying an entire nation.

Reagan's account of the epiphany that provided both the title of his memoir and the answer to the riddle it poses recalls a scene that never occurred in the movie.[61] In Reagan's script of the primal scene of his conversion from actor to politician he is the focus of the shot. But, as Wills points out, "[T]he movie does *not* show Reagan coming to full consciousness in a few seconds. . . . The whole episode is told from [Ann] Sheridan's point of view, through her concern. The camera stays with her. . . . Sheridan, 'not in the shot' according to Reagan, *was* the shot. . . . We have been set up to experience the moment [of recognition] through Ann Sheridan's reaction, which is what we get again after the camera shows him (briefly) shouting in a hoarse voice, 'Where's the *rest* of me?'"[62] In his greatest feat of screen embodiment, Ronald Reagan discovers that he is incomplete, a discontinuous body. Poised on the brink of a run for governor of California, the unfulfilled actor constructs a surrogate past in the form of a damaged body that can only be healed by the actor's performance in the political sphere. The generative scene of this invented past is a simulacrum (a reproduction for which no original exists), a copy that defies ontology by deriving its affective force from the representation of a nonexistent original.

From his performance in *King's Row,* Reagan fashioned a new performance crafted not for movie patrons but for California voters. During his gubernatorial campaign, his performances were pitched to an electorate raised on movies. As an expression of his approach to acting, *Where's the Rest of Me?* implies that as both a film actor and a political performer the connection he strove to achieve was not so much with the character he was playing as with the public whose approval he sought. This impression is reinforced by the lesson Reagan draws from Fraser's teachings: "The process, called empathy, is not bad training for someone who goes into politics (or any other calling). By developing a knack for putting yourself in someone's shoes, it helps you relate better to others and perhaps understand why they think as they do, even though they come from a background much different from yours."[63] Reagan's analysis of his acting technique never moves beyond this vague reference to "a process called empathy." Unlike compassion (with its etymological derivation of feeling pity for and suffering with another, the plight of the other generating corresponding emotions in the self), empathy projects the personality and emotions of the self onto another person in order to render it recognizable to oneself. As a method of relating to others and understanding why they think as they do, the empathetic process Reagan describes has less in common with any of the Stanislavski-based theories or practices that dominated the postwar American acting scene than it does with that other turn of the century theory of mimetic performance, "sympathetic magic."

Sympathetic magic derives from the interaction between what the Cambridge anthropologist James Frazer identified as the two primary principles on which magic is based, *contact* and *similarity*. Frazer joins these principles together under the rubric of sympathetic magic: the capacity of one thing or event to effect another at a distance as a consequence of a similarity that establishes a sympathetic connection between them.[64] Like FDR's fireside chats or the lost limb in *King's Row* whose phantom twitching animates *Where's the Rest of Me?* Reagan's description of the empathic process of putting himself in the place and shoes of another resonates with Frazer's Law of Contact or Contagion, "that things which have once been in contact with each other continue to act on each other at a distance after the physical contact has been severed." Reagan's objective as a cultural and political performer was not to "become" the character (at least not in any sense that Stanislavski or his disciples would recognize) but to re-member it in a performance Peggy Phelan has termed "representation without reproduction."[65] The empathic actor represents its character through a process similar to that of Frazer's magician, who from the "Law of Similarity . . . infers that he can produce any effect he desires merely by imitating it."[66] Unlike Stanislavski's actor, the magician does not derive his effects from a process of *identification* but through an act of *surrogation;* the form of representation Reagan would most often embody in his performances in the political sphere.

The Changing Man

In *Where's the Rest of Me?* Reagan, like Benjamin, is preoccupied with the question of how the arts and crafts of mechanical reproduction condition the relationship between actor and politician. Written on the cusp of his transition from the screen to the statehouse, the title derives from Reagan's contention that as an actor "part of my existence was missing." From a line written by a screenwriter and uttered by a character in a film, Reagan constructs his narrative of an amputated life. "No single line in my career," writes the actor preparing to search for his missing parts in a new profession, "has been as effective in explaining to me what an actor's life must be." The celebrity attendant to his profession was alluring at first, explains Reagan, but over time he began "to feel like a shut-in invalid nursed by publicity." Trapped in an endless procession of "never-never roles," Reagan laments that "[so] much of our profession is taken up with pretending . . . that an actor must spend at least half his waking hours in fantasy, in rehearsal, or shooting." To be only an actor is to be, he concludes, "like I was in *King's Row,* only half a man."[67]

Many of the films of the 1980s considered emblematic of the Reagan era—the *Star Wars* series (1977, 1980, 1983), *Rambo II* (1985), *Back to the Future* (1985), and *Field of Dreams* (1989)—exhibit a similar desire to answer the vexing question posed in the title of Reagan's autobiography by revisiting and revising an unsettled past that troubles an uncertain present. Like Booth and Reagan, these films long for a golden or sepia- tinted age, and their characters share the yearning for liberation from or control over a world in which they feel betrayed by the roles in which they have been cast. Woody Allen's *Zelig,* released in 1983 and set in the 1920s, is one of the most compelling of these celluloid vision quests of the Reagan years. Like Reagan, Leonard Zelig is both a product of a culture of performance and ambivalent about the roles this culture requires him to play. The son of a Yiddish actor, Zelig is a plebeian everyman who is both blessed and cursed by an uncontrollable ability to assume the identity of anyone he encounters. It is this ability that makes him a celebrity.

Doctors cannot agree on a diagnosis for Zelig's condition. One deems it "glandular," a second "neurological," and a third—this is, after all, a Woody Allen film—declares it to be "something he picked up from eating Mexican food." Convinced that his ailment is psychological rather than physiological, a psychiatrist, Eudora Fletcher (Mia Farrow), convinces Zelig to enter therapy. Under hypnosis Zelig reveals that he transforms because it is "safe" to be "like the others." That Zelig ends up in therapy rather than church is a characteristic expression of an era in which a popular psychology of professionally guided "self-help" was, like radio and film, loosening the grip liberal evangelical Protestantism held on the popular imagination. Much as FDR was diagnosed by Adlerian psychologists of the 1930s as a man with an "organ inferiority" who "compensates" for it by developing skills and a lifestyle that enable him to "fit in,"[68] Fletcher addresses Zelig's "inferiority complex" by encouraging him to develop his own personality.

Just as the therapy seems to be working, his half sister and her boyfriend, a former carnival promoter, remove him from the hospital. Sister Ruth and Martin Geist exploit Zelig's celebrity through the licensing of Zelig dolls, clocks, toys, earmuffs, and board games and product endorsements and advertisements for cigarettes and underwear. A book is written and a movie contract signed. But Zelig is "lonely." No longer content to be "a cipher" or exhibited as "a performing freak," he is reunited with Fletcher and goes back into therapy, where, in "the famous White Room sessions," he learns, in Fletcher's words, "to speak his mind, embrace his identity, become a human being."

In depicting Zelig's condition and the notoriety it brings him, the film also documents a formative moment in the emergence of new processes and technologies that would govern the formation of public identities and political fortunes in the United States throughout the century. Shot in a pseudo-documentary style that combines mock interviews with newsreel footage from the 1920s, *Zelig* captures the spectacle of a life lived entirely for the camera, on the front pages of newspapers, and in the public eye. The characters in *Zelig* invariably address themselves to microphones, cameras, or a gathered throng. Caught in the slipstream of the mass-mediated popular culture of the 1920s, Zelig (through his uncanny ability to assume both the bodily form and the psychological characteristics of the people he encounters) morphs his way through the various subject formations and transformations the decade calls forth, from ethnic gangster to black jazz trumpeter, from immigrant Jew to assimilated American, from anonymity to celebrity, from nothingness to being and back again.

To be in this world is to be publicly reproduced. Through the cinematic techne of double exposure, creative editing, and recycled film footage, Zelig materializes alongside iconic figures from the political and popular culture of the day (Babe Ruth and Lou Gehrig, Eugene O'Neill and Clara Bow, Herbert Hoover and Calvin Coolidge). Through proximity and incorporation he absorbs their celebrity just as he assumes the physical and behavioral characteristics of the gangster and the jazz musician. While the trajectory of his transformations traces the mythic arc of American identity from immigration to assimilation, the mass-mediated mode of his public being exemplifies the dominant means and modes of identity formation in the twentieth century. Zelig is a blank screen on which the identities that constitute his social milieu are projected. He is not, however, merely a passive receptor of subjectivities. Through his electronically mediated materialization as a public figure he is also an active conductor of their images. His screen identities—the subjectivities displayed on and through his body—are projected back out into the culture he both represents and mediates through the media coverage of "the changing man." Through the techne that manufacture his celebrity, Zelig spawns commodities, sells products, and achieves a cultural status that endows him with the power to reproduce and circulate emergent identity formations.

Like Clara Bow, Zelig's celebrity comes at a price. In the course of therapy, Zelig and Eudora fall in love. She rejects her attorney fiancé, and the patient and his therapist make plans to marry. Two weeks before the wedding an ex-showgirl claims to be married to Zelig and the mother of his child. Zelig, it turns out, had married her under the influence of another personality—that of an actor. The ensuing scandal turns public opinion against him. The claims multiply, and he is sued for numerous abuses committed by his multiple personalities. Once celebrated for his capacity to be all things to all people, he is now vilified for acting out his potential. The movie studio demands that he return its advance, but he can only come up with half the money. "Outraged," the narrative voice-over reports, "the studio gives him half his life back. They keep the best moments and Zelig gets only his sleeping hours and meal times." Zelig, like Reagan the actor, is only half a man. His "disease" returns and he disappears, never to be heard from again. Or so it seems.

If *Zelig* is a satiric cautionary tale of the twin pitfalls of the invisible private self and the hypervisible public self, then the presidency of Ronald

Reagan is its triumphant sequel. In the Age of Reagan the protean body that governed the nation was incessantly reproduced through the electronic media, and it circulated with an unprecedented ease and ubiquity through the realm of popular culture. For both Zelig and Reagan it is the mass-mediated production and dissemination of the narratives and images of their performing selves that emblematize the virtues and vices of their age. It is the performative dimensions of their celebrity that brand them as representative figures of their time. The one "original" cultural contribution inspired by Zelig's celebrity is "the chameleon," a dance craze that sweeps the nation. Named after the animal that changes its color in order to disappear into its environment, the chameleon also describes the kinetic and shape-shifting performing self, "the colored shadow on the screen" that Reagan, viewing the rushes of his early films, could "barely believe [was] myself."[69] Zelig's chameleon body, like Cohan's dancing body, is the body of the performer, the symbolically requisite body double for the celebrity body of the president electric.

CHAPTER FIVE

The Reagan Brand

There's no business like show business.
—Irving Berlin

The theatrical line of business from which Reagan's image at the 1984 Republican National Convention derives its lineage is that of the somnipractor, Garry Wills's term for all the product salesmen who serve as "the arrangers of other's dreams."[1] Reagan's renomination was a foregone conclusion. His image on the giant video screen was a preview of the eighteen-minute film homage to his first term that premiered later at the convention. The film itself functioned as a teaser for an expanded thirty-minute "documentary" version broadcast by all three networks. Then there were the "Morning Again in America" and "America Is Back" campaign commercials that began airing shortly thereafter. The cumulative

Photo: Ronald Reagan and General Electric Theater, 1954–62. Courtesy Ronald Reagan Library.

effect evoked Guy Debord's insight that the image has become the final form of commodity reification.[2] The convention functioned more as a trade show than a coronation. Reagan's performance was a product launch designed to dazzle the gathered delegates and consumers watching on TV with the new media campaign for the revamped product line that would be marketed through the Reagan brand.

The Reagan Revolution was coterminous with a new theory of corporate management that held that the primary focus of an increasingly postindustrial capitalism was no longer the production of material goods but the production of images of their brands. Naomi Klein identifies the final year of the Reagan presidency as the defining moment in this shift in the core business of corporations, the year when Philip Morris purchased Kraft for 12.6 billion dollars—six times Kraft's paper value. The premium Philip Morris paid to acquire Kraft's brand was not a function of its use value; it was the cost of the word *Kraft*. For tobacco-tainted Philip Morris the symbolic value of Kraft's brand image, it appeared, had a significantly higher value than all of Kraft's fungible assets put together. The disparity between Kraft's net worth and the price it fetched at market, like the disparity between support for Reagan and his policies, was a function of the mimetic value of the brand, a value predicated on the magical capacity of the controllable and transferable image to increase the commercial worth of any product to which it was attached. Addressing the Association of National Advertisers that same year, the chairman of the global advertising firm Ogilvy & Mather preached the new gospel: competing in a commodity marketplace "solely on price, promotion, and trade deals, all of which can easily be duplicated by competition" was a sucker's game. The most effective means of increasing corporate value was branding. In the new calculus of the society of the spectacle, brand promotion was no longer simply a sales strategy; it had become an equity investment.[3]

Images of brands were ubiquitous in the 1980s. Brand logos emerged from the inside of clothing to advertise the wearer's status and the company's image. Corporate sponsorship branded the built environment from cityscapes to sports stadiums, cultural venues to schools. In the music industry, concert tours were opportunities for what the somnipractors termed "live action advertising," and Music Television (MTV) became the paradigm for fully branded media integration. In the movie business, product placement in films was the tip of the iceberg in an industry that increasingly conceptualized the films themselves as branded media properties. Disney, the original "superbrand," launched the first brand superstore, branded holidays, and the ultimate in brand penetration, Celebration, Florida, the first branded town. In sports, Michael Jordan established himself as the first celebrity brand.[4] And in politics there was Ronald Reagan. By the time he became president there were only a handful of people whose image had circulated for as long as or as widely through the communications media, and the Reagan brand was an unparalleled political asset. In the new branded marketplace of the 1980s, Ronald Reagan was the *über*brand.

Brand Loyalty

Beginning with the Nixon administration the decay of electoral allegiances and alliances in place since the New Deal, the decline of party machine politics, and round-the-clock scrutiny by the mass media meant that image crafting, always a critical component of political campaigning, had assumed an unprecedented importance in the art of government itself. The advent of what Sidney Blumenthal termed "the permanent campaign" placed a new premium on an administration's ability to utilize the media in the marketing and public relations campaigns that increasingly determined its ability to influence public opinion, market its policies, and enact its political agenda.[5] While presidents since Theodore Roosevelt had used the presidency as a bully pulpit and since Eisenhower had sought to maximize their television exposure, Nixon's creation of the White House Office of Communications—staffed by public relations, advertising, and media professionals—institutionalized television as a principle technology for governance.

"Going public" became the popular euphemism for circumventing the checks and balances of congressional oversight by using television to rally public opinion in support of political initiatives.[6] The strategic use of television in going public was similar to Franklin Roosevelt's use of radio to generate public support, not so much for the policies themselves as for the president who promoted them. Ray Price, Nixon's chief speechwriter and the mentor of Reagan's communications director, David Gergen, summarized the strategy as "get the voters to like the guy and the battle's two-thirds won." But, as Price makes clear, it was not really "the guy" the public needed to like. It was his image. "The response is to the image, not to the man. . . . It's not the man we have to change, but rather the received impression."[7] In going public, one of the most critical functions of statecraft becomes what might be termed the *mediation of the nation,* the management of a body politic constructed from the competing figural and narrative representations of the electrified bodies that circulate through the networks of the communications matrix. In the new mass-mediated public sphere, the primary task of government became to effectively channel those networks, to master the matrix.

In the political economy of the matrix, the somnipractor assumed the role of empire builder. These new power brokers functioned as political acting coaches, stage managers of presidential productions, and producers of political administrations. In an era in which politics increasingly focused on gauging how specific appeals would "play" on the mass-mediated stage, and following the "spin" attracted more attention than public policy, handlers and spin doctors such as Lee Atwater, Roger Ailes, and Michael Deaver achieved their own niche celebrity among the public cognoscenti. The role of these political dream merchants was similar to what the American "method" acting guru Harold Clurman described as the task of teaching actors a theatrical language. "It was the leader's task," Clurman wrote of his pedagogical method, "to fashion a common language and common point of reference with those whom he hoped to lead." In Reagan a new breed of political star maker had a political actor already conversant with a "common language," one he had acquired from and performed in virtually every venue of electronic media, and a "common form of reference," the mass-mediated celebrity.[8] It was the somnipractors who understood—more than any one else in the Reagan administration—that in addition to "the Speech" the most important asset Reagan acquired during his years with General Electric was the ability to use television to promote a wide variety of products through the magical properties of a fully dramatized brand image.

One measure of the power of the Reagan brand was his administration's ability to deploy it to generate consent for Reagan's presidency in lieu of a popular mandate for his policies. The remarkable disparity in polling figures between public approval for Reagan (for large stretches of his presidency in the range of 60 to 70 percent) and approval of his policies (rarely higher than the low fortieth percentile) has been downplayed by political scientists. Thomas Ferguson and Joel Rogers argue "that significant differentials between performance and personal approval ratings of Presidents are utterly routine, that they always show greater personal approval than performance approval (since Americans, for whatever reason, want to believe that their Presidents are nice guys), and that in fact the differential Reagan enjoyed was proportionately smaller than those of most of his predecessors, not larger."[9] This analysis, however, misses the point by focusing on the statistics as mathematical numbers rather than cultural signs. What *was* significant about the disparity between public support for Reagan and his policies was that Reagan's communications apparatus was so adept at constructing and deploying his image in the media, and media professionals were so unwilling or unable to counter the spin, that a majority of Americans *believed* the disparity to be significant. In Reagan's case, the discrepancy between public approval for his person and his policies *did* reflect an unprecedented phenomenon. Rather than undermining the Reagan administration's political agenda, the much publicized gap between Reagan's personal popularity and public support for his policies actually increased his political capital. Dubbed the "Teflon president"—unaccountable for unpopular policies, impervious to scandal, and until Bitburg and Iran-Contra beyond blame for mismanaged political events—public support for Reagan in spite of opposition to his political agenda was promoted by his administration as a sign of his popular mandate.[10]

Reagan's popularity, however, was not the result of the spontaneous outpouring of affection his handlers touted in the media. In fact, it was as relentlessly choreographed as his ribbon-cutting ceremonies and cowboy photo shoots. The Reagan administration's methods for generating consent where no consensus existed was exemplified in a performative techne its producers termed "the line of the day." At 8:15 most mornings during Reagan's first term, White House Chief of Staff James Baker would convene the "line of the day" meeting. At the meeting (which was regularly attended by communications adviser David Gergen, Deputy Press Secretary Larry Speakes, presidential adviser Richard Darman, and Deputy Chief of Staff Michael Deaver) the discussion revolved around how to "enhance the image of the President," as one participant phrased it. The primary question addressed in these meetings was "What do we want the press to cover today and how?"[11] When consensus was reached and the line of the day crafted, memos were dispatched to every office of government with instructions to feature the line in all interviews with the media and at every event for which there would be media coverage. The line of the day served as a kind of caption for the images of Reagan produced that day by Deaver and broadcast at night on the network news. According to Donald Regan, secretary of the treasury and subsequently Deaver's successor as chief of staff, Deaver "designed each presidential action as a one-minute or two-minute spot on the evening news" and "conceived every presidential appearance in terms of camera angles." In Regan's estimation, Deaver cast Reagan "as a sort of supreme anchorman whose public persona was the most important element of his presidency."[12] Like *Nightline*'s Ted Koppel, Reagan performed the role of the mediator of crises. But as the supreme anchorman, the crisis Reagan repeatedly mediated was one of national destiny, a crisis of representation for which Deaver and Reagan provided images capable of lending narrative coherence and affective resonance to the day's events.

Deaver crafted the image, and the image toed the line. As James Lake, press secretary for the 1984 Reagan-Bush campaign, put it, Reagan was "the ultimate presidential commodity, the right product."[13] But if Reagan was the ultimate presidential product he was also an ideal celebrity salesman. For Lyn Nofziger, a former newspaper reporter and editor and a public relations and political consultant to Reagan since his gubernatorial days, Reagan was "the best candidate. I'm not talking about ability to govern, but the best candidate from the standpoint of understanding instinctively what you have to do to get favorable coverage for the kind of media we have today."[14] The quality that Nofziger credits to instinct was more accurately identified by a former White House aide as "training": "He's an actor. He's used to being directed and produced. He stands where he is supposed to and delivers his lines, he reads beautifully, he knows how to wait for the applause line. You know how some guys are good salesmen but can't ask the customer to give them the order? This guy is good at asking for the order, and getting it."[15] If, as Michael Rogin suggests, "the idol of consumption is the salesman or the object he sells," then surely Reagan qualifies on both counts; his career and his presidency testify to his capacity to play either role.[16] Like Reagan's appearance at the convention and the media campaign it launched, the line of the day exemplified the extended reach of the electronic performance circuit and the affective potency of the body electric.

During his presidency, performances featuring Reagan saturated the airwaves in fifteen-second sound bites, thirty-second and minute-long campaign commercials, thirty-minute promo reels and hour-long news "documentaries." Spin the dial and he was on the Cable News Network (CNN) and the network news, performing roles in old movies or plugging the new James Bond film, as a guest commentator at a sporting event or emceeing all-star galas and celebrity roasts. In its fecund transmission, Reagan's pervasive image accreted into a performative vision of a nation defined by an ongoing process of reinvention, renewal, and rebirth. As these moving images of "Reagan as America" circulated through the mass communications networks that delivered them to us, their autonomy as images eroded, congealing into one continuous serial broadcast: "America in the Age of Reagan."

As in other long-running serial melodramas of the period (I am thinking especially of *Dallas* and *Dynasty*), the Reagan narrative carried certain promises: that Americans' image of both nation and self was, at its root, an aesthetic one, a matter of "lifestyle"; that seemingly intractable social and economic problems could be addressed by stimulating desires that could only be achieved through unbridled consumption; that a government dedicated to promoting access to greater goods rather than the greater good could manufacture consent where no consensus existed; that the incompatible yearnings for progress *and* nostalgia—a desire to live at once in the future *and* the past—could be reconciled; and that with sufficiently compelling story lines, the right casting, and creative cross-marketing anything was possible. The performance of the Reagan melodrama spurned the New Deal verities of market discipline and government regulation of business. In their stead, Reaganism promulgated a "free market" revolution dedicated to the proposition that in politics, as in other commodity-based markets, consumers' purchasing decisions would no longer be limited by the efficacy of the product (Reagan's policies) but stimulated by a desire for the brand (Reagan's image).

Reagan's education in branding began with his arrival in Hollywood. But the political brand began to take shape in 1954 with the coming together of three pioneers of the branded nation: Ronald Reagan, General Electric, and television. Their point of convergence was a television show, *General Electric Television Theater,* broadcast on CBS from 1954 to 1962. The program was an exemplary product of what Lizabeth Cohen has recently defined as "the Consumers' Republic," the post–World War II political economy and culture in which the tasks of reconstructing the national economy and reaffirming democratic values were linked by the shared imperative to promote the expansion of mass consumption.[17] *General Electric Television Theater* promoted a new democratic ideal—the republic of consumption—featuring the citizen-consumer as the protagonist of a heroic drama cosponsored by democracy and capital. Reagan's television celebrity and rise to political prominence is itself a product of this new vision of the imagined community of the nation powered by the body electric in the empire of commodities.

Although it became de rigueur while he was president to diminish Reagan's film career, after appearing as Drake McHugh in *King's Row* his salary, at least, was that of a movie star. Before he could make another picture, however, the United States entered World War II and Reagan's career took a different turn. By 1954, at the age of forty-three and after seventeen years in Hollywood, his film career was effectively over. A series of postwar box office flops, a divorce from Jane Wyman, the decline of the studio system in the wake of the Supreme Court decision in *U.S. v. Paramount* in 1948, and his controversial tenure as president of the Screen Actors Guild had all contributed to derailing his once promising film career.[18] By the early 1950s, Reagan's income from film had dwindled to the point that he began appearing in cameo roles on television, considered at the time to be a sign of a career in decline for established movie actors.

Early 1954 marked the nadir of his acting career, when he accepted a two-week gig in Las Vegas in a variety act at what must have seemed to the struggling actor to be the prophetically named Last Frontier Hotel. It was then, Reagan recalls, that "this television show came riding along.

The Cavalry to the rescue."[19] The cavalry appeared in the person of Taft Schreiber, vice president of Reagan's talent agency, MCA, and the head of its television production company, Revue Productions. Reagan's rescue took the form of a lucrative offer to serve as the "program supervisor," host, and occasional actor for *General Electric Television Theater*, an established but underperforming anthology series on NBC.[20]

The initial lure of television for Reagan was strictly financial. Just a few months before GE offered him the job he had expressed a negative opinion of television—one shared by most film actors of the day—in an article in *Variety*. In the interview, Reagan responded to the critics who had characterized his Vegas gig as the last gasp of a fading film star. "Our business," Reagan told *Variety*, is "the most ruthlessly competitive there is. . . . A producer can be denied financial backing for one failure, an actor can go from [a] $100,000 price tag to unemployment on the supposition that a picture's failure was due to his lack of box office appeal. No one questions whether he can act. In fact, everyone will admit he is a superb actor . . . but, because Joe Shmoe, the moviegoer sat up with a sick friend . . . instead of seeing our hero at the bijou, he faces starvation or a job on television."[21] In his memoirs Reagan claims to have turned down many previous offers to star in television series and lists three reasons why he was wary of the medium. Expressing a concern common among members of the film industry in the early days of television, Reagan feared that playing a recurring character on a TV series "could be the professional kiss of death to a movie actor: The people who owned movie theaters thought nobody would buy a ticket to see someone they could see in their living room for nothing." A second risk, one Reagan had fought to avoid throughout his movie career, was typecasting. Echoing another commonly held view, Reagan contended that after starring in a TV series "audiences—and producers—tended to think of you only as the character you'd played on television." The third reason Reagan gave for his reluctance to cast his lot with television was that "having [his] face beamed into homes across the country every week risked the kind of overexposure that could be fatal to a movie actor's career."[22]

In retrospect there is more than a little irony in Reagan's anxiety about the potential impact of television on his movie career. In fact, it is precisely the reasons Reagan cites for his trepidation—viewers' free access to television, maximum exposure to a mass audience, and the creation of an enduring and familiar persona—that constituted the basis for the celebrity he acquired on *GE Theater* and his viability a decade later as a political candidate. Reagan's concern with being typecast as a result of appearing on television also seems disingenuous in light of a film career that was a model for the way the studio system exploited typecasting in rationalizing the production and marketing of its products. Reagan had long expressed frustration with Warner Brothers' unwillingness to cast him in the leading roles he craved as a western hero. With few exceptions, his film roles had consistently placed him within an industry niche exemplified by his self-professed nickname "Mr. Norm," a genial, midwestern, corn-fed, handsome, American everyman. In this regard *GE Theater* was an ideal vehicle for his not insubstantial but limited skills as a performer.

The show was sponsored by General Electric, but it was owned by MCA. In order to take advantage of their waiver and collect their 10 percent commission from Reagan and the other actors they represented who appeared on the show, MCA installed the advertising agency Barton, Butten, Durstine & Osborne (BBD&O) as producers. The arrangement would prove to be mutually beneficial to all the parties involved. While he would have been loathe to admit it at the time, television's smaller screen and his role as host provided the ideal scale and conditions to feature Reagan's strengths as a performer while minimizing his deficiencies as an actor. In return, GE got exactly what it was looking for from Reagan, a popular embodiment of its corporate image. In retrospect, this union of Ronald Reagan, General Electric, and Hollywood marks a pivotal moment in the relationship between corporate capitalism, consumer culture, and electronic media.

The Corporate Soul

> Corporations have neither bodies to be punished nor souls to be condemned. They therefore do as they like.
>
> —Edward Thurlow

From its inception, the cultivation of a positive public image had been of paramount concern to General Electric, as critical to the corporation's growth as its research labs, home of the alchemical processes by which advances in physics and chemistry were transformed into capital accumulation through commodification. When it was founded at the end of the nineteenth century, GE was not alone in perceiving the production of its corporate image to be another form of alchemy; one that required altering the "natural" properties of the corporation. One of the most significant structural components undergirding the rise of corporate capitalism was the new legal status corporations acquired in a header to the 1886 Supreme Court decision in *Santa Clara County v. Southern Pacific Railroad,* the ruling in which the precedent for the doctrine of "corporate personhood" was established. Henceforth, corporations would be treated as "persons" under the Fourteenth Amendment; a legal entity endowed with all the rights of the individual but with none of the legal responsibilities of human beings.

While their anthropomorphic ontology gave corporations a distinct competitive advantage over other organizations of capital, it also constituted a lurking threat to the corporation's capacity to reproduce its products, its labor force, its markets, and the personification of its public image. What Mark McGurl describes as "the anxiety of embodiment" derives from the paradox at the heart of corporate representation: commerce demands visibility, yet that visibility threatens to reveal the fictitious basis of corporate power, exposing the corporate body to potential injury through public criticism, federal antitrust sanctions, and the actions of organized labor.[23] In other words, the power of corporate capitalism was and is contingent upon the ability of corporations to maximize their control over the production and dissemination of their public persona, while simultaneously minimizing public scrutiny of the animating fiction of personification that enables that power in the first place.

General Electric's evolution from an industrial energy company to a commercial corporate conglomerate illustrates the seminal role of the corporate image in enabling Henry Adams's Four Horsemen of the Apocalypse—mechanical science, market capitalism, mass society, and consumer culture—to generate the second industrial revolution of the twentieth century. In 1876, inspired by the electrical exhibits at the Centennial Exposition in Philadelphia, Thomas Edison opened his laboratory in Menlo Park, New Jersey, where he began to explore and commercialize the possibilities of the dynamo and other electrical devices on display at the exposition. By 1890, he had organized his various ventures into the Edison General Electric Company. Two years later, in a merger with the Thomson-Houston Company, it became the General Electric Company, which along with Westinghouse quickly established itself as the dominant player in a nascent electrical industry that over the next thirty years would integrate electrical technology into virtually every arena of industrial production.

With the post–World War I economic boom and a change in leadership, GE, like many other large industrial corporations, reorganized its operations to enter the expanding mass consumer marketplace. For thirty years as president (1892–1913) and chairman of the board (1913–22), Charles F. Coffin had defined the company's agenda as "simply to make goods and sell them."[24] This the company had done exceedingly well. By the early 1920s, the General Electric Company was marketing nearly four hundred thousand catalog items, making it the world's largest producer of electrical products. Yet the company's public image did not reflect its scientific accomplishments or economic success. Its monopolistic patent practices, quasi-legal holding companies, and coercive financing of public utilities were as responsible for the company's growth as the quality of its research laboratories. Its corporate practices and size and stature in a strategically important industry made the company a constant target of antitrust legislation during the Progressive Era. In addition, while the company dominated the industrial electrical market, its penetration of consumer markets was still relatively insignificant; the only products it sold directly to consumers were fans and light bulbs. Consumers had little contact with the company's products and thus no personal relationship with the corporation that might mitigate its public image as the most visible symbol of the "power trust."

By the 1920s, with the triumph of corporate capitalism and the initial widespread expansion of mass markets for consumer goods, the legal fiction corporations exploited to assert their dominance over the American business landscape placed an increasingly heavy burden on the task of corporate self-representation. In 1922, Coffin and President Edwin W. Rice retired and were replaced by Owen D. Young as chairman and Gerard Swope as president. Swope's immediate concern on becoming president was to broaden the corporate agenda on two fronts: the expansion of General Electric's consumer market and the revamping of its corporate image. To achieve these goals Swope focused on improving company morale and cooperation and promoting consumer trust and loyalty. In the first phase of GE's development it had focused on solving issues related to mass production by training and promoting engineers as the scientific and managerial standard-bearers of its corporate identity. To tackle the issues posed by the imperative to expand its consumer base, GE's new management turned to two recently minted professions, advertising and public relations.

As early as 1897, in response to political pressure to nationalize the electrical industry, GE had created a Publicity Bureau, uniting the functions of advertising and publicity in a single entity to advocate for its interests and educate consumers and employees alike about the irreplaceable industrial and social benefits the company provided. By the time Coffin retired, the Publicity Bureau's 242 full-time employees were overseeing the publication of "catalogues, bulletins, instruction books, technical reports, agents' handbooks," and two company magazines, one for engineers and the other for blue-collar workers. In addition, the bureau produced "a torrent of photographs, posters, calendars, advertising cards, films, brochures, pamphlets, slides, and releases to the newspapers." This onslaught of informational and promotional material—packaged for distinct target markets—was released under a variety of guises to avoid the appearance of a coordinated effort and to deflect attention from the enormous size and power of the corporation. Advertising, too, was product and market specific; the company's various divisions bought and managed their own advertising, which promoted specific products and rarely attached GE's name to the ads.[25]

Swope felt that to become competitive in the rapidly expanding consumer marketplace the company needed to cultivate and publicize a unified identity. To do so he turned to a new breed of corporate engineer, the public relations and advertising professionals who were charged with engineering the corporation's image. In the 1920s—the vexing problems of production having largely been addressed—this new breed of performance theorist began to tackle the problem of how to stimulate consumer interest in the unprecedented volume of products generated by the new efficiencies. Schooled in the techne of mass communication and the same social science discourses as their brethren in corporate management, they eagerly embraced the new media of film and radio. Through their campaigns to educate consumers and expand markets they would inextricably intertwine the technologies of electronic media with the imperatives of corporate capitalism.

In 1922, Swope convened the company's first corporationwide conference on advertising and sales. During the conference, Swope and sixty GE executives entertained proposals for a unified campaign from several of the advertising agencies handling accounts for the company's various divisions. The proposal that articulated Swope's vision most clearly came from a twenty-five-year-old who had made his reputation with a pioneering campaign for General Motors (GM) and was already designing advertising for General Electrics' lamp division. Bruce Barton knew all about the occult and magical powers of faith. As a child, he had witnessed firsthand the earthly benefits of an entrepreneurial faith. His father was a Tennessee circuit rider who had risen through the ranks to become the moderator of the National Council of Congregational Churches. Raised on evangelical Protestantism, Barton's harnessing of the tenets of his faith to the new techne of public relations and advertising would make him the leading business evangelist of the day.

Barton crafted corporate advertising and image-building campaigns that defined the transition from the production-driven industrial landscape forged by the money trusts and Taylorism to a consumer-oriented economy characterized by the institutionalization of corporate liberalism and Fordism. A prolific author of inspirational literature, he promoted advertising as a revelation and declaration of the gospel of business. His best-selling book on Jesus (*The Man Nobody Knows*) characterized Jesus as the founder of "modern business" and the consummate promoter of God's word. The sequel (*The Book Nobody Knows*) cited the New Testament as the theological basis for sanctifying the new consumer capitalism. For Barton, salesmanship in general and advertising in particular were, like Jesus' ministry, evangelical missions that spread the good news that work was worship, consumerism was holy, and corporations were coworkers of "the Almighty in the great enterprise which he has initiated but which He can never finish without the help of men."[26] American capitalism was

God-given, but in order to thrive it was, like the nation, in constant need of representation.

In Barton's theology, advertising was a sacred calling primarily concerned with the revelation of the corporate soul. Promoting the soul of the corporation appealed to Swope and Young, who, like Barton, were convinced that corporations needed to focus on addressing their image problem. Barton's proposal was that if GE was to become as important to consumers as it was in the industrial arena it would have to overcome its fear of visibility and anxiety over embodiment. The biggest obstacle to future growth, Barton argued, was no longer public hostility toward a monopolistic trust but consumer indifference to an anonymous conglomerate. The company's image needed to be strategized and promoted not obfuscated and obscured. Like Louis Howe's strategy for electing FDR in 1912, Barton advocated developing a brand image of the corporation/candidate that authorized the endorsement of a variety of targeted products/policies through a publicity campaign that saturated the consumer/constituent marketplace. "Reputation is repetition," Barton wrote to Swope, using language that could have come from Howe.[27]

Barton was charged with marketing GE's new target image to its consumers and employees. Combining an identity-building national campaign for an "electrical consciousness" with an internal company campaign for a "corporate consciousness," Barton introduced the concept of a "corporate culture," a collective corporate identity that embodied and manifested the corporate soul.[28] To effectively disseminate GE's new consumer-friendly target image, which emphasized merchandising and public service, Barton insisted that GE's monogram appear on every product and in every advertisement. In a series of print ads focusing on GE's contributions to the development of electrical power and electricity's contribution to "human progress," Barton crafted a campaign focused not merely on hawking light bulbs but on claiming credit for light itself. In a speech that, like his ad campaigns, mixed Protestant theology and Barnumesque chutzpah, Barton told GE employees that they did not merely manufacture electrical products. Instead, he told them, they were "engaged in the great profession of lighting the world," operating under a charter "from the beginning of time . . . . recorded in the four words, 'Let there be light.' "[29] By sponsoring public service advertising highlighting discoveries made in GE's research labs, Barton positioned the company as "the headquarters of progress," successfully transforming GE's negative image as a symbol of the money trusts into a positive image as a familiar symbol of consumer trust.[30]

The economics of image building dictated that neither repetition nor reputation came cheap. General Electric's advertising budget grew by 600 percent between 1922 and 1930, rising to over twelve million dollars a year. Assessing the effects of the company's investment in "consumer education" and characterizing each advertising "message" as a unit of repetition, one GE public relations officer observed that "an average of a million dollars a month made it possible to circulate during the year, through newspapers and magazines, more than five billion messages—approximately 200 for every family."[31] Repetition and saturation were also the impetus behind GE's participation in radio, which not only increased the consumption of and desire for access to electricity but also served as a new medium for advertising. General Electric was a founding member of the radio trust, and its stations in Schenectady, Denver, and Oakland together reached most of the radio listeners in the United States. Radio generated larger audiences than any single newspaper and captured the ears of many whose eyes rarely drifted toward print. Promoting the medium as well as the message, the two million dollars GE spent on radio advertising between 1927 and 1930 further solidified the impression that it not only sold electrical products but was the corporate embodiment of the bright future that would be lit and powered by electricity.

Lizabeth Cohen has argued that the foundation of the "consumer's republic" was laid in the 1930s by New Deal policies and grassroots activism that created the figure of the "citizen consumer" as an economic, social, and political expression of the benefits of encouraging the mass consumption of consumer goods as a means of ending the Great Depression. Barton's transformation of General Electric's corporate image, however, suggests that the critical innovation enabling the transition from a production-based economy to a consumer-oriented one began with the development of corporate branding in the 1920s. Professional advertisers, no longer content to merely link producers and consumers in the marketplace, utilized theology, psychology, and sociology to devise and coordinate public relations campaigns that shaped corporate identity and mediated consumer behavior. As pioneers of the performance techne that would transform American politics in the 1930s, somnipractors such as Barton possessed the essential pedagogical tools Franklin Roosevelt alluded to when he declared advertising to be "essentially a form of education" on which "the progress of civilization depended."[32]

Electrifying Democracy

Perhaps the definitive example of how corporate capitalism utilized the electronic media to brand the public sphere in the 1920s was the staging of Light's Golden Jubilee, an event commemorating the fiftieth anniversary of Edison's invention of the electric light bulb. Publicized as a celebration of Edison's invention, the electrical corporations that sponsored the event conceived it as a launch party for an international campaign promoting electrical consumer goods for the working class. When Edison, the most commercially savvy of scientists, ironically expressed concern that GE would commercialize the celebration, his admirer Henry Ford offered to host the event near his headquarters in Dearborn, Michigan. To ensure the fulfillment of its own agenda, GE hired Edward Bernays to make the jubilee the first example of what is commonly referred to today as a "global media event."

Bernays's career speaks to the electronic media's incorporation of the various performance traditions of education, entertainment and "uplift" spread by the Circuit Chautauqua. Along with Barton and Ivy Lee, Bernays, the self-professed father of public relations, was the most influential corporate publicist of the 1920s. He began his career in the theater in 1913 promoting Eugene Brieux's *Damaged Goods,* a French play about a man with syphilis who fathers a syphilitic child. Exploiting the controversial topic to generate publicity for the production, Bernays made syphilis a cause célèbre, turning a play the reviewer for the *New York American* described as "dull and almost unendurable" into a New York hit that moved to the National Theater in Washington, where it was seen by Supreme Court justices, congressmen, and members of Woodrow Wilson's cabinet. Hired as a press agent and publicist by the top New York theatrical booking agents, Klaw and Erlanger, Bernays was responsible for U.S. tours that introduced Sergei Diaghilev's Ballets Russes and Enrico

Caruso to Americans and identified an untapped market for ballet, modern dance, and opera. During World War I, he worked for George Creel's groundbreaking Committee on Public Information (CPI); a cadre of newspaper, advertising, and publicity professionals who constructed an unparalleled public relations apparatus in support of the war effort.[33] "Never before in history," wrote the historians Charles and Mary Beard, "had such a campaign of education been organized; never before had American citizens realized how thoroughly, how irresistibly modern government could impose its own ideals on the nation."[34]

During the 1920s, Bernays applied CPI's techniques for altering individual and social behavior to the task of "crystallizing public opinion" in the service of expanding consumer markets. Influenced by Sigmund Freud's research on the unconscious roots of human behavior, Bernays (who was Freud's nephew) perceived publicity as, in the words of another prominent publicist of the day, "essentially a matter of mass psychology."[35] Bernays also exploited the insights of social psychologists, including Gabriel Tardé, who conceived of the modern "public" as essentially "a spiritual collectivity, a dispersion of individuals who are physically separated and whose cohesion is entirely mental."[36] In the virtual public sphere constituted by newspapers, radio, and film, people's attitudes and behavior were constantly influenced by these media, which social psychologists conceived as functioning like "cognitive connecting points joining an extensive highway of perception."[37] Reflecting on a campaign for the American Tobacco Company in which he successfully shattered social taboos and dramatically increased the number of female smokers, Bernays observed that "age old customs . . . could be broken down by a dramatic appeal, disseminated by the networks of media."[38]

Bernays's campaign began six months before the jubilee itself with the release of souvenir editions of the *New York Herald* from 1879 announcing Edison's discovery. He enlisted magazines to publish features and pictorials heralding the jubilee. He convinced the post office to issue a commemorative stamp depicting Edison's lamp with electrical rays emanating from its light. George M. Cohan contributed a song, "Edison—The Miracle Man," and sheet music was distributed worldwide. Mayors and governors issued proclamations to celebrate Light's Golden Jubilee. Universities offered lectures on Edison and the implications of his discovery. Librarians displayed books about Edison. Educational groups conducted essay contests. Museum heads arranged exhibits that would illustrate the history of light.

Budding young scientists from forty-eight states were brought to Edison's Menlo Park laboratory. "Every day for a week," wrote the *Nation,* "these lads—aided by the forethought of the publicity man in arranging for the simultaneous presence of Messrs. Edison, Eastman, Ford, and Lindbergh—made the front pages. Every day the thought was subtly instilled in impressionable minds that the electric-light companies yearned to help bright boys and to achieve more inventions, all for the benefit of the dear old Ultimate Consumer."[39] Through Bernays's influence, virtually every extant medium of education and communication was enlisted to give the impression that Edison, his light, and by extension the electrical industry were national treasures as vital to the health and prosperity of the country as the ideals of democracy itself.

The jubilee accentuated the connection between electricity and democracy by utilizing performance and celebrity as excellent substitutes for what they were produced to represent. Arriving in Detroit for the festivities on a facsimile of a train Edison had worked on, President Herbert Hoover was greeted by Bernays and introduced to the other attendees, who included captains of finance and industry (J. P. Morgan Jr., John D. Rockefeller Jr., and Owen D. Young), renowned scientists (Marie Curie and Orville Wright) and other prominent Americans. After a banquet served in a reproduction of Independence Hall that Ford had erected for the occasion, Edison, Ford, and Hoover were whisked off to Ford's historical theme park, Greenfield Village, where he dedicated the Edison Institute of Technology (later renamed the Henry Ford Museum), his personal tribute to Edison as an American innovator. There, in the reconstructed Menlo Park Laboratory, which Ford had moved to Michigan for the occasion, Edison reenacted the lighting of his lamp for millions of radio listeners around the country. "Will it light? Will it burn?" announcer Graham McNamee breathlessly intoned as millions of people huddled in darkness around their radios waiting for Edison's successful re-creation as a cue to turn on their lights. "Oh you could hear a pin drop in this long room," McNamee continued, extending the drama. "Now the group is once more about the old vacuum pump. Mr. Edison has two wires in his hand; now he is reaching up to the old lamp; now he is making the connection. It lights!"[40] As the museum building lit up, a replica of the Liberty Bell cast from the same mold tolled in the belfry. The jubilee's various replicas, reproductions, reconstructions, reenactments, and facsimiles of Americana—a cornucopia of excellent substitutes for the thing itself—was the quintessential expression of a culture of performance in which democracy itself was represented as a product of the fiat of electricity.

The jubilee reinforced Bruce Barton's conviction that big business had not only solved its production problems but through coordinated public relations and advertising campaigns had also ameliorated its image problem, successfully identifying size with service, corporate culture with innovation, and the corporation with national prosperity and American democracy. Three days after the jubilee the stock market crashed. The Depression that ensued would shake Americans' faith in corporations. To restore this faith and reanimate the machinery of consumption would require the development of a new electronic media with an unprecedented capacity for branding the corporation and the nation.

Being Televised

Of the various media that have contributed to the dominance of corporate capitalism by alleviating the anxiety of embodiment, it is television that has most effectively addressed the corporate dilemma of self-representation. Unlike the movie industry, television has been a corporate medium from its inception. Unlike radio, which could only transmit the corporate voice, the overwhelmingly visual experience of *watching* television made it an ideal medium for promoting the corporate image, mitigating the pitfalls of visibility, and easing the anxiety of embodiment. General Electric had long been interested in television. Edison, as early as 1891 while working on the kinetoscope, boasted that he was on the verge of achieving the direct transmission of live events into the home. The technological obstacles, however, would prove to be more significant than Edison imagined. It took another half century before the Radio Corporation of American (RCA) and its broadcasting wing, NBC—both founded by GE and its partners in the radio trust—began regular television broadcasting at the 1939 New York World's Fair.

Beginning with the Philadelphia Exposition of 1876, which inspired Edison to establish his first research laboratory, American industrial and trade exhibitions had consistently linked the national destiny and industrial progress to electrical power. The 1939 New York World's Fair, however, set a new standard for the reification of electricity and the corporate embodiment of its fiat. The fair's theme, "The World of Tomorrow," was designed to restore faith in a corporate sector increasingly perceived to bear responsibility for a decade of economic deprivation and social unrest. The fair's most popular attractions were exhibits sponsored by the leading companies (GE, General Motors, Eastman Kodak, American Telephone and Telegraph [AT&T], and RCA) in the fastest-growing industries (automobile manufacturing, electricity and electronics, mass media, and telecommunications). The exhibits propagated a shared vision of social reconstruction in which the electrified commodities produced by the corporations were promoted as guarantors of a more prosperous and democratic future. The architecture, exhibits, and multimedia spectacles combined to create a massive *teatrum mundi* in which electricity was not only the most prominent technology on display but also the means by which visitors would enter and experience "The World of Tomorrow."

As a symbolic window on the future, television's commercial debut at the fair linked the new medium to the brave new world of consumer culture promoted by the corporate exhibitions. Televisions situated throughout the fairgrounds broadcast the opening ceremonies in which Franklin Roosevelt welcomed visitors and Albert Einstein threw the switch to electrify the dazzling lighting systems that would illuminate America's future. Visitors were transported via two electric staircases from the base of the Trylon, a seven-hundred-foot triangular spire, and into the Perisphere, a two-hundred-foot globe theater. Here, from two electrically powered revolving platforms suspended just below the "equator" of the great sphere, visitors viewed Democracity, Henry Dreyfuss's massive model of a core city and its exurban ring rendered in perfect harmony. While the balconies rotated slowly and the lights dimmed to suggest dusk, symphonic music piped through loudspeakers filled the globe and a great chorus heralded the approach of various incarnations of the American working man displayed on the dome by movie projectors hidden in the balconies. The narration provided by the popular radio newscaster H. V. Kaltenborn lent an authoritative voice to the stirring music and populist imagery designed to obscure the conflicts between labor and capital that threatened the continued coexistence of capitalism and democracy. The six-minute performance concluded with a series of *tableaux vivant* projections of heroic farmers and industrial workers. These people, as Kaltenborn's inspirational oratory made clear, represented the diversity of American society, and their cooperation would lead to a better life in the new Democracity.

The most popular exhibit at the fair was Norman Bel Geddes' design for the General Motors pavilion, which reinforced the vital role of electricity in the imagineering of a post-Depression imagi-nation. Bel Geddes' Futurama transported its passengers into the America of 1960, enabling them to ride one of six hundred electrically propelled chairs at simulated speeds of up to a hundred miles per hour while suspended over a 36,000-square-foot scale model of the United States. The accompanying narrative, amplified over loudspeakers attached to each chair, extolled the virtues of a future in which "abundant sunshine, fresh air, [and] fine green parkways" would provide access to a world of abundance in which the massive skyscrapers and cornucopian farms of Futurama would be connected by shiny seven-lane highways. At the conclusion of the ride, visitors were returned to 1939 and deposited in a GM showroom where they were handed a souvenir button that read "I have seen the future."[41]

Significantly, the mise-en-scène for the futuristic visions of Democracity and Futurama—visions of the city and country and labor and capital harmoniously united through the spectacular technologies made possible by electricity—was neither urban nor rural. As any visitor strolling through the fair's Town of Tomorrow could not help but conclude, the future would be suburban. Walking the streets of tomorrow town it would be easy to conclude that with a few quirky exceptions the future promised merely newer versions of the same old colonials and ranches. To enter these unexceptional structures, however, was to confront a brave new world of consumer convenience that less than a decade in the future would define the lure of the suburban life and lifestyle. General Electric's contribution to tomorrow town was an "all electric home" complete with a "Magic Kitchen that moves, talks and tells a timely story."[42] The story it told, like that of the architecture, landscaping, and layout of the other fifteen demonstration homes on display, was that the American future would be lived somewhere between the urban squalor and rural poverty that framed the social imaginary of the Depression. In their own humble way, these electrical appliances foreshadowed a future as breathtakingly new as anything found in Democracity or Futurama. Looking out the window of the Magic Kitchen, one could almost see the postwar suburbs springing forth; the rows of single-family homes like tranquil islands dotting a verdant sea of impossibly green lawns, each lavishly equipped with electrically powered devices that promised to fulfill the fantasies of leisure and abundance the Depression had suppressed.

The most remarkable technology introduced at the fair, and the one that most presciently mirrored the world of the future, was television. "Now we add radio sight to sound," declared David Sarnoff, speaking from the RCA pavilion at the fair, and "it is with a feeling of humbleness that I come to this moment of announcing the birth of a new art so important in its implications that it is bound to affect all society . . . an art which shines like a torch in a troubled world . . . a creative force we must learn to utilize for the benefit of all mankind."[43] As roving camera crews from NBC canvassed the fairgrounds documenting its marvels, visitors shared their opinions of the future on a set the network had constructed to demonstrate the magic of television. The buttons given to the people who recorded their impressions of the future on camera spoke to the novelty of the new medium, the promise of the world of tomorrow, and the new subjectivity that together they would engender. The simple message inscribed on the buttons depicted an act that would transform their lives: "I have been televised."

Three months after the fair opened, the outbreak of World War II put the future on hold, at least temporarily. While commercial television broadcasting was suspended in the United States during the war, television's role in postwar America was the subject of discussion before the war ended. Speaking to an audience of media professionals in 1944, T. F. Joyce—the general manager of RCA's Radio-Phonograph-Television Department—made the case for television's future prominence in the conversion from war to peace. "A nationwide television system is the medium which can arouse the spirit and will of the people," Joyce told his fellow somnipractors. "Through skillful use of a nationwide television system, American political, business, labor, religious and social leadership can create in the hearts and minds of America's 134,000,000 people the desire to bring about the peace, security, and plenty that is the dream of every citizen."[44] Begging the question of why a desire for peace, security, and plenty needed to be created when it was already the dream of every citizen, Joyce was not alone in his enthusiasm for television's potential as an instrument of leadership. His description of the role of the new medium in the postwar production of desire and the marketing of dreams was a characteristic expression of a socioeconomic order anxiously anticipating the transition from a booming wartime economy and searching for ways to guarantee that peace would not result in another depression.

After the war itself the most anxiety-producing issue for Americans was how to afford tomorrow town. As Cohen demonstrates in *The Consumer's Republic*, the wartime dreams and desires that dominated Americans' vision of postwar security and prosperity were centered on the private home, typically suburban, and "fully equipped with consumer durables."[45] While reaping the benefits of converting its factories to military production during the war, GE was already positioning itself as a principal beneficiary of the housing boom that would serve as the engine of the postwar economy. In a typical GE wartime ad that ran in the *Saturday Evening Post* on 5 June 1943, a soldier sits on a park bench with his adoring gal, sketching a starter home in the sand with a stick. The home is, as the copy informs us, "A promise of gloriously happy days to come . . . when Victory is won." Reminiscent of GE's Norman Rockwell illustrated and Bruce Barton authored ads of the 1920s linking Protestant theology to GE's light bulb as the bearer of light into darkness, the "victory home" campaign represents Protestant eschatology but with a twist. Promising future rewards for present sacrifices, the ad does not ask the young couple to defer their dreams until after death but only until victory is achieved. Then—through the "new comforts, new conveniences, and new economies" of "electrical living"—their victory home will provide them with paradise on earth. The advertisement's cross promotion of a dizzying array of consumer products and services—household appliances, war bonds, radio programs, and appliance manuals—is synthesized by GE's corporate logo with its patriotic and democratic "promise" of a new kind of home available to all, with "better living built in."

By 1946, the swift fulfillment of GE's promise had become a national priority. Fifteen years of economic instability and war had resulted in the relocation and dislocation of millions of Americans and an acute housing shortage that would be exacerbated by the return of the troops. The most visible fruits of victory were not immediate prosperity and plenty but the worst outbreak of labor unrest in history and a crippling housing shortage that *Fortune* magazine, in a special issue devoted to the crisis, declared to be the worst "since 1607 when John Smith wondered where he would spend his first night in Virginia."[46] In the same issue, *Fortune* editor Eric Hodgins, in a short story that introduced Americans to the postwar suburb, offered a potential resolution to both the labor and housing crises. In "Mr. Blandings Builds His Castle," Jim and Muriel Blandings solve their housing crisis by fleeing a dirty, overcrowded New York City and their cramped rental apartment for what the real estate ad that inspires their exodus describes as the "sylvan charm" of the "peaceful Connecticut countryside" and the "dream house" that only suburban home ownership can provide. Later that year, "under the more American and democratic title" *Mr. Blandings Builds His Dream House,* Hodgins's story became a best-selling novel, followed in 1948 by a movie starring Cary Grant and Myrna Loy.[47]

In a spectacle of imagineering reminiscent of the Town of Tomorrow, the promotional campaign for the film featured the construction of seventy-three "Blandings Dream Houses" across the country. Built with labor, materials, and furnishings donated by companies with a vested interest in stimulating the dream of home ownership, they were raffled off to publicize the film. Prominent among the corporate donors was General Electric, whose new "all-electric kitchen" was featured in the film and installed in all the houses.[48]

The Blanding's Dream House campaign typified the new postwar dynamic between corporate capitalism and electronic media. An expanding economy and the introduction of readily available consumer credit and low-rate mortgages meant that an unprecedented number of Americans could now afford home ownership. The Blandings campaign made it clear that Hollywood would have something to say about what kind of homes they would buy and how they would be outfitted. When a Kansas City developer, J. C. Nichols, proved he could build the same house for less than

Blandings paid, the orders poured in. Who wouldn't want to live in Cary Grant's dream house, and who could resist such a bargain? If it cost a bit more than was prudent, there was always credit. And besides, a dream house was, as Blandings explains in the film, "like a fine painting. You buy it with your heart, not your head. You don't ask, how much was the paint, how much was the canvas. You look at it and you say 'it is beautiful—I want it.' And if it costs a few more pennies, you pay it and gladly, because you love it and you can't measure things you love in dollars and cents."[49] The Blandings campaign demonstrated that electronic media was more than merely another venue for selling products; that its influence in manufacturing dreams and marketing desire made it a critical collaborator in what Bernays called the "engineering of consent" for the consumer's republic.[50]

To fully realize the synergies of the electronic media and consumer capitalism, however, would require the widespread deployment of the little box that was just then being installed in the paradigmatic mass-produced suburb of Levittown, Long Island, the first planned community to offer homes complete with a built-in television set.[51] Nowhere was the emerging postwar calculus that equated television and suburban home ownership with economic prosperity and national security more evident than in Levittown. In the September 1948 issue of *Harper's*, the developer of Levittown, William Levitt, famously summarized the relationship between home ownership and democracy: "No man who owns his own house and lot can be a communist. . . . He has too much to do."[52] Over the next decade the dominant corporate message was that one of the most patriotic things the suburban home owner could do was to watch television and purchase the products it displayed.

Total Electric Living

The debut of the *General Electric Television Theater* in 1953 marked a new approach for utilizing television to resolve the challenges and exploit the opportunities posed by the new business landscape created by the postwar economic boom. Wartime production had quadrupled GE's sales volume, and the postwar expansion of the market for electrical and related products increased the size of the company beyond what its administrative structure could handle. In response, GE's president, Ralph Cordiner, initiated the most sweeping change in the management of the company since Swope's innovations in the 1920s. Cordiner radically decentralized the company's operations by restructuring GE from eight profit and loss groups into more than a hundred and gave departmental general managers unprecedented responsibility for the new groups. The relative autonomy of the branch offices and factories of GE's far-flung empire resulted in increased economies of speed by localizing decision making and reducing bureaucratic drag. Decentralization, however, raised a new set of challenges. Employees far removed from the corporate metropole often felt like colonial subjects whose loyalties and ambitions were increasingly localized and often at odds with the larger corporate agenda. Similarly, the different and often conflicting requirements for marketing a refrigerator as opposed to a jet engine meant that GE's various divisions were often competing for resources in ways that brought them into conflict with each other and the corporation itself. In addition, the new corporate structure did little to alleviate the increased regulatory scrutiny of GE's corporate practices stimulated by its increased size and stature in strategically important industries. Finally, and perhaps most significant, decentralization threatened the carefully crafted corporate image that united GE's diverse holdings and products.

As with Swope in the 1920s, Cordiner's solution was a public relations campaign that sought to ameliorate divisional rivalries, mollify antitrust regulators, stimulate employees' identification with the corporation, and invigorate its public image. Implicit in GE's public relations strategies of the 1920s and 1950s was the recognition that large corporations, like nations, are largely imagined communities. Confronted with a crisis in corporate self-representation, in both instances the company's president sought the assistance of public relations professionals to define and disseminate a new corporate identity. This identity was constructed to represent for GE's workers and consumers alike what the nation represented for its citizens, what Benedict Anderson defines as "the image of their communion." For both Swope and Cordiner the solution to the paradox of corporate self-representation was to promote a belief in the scientific and magical power of electricity as the source of human progress, to inspire faith in a better way of life made possible by the products derived from electricity, and to instill in the public imagination the image of GE as the embodiment of that faith.

For Cordiner, the primary vehicle for corporate image crafting would be television, most notably *General Electric Television Theater*, the corporation's first "all-company project," sponsored not by a particular GE product line or division but by its Department of Public Relations Services.[53] Before *GE Theater*, as it came to be known, the company, like most corporations, had approached television as merely another platform for advertising its products. Its early attempts at company-sponsored television programming had been dismal failures. In the fall of 1948, its first foray into commercial television, the variety show *The Dennis James Carnival*, was canceled after the first broadcast. Its replacement, *Riddle Me This*, a quiz show, lasted just twelve weeks.[54] In April 1949, GE tried again with a musical variety program, the *Fred Waring Show*. Waring, a popular bandleader, had already made an indispensable contribution to consumer culture with his invention of the blender that bears his name, but he proved less successful as a television personality, limping along for five years with mediocre ratings and little benefit to his sponsor. Rather than promoting the individual products manufactured by its disparate divisions as its previous TV programming had done, *GE Theater* was conceived, in the spirit of Barton's revelation of the corporate soul, as a vehicle for merchandising brand awareness, corporate identity, and GE's target image as the leading innovator of the electrically enhanced technologies, commodities, and lifestyle that powered the postwar American economy.[55]

Cordiner's decision to focus on television as the best medium in which to represent GE's new corporate soul reflected the speed at which television entered American homes after World War II. In 1947, there were only about fourteen thousand television sets in the United States. By January of 1952, the Nielsen ratings for the first time registered more televisions than radios in use during prime-time hours. That spring—after the FCC lifted a four-year freeze on licensing new stations—stores selling televisions began opening at the rate of a thousand a month. By 1954, the year Reagan began hosting *GE Theater*, the number of televisions had more than doubled to almost thirty-two million. By the time Reagan left the show in 1962, there were televisions was in 90 percent of American homes, the average American watched five hours of television per day, and TV had replaced movies as American's dominant leisure-time activity. Advertising was the sine qua non of television, and it wasn't long before television became the leading venue for promoting the postwar expansion of consumer markets. By 1952, it had overtaken radio in advertising revenue, and by 1955 it exceeded magazines and newspapers in national advertising.[56] The singular importance of television to the unprecedented expansion of the American economy in the 1950s was summarized in a 1960 NBC Research Department report, which stated, "In virtually all industries the emphasis in the battle for profits has shifted from the factory to the marketplace. . . [and] marketing activities are the single most important influence on profits."[57] The effectiveness of television as a marketing tool was unprecedented. But fully exploiting its potential as a medium for the revelation of the corporate soul would require cultivation of the body electric.

While Cordiner's strategy for television would ultimately prove successful, the initial response to the anthology format was not what GE had hoped. It was not until the decision was made in the second season to emphasize "consistent company voice advertising" and Reagan was hired that the program became a hit.[58] When Reagan began hosting *GE Theater* in September 1954 it ranked a mediocre nineteenth in the Nielsen ratings. By December, after only four months with Reagan as host, the revamped show had climbed to tenth in the ratings and was the most watched weekly dramatic program on television. The washed-up film actor was an instant TV star. Although the ratings peaked during the next season, when the show ranked third among all programs on television, for the duration of its run it consistently placed first in its desirable time slot, nine o'clock on Sunday night, between the *Ed Sullivan Show* and *Alfred Hitchcock Presents.*[59]

Reagan's self-described role on the program was that of a "continuing personality on which to hang the production and advertising of the show."[60] As host, he was a constant presence, unifying the disparate offerings—adaptations of popular plays, short stories, novels, magazine fiction, and motion pictures—by introducing and concluding each program. In addition to Reagan, Don Herbert, already a recognizable TV personality as the star of *Watch Mr. Wizard,* would periodically appear during the intermission between the show's two acts as the General Electric

Progress Reporter to report on recent developments from "the house of magic," the nickname coined in a 1930s ad campaign to describe GE's research and development laboratory. Eschewing television's standard programming format, derived from radio, in which the program's ostensible "content" was punctuated at regular intervals by product advertisements, *GE Theater* utilized the intermission as an opportunity to inform the public about the company's latest advances in science and technology rather than to advertise specific products. By blurring the boundaries between entertainment and marketing and presenting corporate promotion in the guise of consumer education, the show introduced a new strategy for exploiting television as a unique medium for *"projecting an image* to a public that never assembled as such."[61]

The benefits he accrued from his association with GE were immediately apparent to Reagan. "From my own viewpoint," he told the *Hollywood Reporter* less than a year after assuming his new job, "my kind of an association with a big business firm not only adds half or better to the economic value of my name, but provides a degree of security entirely foreign to the movie business, which is ruled so much by suicidal fluctuations, fads and whims."[62] But what did GE's association with Reagan add to the economic value and security of *its* name? Reagan's role on the program reflected an emerging consensus among advertisers and media analysts that television's new language of the image required careful attention to the person selected to represent the corporation on TV. In his 1955 report for AT&T on the role of the corporate spokesman on television, the media consultant Chester Burger summarized the new thinking: "The person you choose will represent the telephone company to thousands of viewers. His title or official position with the company will be less important to the company . . . and the audience than the impression he makes." Television, Burger instructed, "has its own language, its own grammar," requiring the corporate message to be conveyed "through images rather than words." On television, *"The pictures don't illustrate the story; they are the story.* The narration merely helps the pictures."[63] Thanks to the movies, Reagan had already acquired brand awareness as "Mr. Norm," a persona he easily adapted into the affable electrical everyman who became the embodiment of GE's corporate image. In lieu of commercials promoting GE's products, Reagan, like the corporate logo that inevitably appeared whenever he was onscreen, performatively reiterated the corporate image, branding Reagan as, in the words of *TV Guide,* "the ambassador of things mechanical."[64]

On television, serving as the ambassador of mechanical reproduction, Reagan brought an aura of mass-mediated celebrity to bear on the production of GE's target image as expressed in its new postwar slogan, "Progress is our most important product." The scaffolding of this new celebrity was constructed shortly after Reagan took over as host. Don Herbert's "progress reports" introducing viewers to GE's contributions in "Jet Engine Advancement," "Turbosupercharger Progress," "Atomic Safety Devices," and the like, recorded such impressive "impact scores" in audience recall that the polling firm of Gallup-Robinson declared *GE Theater* to be "the leading institutional campaign on television for selling ideas to the public." The highest score Gallup-Robinson had recorded to date was for "Kitchen of the Future," inspiring GE to launch a campaign to promote its domestic products by encouraging home owners to "Live Better Electrically."[65] In conjunction with its campaign to promote "Total Electric Living," GE equipped the modern ranch-style house Reagan was building in Pacific Palisades with the latest technology developed by the house of magic: "everything electric," Reagan quipped, "except a chair."[66] In return, Reagan opened his home and offered his family to the show as a testament to the virtues of living better electrically. During his second season as host, he periodically offered viewers a tour of his "total electric" house. As a venue for living better electrically, the Reagan's home became the setting for TV's first reality series. Like the Blandings dream houses, the Reagans' home modeled the benefits of the new suburban lifestyle as a show house for the consumer's republic.

The first segment, shot while the house was still under construction, was an unabashed promotion of the new lifestyle available to electrically savvy consumers.[67] The Reagans and their electrical contractor toured the shell of their new house, demonstrating how to wire a home for "full house power." While the contractor patiently detailed the technical specifications required to reap the benefits of GE's products, Reagan enthusiastically extolled the virtues of the new technology. Nancy, in the role of the naive housewife, posed the questions on the minds of average viewers yet to be initiated into the mysteries of total electric living. After much discussion of the benefits of sufficient wiring and abundant circuits and outlets, an increasingly impatient Nancy delivered the ideological hook. Following her husband's particularly condescending explanation that *full house power* means "enough electric power in every one of your circuits, and enough circuits and outlets so that no one of them ever gets overloaded," Nancy cut to the chase. "Well," she declared, speaking to and for the members of the TV audience, who were no doubt bored or confused by all this talk of circuits and outlets and wiring, "I'm glad we have it. Because we're going to have some wonderful electric equipment and we want to have all the entertainment and pleasure and comfort out of that equipment that we can. I'm sure that's what you want out of your appliances too."

As television's first all-electric family, the Reagans modeled the electrically generated virtues of entertainment and pleasure and comfort, keywords of what Thomas Hine has termed the "populuxe" lifestyle.[68] During the initial postwar period, corporations reacted to what Hine describes as the "the strongest consumer economy the world had ever seen" by focusing on speed and efficiency in bringing affordable products to market. Hine identifies 1954, the year Reagan signed on with GE, as the beginning of the "populuxe decade," the year corporations transformed their sales focus and marketing strategies to induce consumers to spend their growing disposable incomes on products that had previously been considered luxury items. The term *populuxe,* Hine explains, like the torrent of newly affordable consumer gadgets, conjured "an ineffable emotion" by infusing the popular with the trappings of luxury.[69] While American suburbanites never fully endorsed Le Corbusier's functional modernist dictum that a house is a "machine for living in," they eagerly embraced the populuxe fantasy of the modern home chock-full of "machines to live with."[70] Like the houses of tomorrow town, the magic of the homes built during the populuxe era was not to be found in their architecture but in the cornucopia of "space-age" devices contained within. In what Hine characterizes as a "reversal of the age-old pattern in which seats of government and houses of worship received the highest craftsmanship and ornamentation a society could produce while the individual house was relatively bare," the suburban house became a showcase for a design aesthetic derived not from European modernism but from the democratic promise of American capitalism.[71] More than mere conveniences, the machines GE installed in the Reagans' new home symbolized the achievement of a style of living—a level of entertainment, pleasure, and comfort—previously unaffordable for all but the very wealthy.

In subsequent programs, the Reagans' new home served as a mise-en-scène for the multiple virtues of an electrically enhanced lifestyle. As hosts, the Reagans' job was to sell the idea that GE's cutting-edge electrical technology provided mastery over nature and democratic access to an aristocratic way of life. Inserted in the intermission between the two acts of the weekly drama, the segments on the Reagans' new home demonstrated how total electric living provided a utopian resolution to the ideological tensions of American Exceptionalism. Introducing a 1957 episode entitled "Too Good with a Gun," Reagan picks up a prop six-shooter and spins the cylinder.[72] "A man's talents may be used for good or evil," Reagan comments in a characteristic formulation of cold war existentialism. "Exceptional talents only widen the possibilities for both. Nowhere was this better illustrated than in the young communities of the American West some eighty years ago. Our story tonight takes place in such a community where men were struggling towards that stability and peace so badly needed." At the end of the first act, Slick Everret, the bully who has disrupted the peaceful town ("where most men's guns are so rusty they don't shoot") lies dead in the street, shot by a reluctant gunfighter who is too good with a gun to escape the death and destruction that results from his unique talent.

Cross-fade to Mr. Wizard, who announces, "Tonight we're going visiting at the Ronald Reagans' again, in their new home, to see how their many wonderful electric servants are helping them, just as they'll help you, 'Live Better Electrically.'" Cut to Ronald, Nancy, and four-year-old Patti, who are sitting at the breakfast table eating a "perfect meal" made by Nancy's electric servants. The English muffins, they inform the viewer, were prepared in their new toaster, and the cheese on top was melted in their toaster oven. The "steady heat and automatic timing" of their new electric skillet, Nancy explains, "makes a tricky dish like soufflé "easy and safe to make."

"My electric appliances do everything," purrs Nancy.

"What's elesses aplotz?" asks little Patti.

"They're all the things around the house that make Mommy's work easier."

"Tell you what, Patti," Dad chimes in enthusiastically. "Let's see how many electric appliances we can find around the house."

They all troop into the kitchen, where a game of "name that appliance" turns up a clock, a mixer, a vacuum cleaner, "Mommy's iron," a waffle iron, and a grill:

> NANCY: One at a time or all together [the electric servants] make quite a difference in the way we live. That's why every housewife wants them, the latest models with the newest improvements.
>
> RONNIE: Because she knows that you really begin to live when you "live better . . .
>
> PATTI: . . . Eletriffly.

Through the alchemical talents of the GE scientists at the house of magic and the dream merchants at *GE Theater,* the deadly talents employed by the reluctant gunfighter to settle the frontier have been domesticated to provide the stability and peace that cold war American communities still craved. Suburban husbands need not fear that their retreat from the urban frontier has left them with "guns so rusty they won't shoot," imperiling their families, property, or manhood. Liberty, equality, and happiness are available to all through a revolution that no longer requires the squeeze of a trigger, just the flick of a switch. Entertainment and pleasure and comfort—the attributes of an electrically enhanced lifestyle—were the utopian virtues of a consumer's republic in which everyone could, at the very least, *imagine* living better electrically.

Another heavily promoted benefit of the virtues of total electric living was the introduction into the home of new technologies of mechanical reproduction. In a segment touting the entertainment systems provided for them by GE, Reagan describes traveling a hundred miles to Chicago as a child to see his first play.[73] "Think how much different it is today. . . . Here at our new home if we want entertainment," he demonstrates, proudly opening his TV cabinet, "all we do is flick a switch and electricity brings it to us." Opening the sliding glass door to his patio, he reveals a spectacular view of Los Angeles and the Pacific and "a portable television set" the Reagan's use to watch TV "on the patio or by the pool." Encouraging the viewer to "enjoy the ball game, see the latest news of the world, see the great stars of the theater," Reagan makes it clear that television has replaced Mugs's dramatization and pageant work as the ideal substitute for firsthand knowledge of the world.

Like their television, Nancy informs us, her new transistor radio, sheathed in a "real top-grain leather" case, "can be a great deal of company. And it can go even more places, around the home or on picnics or on fishing trips." Demonstrating another "important source of entertainment," Reagan unveils their "projection machine for home movies," which is hidden in an alcove covered by a framed painting of a sailboat. Opening yet another wall cabinet, Nancy demonstrates their "new high fidelity."

"Remember what a difference there used to be between home listening and the concert hall?" Reagan remarks.

"It's almost as if the orchestra were playing right here in the living room," Nancy chimes in.

Slipping his arm around his wife's waist, Reagan seals the deal: "As you can see we're enjoying all the entertainment electricity can bring us. So can you. There's no trick to it. It's just a matter of starting in easy stages, one item at a time. The first thing you know, you and your family will begin to [Nancy joins in for the chorus] 'Live Better Electrically.'" Like the patio doors and picture windows that frame the view of an arid desert transformed into a thriving metropolis through the auspices of capitalism and mass media, their entertainment technologies enable the Reagans to imaginatively picture the pleasures available by living better electrically without ever leaving the comfort of their home. Why would anybody want to leave the house when the whole world can be made accessible merely by purchasing these products "in easy stages" with the credit conveniently provided by GE through the GE Credit Corporation.

While the vast majority of television shows were still broadcast in black and white, the Reagan's television set offered a vision of the future through the "pleasure and excitement" of color. In a subsequent house tour that touted the virtues of "modern light conditioning," the Reagans stressed the importance of introducing color into the home through lighting to create "a more livable house."[74] The reasons they give for doing so materialize the imaginative dimensions of the consumer's republic, as well as the utopian promise of total electric living. The adjectives Nancy uses to describe the Reagans' various lighting devices—*eye-catching, marvelous, interesting*—are those of a world made familiar to the viewer by the entertainment technologies scattered throughout the house. The multicolored house made possible by the colored lights that Nancy can "change" and "mix" to "get different effects" by "turning the knobs of [a] dimmer" is an ideal modeled on the saturated Technicolor effects of 1950s movies, which tried to distinguish themselves from black and white television shows by cranking up the color. Nancy, a former film actress, informs us that these colors are not only yellow, blue, and pink but also "warm" and "cool," and "flattering." They produce a light that does not simply illuminate the home but alters its "mood," enabling the Reagans "to see better and look better and live better in our home." Of course, most viewers can't see the colors Nancy describes. They don't yet own a color TV. But they know what she means. Even in black and white they recognize what it means to be warm or cool. They want *their* lights to flatter *them.* They want their lights to make them eye-catching and interesting and to "do marvelous things" for them. They know and want these things because radio, film, and television have stimulated their imaginations and desires by teaching them new ways to imagine how they might look, sound, and feel.

On *GE Theater,* Ronald Reagan was introduced to the first TV generation. Through television, he would become one of the most visible patriots of the empire created by the cold war consumer's revolution. "I am seen by more people in one week [on television]," he marveled, "than I am in a full year in movie theaters."[75] By 1958, according to one survey, Reagan was one of the most recognized men in the country. He would prove to be so effective as a celebrity salesman that a joke began to make the rounds in Hollywood that after listening to his spiel for GE's nuclear arsenal one viewer remarked, "I didn't really need a submarine, but I've got one now."[76] Through television, Mr. Norm had become the popular embodiment of the virtues of living better electrically. Television established Reagan as a new kind of celebrity archetype peculiar to the medium, not the western hero he had aspired to become as a film actor but a corporate icon, "the Actor in the Gray Flannel Suit" as the film industry took to calling him, "as intimately identified with the corporation as its advertising slogan or trademark logo."[77] This new and improved body electric was coterminous with the advent of television and reflects television's genealogy as a medium and industry shaped from the outset by the imperatives of corporate capitalism and the performance of mass-mediated celebrity. Reagan's television celebrity and political prominence were both a product and an embodiment of this new vision of the imagined community of the nation powered by the body electric.

The Biggest Fan in the World

As had been the case with radio and film, Reagan's entry into television occurred during its formative golden age. With television, however, Reagan also contributed to laying the foundation on which the medium would be built. By the early 1950s, as Reagan's film career was winding down, the balance of power in Hollywood was shifting. In 1948, in the antitrust case *United States v. Paramount Pictures,* the Supreme Court ruled unanimously that the "Big Five" studios must divorce their theater exhibition holdings from the production and distribution ends of their businesses and cease their practice of block-booking films. While the dismantling of the studio system made film stars "proprietors of their own image," it didn't take long for them to receive help in managing their property. As the studios reluctantly loosened their grip on their stars, a semiautonomous, "independent" publicity profession emerged to take over the studio functions of cultivating "talent" and selecting which human and literary "properties" to develop. It was during this period that talent agents "began to be important power brokers, and the packages they offered—a writer, a script, a star or two, sometimes a director—became (and remain) the currency of the industry."[78] The restructuring of the Hollywood studio system enhanced the profile of performer-oriented somnipractors such as the talent agent, who could now, in Raymond Chandler's caustic summary, "create packaging corporations which delivered complete shows to the networks or the advertising agencies [and load] them with talent, which sometimes under another corporate name, he represented as an agent. He took his commission for getting you a job, and then he sold the job itself for an additional profit."[79]

Chandler's scenario perfectly describes MCA's arrangement with BBD&O to produce *GE Theater*. While the arrival of the cavalry that rescued Reagan from a floundering film career may have been dramatic, its source could hardly have been as unexpected as Reagan recalls. In 1952, as president of the Screen Actors Guild, Reagan had negotiated an unprecedented blanket waiver, making MCA—headed by Reagan's longtime agent, Lew Wasserman—the only talent agency permitted to produce its own shows for television. Thanks to Reagan's waiver, MCA, in exchange for granting guild members residuals when no other production companies would, became the only company granted unlimited rights to both produce television shows and represent the labor that made them. By the time Reagan left the show in 1962, the original talent agency accounted for only 10 percent of MCA's income. Less than a decade after receiving the waiver, it had parlayed the huge competitive advantage Reagan had negotiated for it into a horizontally and vertically integrated entertainment conglomerate that controlled over 40 percent of prime-time television and 60 percent of the entertainment industry as a whole.[80]

By 1961, MCA's astonishing growth had drawn the attention of the Justice Department. Eight separate antitrust investigations probed the legality of the company's dealings, including the waiver Reagan had granted. Testifying before a federal grand jury in Hollywood in 1962, Reagan answered questions regarding how he might have profited from the waiver. His sketchy memory of the details surrounding his negotiations with MCA was convenient, and his disavowal of any benefits he or MCA might have derived from the waiver was unconvincing. His testimony as to his value to GE, however, was not so farfetched. Dismissing the insinuations that his job with GE represented a quid pro quo arrangement with MCA, Reagan proposed an alternative reason why he felt more secure as an employee of General Electric than he ever had while working at Warner Brothers: "General Electric was having me go on tours. Each year I go on tours all over the country and make speeches. . . . It was never done by anyone else in the television business so it was apparent that I had a value, a relationship to General Electric that was probably sufficient above and beyond the show, that if the show wasn't successful they would still retain me."[81] In later years, Reagan would characterize his value to General Electric as a "kind of goodwill ambassador from the home office," whose tours played a "supporting role in an extraordinary experiment by American industry." While Reagan's description of the larger experiment is sketchy, his plant tours were designed to ameliorate the tensions produced by Cordiner's new decentralized management structure and to forge "a closer link between the plants and the communities where they were located."[82] Like Dick Falkner in *That Printer of Udell's*, Reagan had begun to apply the skills he had acquired as an orator to "a field of wider usefulness."

The tours were also the venue for fusing Reagan's embodiment of the corporation's public image into the body electric that would define him as a political performer. The idea for the plant tours originated with Earl Dunkel, another somnipractor whose ideas would influence the career of the future president. Dunkel, a former newspaperman, started at GE as a "communicator," was promoted to advertising account supervisor, and when Reagan joined the company was assigned the task of "audience promotion" for the television show.[83] The show represented a new direction in corporate promotion, and not everyone in the company was sold on the concept. The initial objective of the tour as Dunkel conceived it "was to have [Reagan] meet and charm . . . GE vice presidents all over the country so they would stay off our backs long enough for us to get the program moving." Because GE had approximately seven hundred thousand employees, the tour, in addition to serving as "an employee communication device," would also function as "an audience promotion device."[84] Initially, Reagan's plant visits consisted largely of meet and greets with production line workers. It didn't take long for regional managers to recognize the community relations benefits of his celebrity, however, and they began asking Reagan to deliver a few remarks at their clubs and civic organizations. What began with fielding questions about what it was like to kiss Ann Sheridan evolved into lengthy speeches defending Hollywood, promoting corporate values and the free enterprise system, and warning against the threat to liberty and property of excessive taxation, big government, and the communist menace.

Over the next eight years, touring between six and sixteen weeks a year, Reagan honed his elocutionary skills and prepared the ground for his entry into politics. Making as many as fourteen speeches a day, Reagan, by his own estimation, spent 250,000 minutes in front of a microphone.[85] He peddled his message to over a quarter million workers in GE factories in forty-two states and "to local chambers of commerce, school boards, garden clubs, union halls, and Rotary meetings. He plugged it on promotional tours to city councils and to conventioneers. He hawked it to Shriners, to Masons, to Knights of Columbus. He marketed it to the Kiwanis, the Lions, the Elks, the American Legion."[86] In the process, Reagan achieved a visibility far greater than he ever had as a movie actor.

As a preparation for politics, the tours presented Reagan with an invaluable opportunity to educate himself in the ways and means of sympathetic magic. On tour, Reagan, who had always appreciated his audience, was able to observe firsthand what that audience cared about, what it believed in, and how it worked. Hours spent on the factory floor, in auditoriums and in banquet halls, speaking with and delivering speeches to a cross-section of the American electorate, served as rehearsals for the kind of performances required in political campaigning. Unlike many celebrity speakers, who attend the event they are hired to address just long enough to speak, shake a few hands, and sign a few autographs, Reagan used cocktail and banquet time to size up his audience. His memories of the General Electric years were inevitably summarized in anecdotes affirming his conviction that, as he asserts in *Where's the Rest of Me?* "no barnstorming politician ever met the people on quite such a common footing." In his live performances on tour, Reagan was able to recapture the sense he had felt while addressing the striking students at Eureka, the sense that he was "together" with his audience. "Sometimes," he wrote, "I had an awesome, shivering feeling that America was making a personal appearance for me, and it made me the biggest fan in the world."[87]

As the most visible representative of the company that had manufactured the biggest fan in the world, Reagan cultivated a relationship of mutual fandom with his audience that would become a critical component of his future political success. Throughout his political career, he rarely pandered to his audience or altered his beliefs in response to public opinion; his repudiation of his New Deal roots and growing neoconservatism remained steadfast. On tour for GE, however, he learned how to tailor his presentation of the ideas that his education had bestowed on him to his audience. Previews and tours of the provinces were where the performance was crafted, the production's rough edges smoothed and polished, and the brand tested for television. Reagan would then adapt the audience-tested talks he gave on tour into a controllable and transferable form, a distillation of his best material, variations of which he would give for the rest of his life. Codified as "the Speech," his stirring rendition of the script in a televised address in support of Barry Goldwater's presidential candidacy made him, in journalist David Broder's words, "a political star overnight."[88] With his star-making television debut as a prime-time politician, Reagan had, as he recounts in the final words of *Where's the Rest of Me?* "found the rest of me."

As a TV star, corporate spokesman, and barnstorming ideologue, Reagan became the electronic media's answer to the nation-building role of the nineteenth-century stage actor. Schooled in the entertainment industry, Reagan had learned the theatrical and political lesson *Dracula* author Bram Stoker had gleaned as actor Henry Irving's business manager. "Without an audience in sympathy," Stoker noted of the most widely emulated performer of his day, "no actor can do his best."[89] Plugging the GE brand, Reagan acquired the techne that enabled him to, as W. D. King writes of Irving, "foster elite expectations without recourse to class prejudice and without disrupting the essentially middle-class base of his audience."[90] Through his television celebrity and house tours, Reagan connected his audience to the new imagi-nation of the consumer's republic. The populuxe desires fostered by his performances were not limited to the worldly goods available through GE's credit division. Over the course of his career as a performer, Reagan cultivated associations with prominent members of the social and cultural elite and, like Irving, "took care that the bulk of the crowd should feel at one with them, contiguous with eminence and wealth and authority."[91] Much as Irving was credited with generating a "revolution in the attitude of the English people towards the calling of the actor" that coincided with "a revolution in the attitude of the English people towards itself as an audience," Reagan would transform middle-class Americans' attitudes toward the actor as a player on the political stage at the same moment that television was transforming Americans' ideas about themselves as an audience of social actors.[92]

By the mid-1960s, the virtues of living better electrically would be challenged by a counterculture advocating an antimaterialist lifestyle and secession from the republic of consumption. Its rallying cry advocated better living not through electricity but through chemistry. Its mantra, "tune in, turn on, drop out," was not a celebration of the couch potato but a defiant rejection of the teachings of television and its spectacle of mass consumption. Yet by the late 1970s this TV generation, raised in the suburbs and on television and schooled in the values of the consumer's republic, would elect Ronald Reagan president. One of the reasons why Reagan's career change was successful is that the unionized factory workers and suburban warriors that constituted the Reagan Revolution did not perceive him to be a politician.[93] He had let them into his house and sold them his appliances. They viewed him and knew him as the celebrity who had taught them that progress was our most important product and how to live better electrically. He wasn't the actor who shot Lincoln. He was the "progress" man. It was a curious appellation, to be sure, for the standard-bearer of a conservative revolution. But that was the point. That's why it worked: progress *and* nostalgia, ideology *and* utopia, no taxation but plenty of representation. These were the promises made by Mr. Norm, the Great Communicator, and the Ambassador of Things Mechanical. The nicknames, monikers, and epithets flowed easily with Ronald Reagan, and they all sounded like the titles of movies or television shows. The temptation is to dismiss the verbiage as hype, an advertising pitch, a product of the inflated claims made for celebrities, or just good public relations. It was all those things. Yet Reagan was not only a product of and a salesman for the consumer's republic he represented it all the way to the White House. The relationship among Reagan, GE, and television in the 1950s suggests that the story of the Reagan Revolution cannot be adequately explained, as it characteristically is, by the waning of postwar liberalism's lure and the rise of a new conservatism. To fully appreciate the legacy of Reaganism requires heeding the capacity of corporate capitalism and mass mediation to shape the body politic through the body electric.

CHAPTER SIX

The Rights of Memory

I have some rights of memory in this kingdom,
    Which now to claim my vantage doth invite me.

    —Fortinbras, *Hamlet*

When Polonius is slain, Claudius sends Rosencrantz and Guildenstern to interrogate Hamlet. "My lord, you must tell us," entreats Rosencrantz, "where the body is, and go with us to the king." Hamlet replies, "The King is with the body / But the body is not with the king / The king is a thing."[1] Hamlet's formulation of the thingness of kingness derives its ontic calculus from a political economy that traffics in bodies and bodies of memory. The kingdom of Denmark is at stake, and the bodies are not with the king. Apparitions, usurpers, unwilling heirs, and foreigners contend for a throne

---

Photo: En route to the U.S. Capitol, a riderless horse bears the riding boots of Ronald Reagan as it is led behind a procession of the former President's casket. Photo © Brooks Kraft/Corbis.

whose rightful occupancy is in dispute until carnal, bloody, and unnatural acts eliminate all claimants save Fortinbras, who in his first act as king orders his troops to "take up the bodies" lying in his path to the throne. In taking up the bodies, Fortinbras enacts his claim to power as a ritual of remembrance. Fortinbras's *rights* of memory are predicated on a common cultural understanding that it is through his performance of the *rites* of memory that the would-be king legitimates his claim to power by embodying the memorial authority of the dead.

Like Fortinbras, Ronald Reagan came to power at a time of national crisis. Beginning with the return of the hostages from Iran on the day of Reagan's inauguration, his presidency, too, oriented itself around the reclamation of bodies. The hostages were a source of national shame, symbols of America's declining global power, and their return was a propitious augury for a presidency constituted on the proposition that under its watch "America was back." Playing Fortinbras to Jimmy Carter's malaise-ridden Hamlet, Reagan proceeded to take up the bodies from the killing fields and movie screens of American cultural memory and to remember them in the service of his political agenda. These bodies of memory refute the now clichéd and still inaccurate description of the Reagan years as a period during which the nation and its citizens suffered from "collective amnesia." Memory in the 1980s—as Foucault writes of sexuality during the Enlightenment—was not repressed but selectively and ardently produced and at a remarkable rate and volume.

The governmentality of Reaganism was made manifest through his administration's staging of Reagan's rights of memory. Reagan's personal and political authority as head of state was constructed around these performances, in which his body electric was deployed as a medium for recollecting and re-forming the damaged body of the American polity. Joseph Roach defines this process of cultural reformation and reproduction as one of "surrogation" in which "actual or perceived vacancies occur in the network of relations that constitute the social fabric" and a substitute emerges to fill the cavity in the network. Successful surrogation, as Roach defines it, requires "selective memory" and "public enactments of forgetting" in order for the substitute to successfully, if always incompletely, stand in for the absent original. It is this triangular interaction among bodies and mimesis and memory, Roach contends, that we most often refer to when we use the word *performance*.[2]

The funeral procession made its way slowly down Pennsylvania Avenue toward the Capitol rotunda. Six horses accompanied the black artillery caisson bearing the flag-draped casket. Behind the caisson was another horse, this one with an empty saddle and a pair of riding boots reversed in the stirrups. Of all the props employed to usher Ronald Reagan into history, the worn boots, Reagan's favorite pair, received the most commentary in the reviews of what was surely the lengthiest funeral tour in recent memory. Derisively referred to in the early days of his administration as "the cowboy president," Reagan's restoration of the tarnished cowboy image was attested to by the reverential attention bestowed on the boots nestled in the stirrups of Sergeant York, a retired New Jersey racehorse. In the symbolic continuum of Reagan's presidential roles, from the cowboy to the cold warrior to cinematic soldiers like the one for which the horse was named, the empty boots served as an effigy for a political actor of a popular line of business common to every form of performance: the mediator of cultural memory.

In the American performance genealogy that connects the patriot to the Deerslayer to Sergeant York to Rambo, the American warrior has proved a particularly durable line of business for the transmission and transformation of cultural memory, what Marita Sturken defines as the "field of cultural negotiation through which different stories vie for a place in history."[3] As a political ritual, the state funeral is a performance that intervenes in the production of cultural memory through a syncretic blend of ancient and invented traditions. The empty boots are a relatively recent addition to a much older custom that dates from the Roman Republic. When a Roman soldier died his horse was led behind his coffin in the funeral procession as a sign that the warrior would ride no more among the living. After the marchers reached the cemetery, the soldier's horse would be killed and buried with him. This ritual served as both a tribute to the warrior's service to the empire and a guarantor that the horse, trained to serve its owner, would never be ridden by another. Over time, the practice of killing and burying the horse was abandoned, replaced by the empty boots, signifying that their owner was gone. Placing the boots backward in the stirrups was thought to ensure that no one else would ever ride the horse again.

In the rituals of national mourning, however, the significance of the empty boots is predicated on a paradox: What is irretrievably lost must somehow be replaced. Moreover, in the economy of cultural memory the more important the social role played by the departed the more immutable the loss *and* the more critical it is that a substitute be found to fill the social cavity created by his or her absence. In memorializing the fallen leader, the ritual of mourning simultaneously and necessarily calls forth a replacement capable of recapitating a body politic that has literally lost its head. As Roach reminds us, however, the process of surrogation is (like the absent presence of performance itself) necessarily incomplete, haunted as it is by the ones the surrogates seek to replace. Like Fortinbras, for the surrogate to establish its "rights of memory" and lay claim to its "vantage" it must establish authority over the dead as well as the quick, ever mindful of Roach's dictum that "memory is a process that depends crucially on forgetting."[4] In the performance context of the state funeral, the rites of memory are also by necessity rituals of forgetting. The political stage must be cleared, the leader re-placed offstage, and a new mise-en-scène of state power created to inaugurate the new political formation. As such, the *rites* of memory inevitably reproduce or reconstitute the *rights* of memory, the criteria by which the living nominate a stand-in to take up the reins from and fill the boots of those who have gone before.

The paradox of the empty boots is emblematic of the seminal political role played by performances of memory during the Reagan presidency. In death, as in his presidency, Ronald Reagan embodied the imagined community of the nation through the staging of these rites of national memory. In what follows I am primarily concerned with that genre of memory as performance that, like Reagan's funeral, reproduces or transforms the body politic through the staging of lost, damaged, and absent bodies as *bodies of memory.* These rituals of lamentation and surrogation helped to form the political imaginary of the Reagan presidency and served as a primary means of claiming its rights of memory and asserting its political vantage.

The political ontology of what I am calling bodies of memory is akin to what Judith Butler in *Bodies that Matter* defines as the materialized effects of power, material products of "the reiterative and citational practice by which discourse produces the effects that it names," or, more simply, "performativity."[5] Through citation and repetition, Butler asserts, certain performative practices generate *"a process of materialization that stabilizes over time to produce the effect of boundary, fixity, and surface we call matter."*[6] Bodies of memory are bodies that matter. They are products of the performative processes through which Reaganism fashioned culturally potent bodies into symbolic entities capable of regulating social behavior and mobilizing political constituencies. Much as *Where's the Rest of Me?* answers the question posed in its title by narrating the transformation of the amputee actor into the wholeness of the political performer, Ronald Reagan authorized and legitimated his presidential role through the transformation of materially and symbolically damaged bodies into rejuvenated political subjects and subjectivities.

As a measure of the prominence of bodies of memory during the Reagan years, we need look no farther than the most closely followed news stories of the 1980s. As ranked by that bellwether of the national psyche, *TV Guide,* the most affectively compelling events of the Reagan presidency—Little Jessica McClure stuck in a well in Texas, the Trans World Airlines hostage crisis in Beirut, the *Challenger* explosion, the air strike against Libya, and the Chernobyl meltdown—can all be classified under the genre of catastrophe.[7] As indices of the political unconscious, these stories form a signifying chain of bodies in jeopardy, encumbered bodies, trapped, captive, ailing, absent, or presumed dead. A host of American bodies "gone missin,'" as Huck says of Jim after one of his periodic sojourns off the raft. The presidency of Ronald Reagan was predicated on the mimetic and political re-membering of these catastrophic bodies. Some bodies in the Age of Reagan, like Jessica McClure's, attracted powerful but fleeting emotional attachments and were composed and decomposed within mass-mediated culture in response to shifting sociopolitical winds. Others, like the "welfare queen," became bodies that mattered through their capacity to alter the composition of the body politic, disenfranchising, by dematerializing, a class of bodies they were constructed to represent. A very few bodies, like Reagan's, combined the qualities that attracted deep affective investments with the chameleon-like ability to performatively enact a body politic they both reproduced and re-formed in their image. The Reagan administration took up these politically potent bodies, circulating and channeling them through the matrix of the electronic media as a means of representing and reconstituting the body and boundary of the state as dictated by political exigencies. As president, the skills Reagan acquired in his previous careers as a performer of cultural memory would be applied to a damaged political body reeling from the specters of Vietnam, Watergate, the Iranian hostage crisis, and a crippled economy; which taken together seemed to signal the end of the American Century. The means for re-membering these damaged bodies politic was the performance of the rites of memory, which in the Age of Reagan assumed the form of a strategic technology of government.

To begin to assess how the stagecraft of the Reagan administration produced its statecraft, I first turn to *Hamlet* for the lessons it reveals about the shared role of players, kings, and ghosts as featured performers in the stagings of memory and mourning that represent the state to its imagined community. I then apply *Hamlet's* lessons regarding the relationship between memory and performance in the production of the state to the performative turn in American politics signaled by the election of the nation's first actor president. Here I am interested in excavating what I call the politics of *playing dead*. Finally, I examine the controversy surrounding Reagan's attempt to commemorate the World War II dead buried in the Kolmeshöhe cemetery in Bitburg, Germany, as a case study of the political stakes invested in his role as a performer of the rites of national memory and the limitations on state power when it transgresses the territorial boundaries that mark the outer limits of the rights of memory.

Three Things

> The King is a thing.
> The play's the thing / Wherein I'll catch the conscience of the king.
> What, has this thing appear'd again tonight?

In *Hamlet,* three *things* define the temporal and spatial limits of the Danish state. Each—ghost, player, and king—exerts its representational authority through its capacity to enact or transgress the borders between past and present, matter and spirit, life and death. As such, these things embody the boundaries of being and knowing that shape the plot of the play and the political economy of its world. "What, has this thing appear'd again tonight?" asks Horatio as the play begins, referring to the apparition Marcellus has entreated him to both "approve" and "speak to." "I have seen nothing," replies Barnardo, completing the conundrum that will animate Hamlet's desperate need to apprehend the identity of the Ghost.[8] By the end of the first act, Marcellus, Barnardo, Horatio, and Hamlet have all encountered the Ghost and are agreed that it looks and sounds both "most" and "very" like the dead king. Yet this similarity is insufficient to clarify Hamlet's need to know—with a deadly accuracy—what this *thing* is in order that he may weigh his obligation and perform the requisite rites of mourning.[9]

Enter the players. Until their arrival, Hamlet still entertains the possibility that the thing that has appeared as his father's spirit "[m]ay be a devil," for "the devil hath power [t]'assume a pleasing shape."[10] Having only the word of a ghost, Hamlet seeks more reliable evidence of Claudius's guilt. But this desire for material confirmation pushes Hamlet farther into the realm of spirits, memory, and death. While Hamlet rhetorically links the players to history (as "the abstract and brief chronicles of the time") and their craft to verisimilitude ("to hold as 'twere the mirror up to nature"), both their art and the task he assigns them are those of semblance and conjuration. Like a devil or a ghost, the players are shape-shifters whose *thingy* qualities enable them to become grave diggers capable of unearthing through their performance of memory not merely what has passed or the likeness of nature but the generative deed that will adjudicate the rights of memory.

It is the capacity of performance to compel the living to acknowledge the dead that leads Hamlet to his fateful decision to "have these players / Play something like the murder of my father."[11] Marvin Carlson notes that "the evocative phrase *something like* not only admits the inevitable slippage in all repetition but at the same time acknowledges the congruence that still haunts the new performance."[12] Here Carlson points to a second paradox endemic to all performances of mourning; while the invocation of memory is constrained by the inevitable slippage of repetition, the congruence between performance and memory always contains the potential to haunt its audience. It is this congruence that leads Hamlet to stage the murder of his father as a means of solving the mystery of his father's death and establishing the rights of memory to the Danish throne. To truly know the identity of the Ghost, Hamlet must apprehend it through performance. "The play's the thing," he declares at the end of the second act, "Wherein I'll catch the conscience of the king."[13] To catch the conscience of a king, Hamlet employs a cry of players to elicit Claudius's cry of guilt, confirming the Ghost's cry of murder and sealing Hamlet's obligation to obey the Ghost's injunction to both remember and revenge.

A seminal work of early modern political theory, *Hamlet* ghosts Reagan's postmodern presidency. The central role of actor and specter in the struggles for power in Hamlet's Denmark—as in Shakespeare's England—reflects a political reality embedded in the social fiction at the heart of the doctrine of divine kingship. When Polonius is slain, Claudius sends Rosencrantz and Guildenstern to interrogate Hamlet. "My lord, you must tell us," entreats Rosencrantz, "where the body is, and go with us to the king." Hamlet replies, "The King is with the body, but the body is not with the king. The king is a thing."[14] Hamlet's koan cannot be parsed by his classmates, which indicates that their studies at Wittenburg did not include political theory. In Elizabethan England, the monarchy's doctrine of legitimation held that the king possessed two bodies, the *body natural* and the *body politic*. While the king's body natural was subject to the same slings and arrows that bedeviled other mortals, the body politic—"a body that cannot be seen or handled" but "contains the Office, Government, and Majesty" of the king—marked the inviolate continuity of the state.[15]

Hamlet is certainly correct, then, in countering Guildenstern's epistemological confusion ("A thing, my lord?") with ontological clarity ("Of nothing").[16] In Elsinore, as in London, the monarch was, as Pierre Bourdieu puts it, "an entirely real substitute for an entirely symbolic being." Through the performative processes of "political fetishism," as Bourdieu characterizes the sympathetic magic by which the monarch embodied the body politic, "the representative makes the group he represents."[17] Probing the metaphysical mystery of how the monarch "makes" his political body, Hamlet poses an acting question. How is it, he wonders, that a player enacting Hecuba's sorrow at Priam's slaughter,

> *But in a fiction, in a dream of passion,*
> *Could force his soul so to his own conceit*
> *That from her working all his visage wann'd,*
> *Tears in his eyes, distraction in's aspect,*
> *A broken voice, and his whole function suiting*
> *With forms to his own conceit? And all for nothing.*[18]

Like the theatrical embodiment symbolized in the Catholic doctrine of transubstantiation, making a body politic requires staging an affectively compelling "dream of passion" capable of representing those whom the political leader would embody. This passion play is dramatized through the ritual performance of death, incarnation, and resurrection in the service of a political theology in which one becomes all . . . and all for nothing.

Of paramount importance with regard to the Reagan presidency is the fact that in *Hamlet* the techniques and processes by which political actors strive to become the thing that is a king are intimately connected to the credible enactment of the rites of memory, rituals through which the would-be king makes his body politic by performing the rights of memory. The performative construction of these bodies of memory was Reagan's stock-in-trade as a political actor. The Reagan Revolution did not, as many a friend and foe have charged, single-handedly topple the New Deal order. Something was already rotten in the welfare state, and the poisoned bodies of liberalism had already begun falling by the time Reagan arrived on the scene. The question facing Reagan when he assumed the presidency was the same one Fortinbras confronts at the end of *Hamlet:* What is to do be done with all the fallen bodies? Like Fortinbras when he assumes the Danish throne, Reagan's claim to power was predicated on his performative skill in taking up the bodies and animating them in the production of his rights of memory.

The Sanction of Death

Prior to the bloody denouement, much of the action in *Hamlet* derives from rituals staged to establish the rights of memory by catching the conscience of those who would be king. In these social dramas designed to establish the moral and memorial basis of political authority, the performances of players, ghosts, and kings derive their potency from a common source; they all borrow their authority from the dead. "Death" wrote Walter Benjamin, "is the sanction of everything that the storyteller can tell. He has borrowed his authority from death." In his essay on the storyteller, Benjamin identifies a parallel between the decline of the art of storytelling and the development of nineteenth-century bourgeois institutions that removed the dying and the dead from public life, public spaces, and public visibility, pushing them "further and further out of the perceptual world of the living." The segregation of the dead, he argues, made the moderns "dry dwellers of eternity" unacquainted with death and dying and possessed of diminished resources for conveying "the communicability of experience."[19] Ronald Reagan, "the Great Communicator," claimed the sanction of death as the authoritative basis for his political narratives of rebirth and renewal. During his presidency, Reagan's re-membered or invented stories of the dead served as a principal means of claiming his rights of memory.

Reagan's capacity and predilection for representing the dead derives from the skills he mastered prior to his career in politics. "No actor can ask for more," he wrote of his death scene in the Eureka College production of *Aria Da Capo*, "Dying is the way to live in the theater." Playing dead was his entrée to a lifetime of animating and incarnating bodies. One of the principal techniques Reagan employed to exploit the political benefits of playing dead was his strategic deployment of hagiographic narratives. Hagiography traditionally refers to the study or writing of the lives of the saints. In the political imaginary of the Reagan presidency, however, all manner of subjects were represented hagiographically. His favorite hagiographic narrative was what I will refer to as the parable of the hagioplebe. In this parable, which he evoked in various forms in numerous presidential performances, an "average" American embodies an idealized America through a heroic act of self-sacrifice. The hero was almost always male and usually dead or fictive. The appeal to the uncommon virtue of the common man is a hallowed tradition in American politics, but in Reagan's employment it takes on the visage of a primary narcissism. The figure in the parable is always Reagan's own: Zelig Unbound.

The figure of the hagioplebe first appears in the peroration of Reagan's first inaugural address. Describing the mythic domain he is entering, Reagan reminded his audience that for the first time in history an inaugural ceremony was being performed on the West Front of the Capitol. "Standing here one faces a magnificent vista," he intoned. "At the end of this open mall are those shrines to the giants on whose shoulders we stand."[20] With the adjectives *monumental, stately,* and *dignified,* he pays homage to the memory of Washington, Jefferson, and Lincoln, respectively. This is the traditional inaugural tipping of the hat to the Founding Fathers, here shrewdly staged to encourage the maximum televisual connection between Reagan and his illustrious predecessors. But Reagan's staging allows him to make an even more innovative geographic and hagiographic leap. Shifting his audience's and the camera's gaze away from the "monuments to heroism" and across the Potomac River, Reagan asked his audience to train their gaze "on the far shore," on Arlington National Cemetery, "with its row upon row of simple white markers." Here, across the river from the monuments of American history, he fixed our gaze on its unsung heroes, anonymous bodies lost in battle. I remember even now, despite my feelings of impending doom, being moved by his gesture.

In the final act of his inaugural address, Reagan takes up the body of one of Arlington's denizens, Martin Treptow, "a small town barber" killed in World War I. "We're told," Reagan told us, "that *on his body* was found a diary. On the flyleaf under the heading 'My Pledge,' [Treptow] had written these words: 'America must win this war.' Therefore I will work, I will save, I will sacrifice, I will endure, I will fight cheerfully and do my utmost, as if the issue of the whole struggle depended on me alone." Treptow's words are a condensation of the credo Reagan conveyed in the body of his address and enacted during his presidency. Taking up Treptow's body, Reagan casts himself simultaneously as the rightful heir to Treptow's legacy and the incarnation of Treptow's pledge. Reagan's vision for America, outlined earlier in the address, is authoritatively situated in a mythic lineage drawn from both sides of the river, the stately monuments and the simple white markers. Reagan's inaugural address assumes the form of a eulogy in which he invokes the power of the performer and the corpse to summon an imagined community into being.

Like Westminster Abbey, where Betterton's body was interned amid the royal dead, Arlington's location across the river from the White House is symbolically resonant. Arlington's warrior's, too, are players in "a particular kind of secular devotion" that "enact[s] the memorial constitution of the body politic."[21] However, in a stunning inversion of Roach's description of how surrogation functions in a modernizing society, Reagan's taking up of Treptow's body demonstrates how, in a thoroughly dramatized society, the president of the United States can claim his rights as the caretaker of cultural memory through the performed effigy of the actor. The parable of the hagioplebe illustrates how, in the journey from the early modern to the postmodern state, the techne of the body electric comes to supersede the absolutist claims of the sovereign. The actor no longer rules as the "mimic king" of the English stage. In the role of a lifetime, the performer represents the nation from the White House itself. From this stage Reagan's body electric mimetically reproduced a surrogate past, utilizing the techniques and technologies absorbed through years of training in the professions that define American cultural memory. As his subsequent presidential performances attested, under the fiat of electricity the primary way certain stories are placed in and as history is through the performance circuits of electronic media.

The story of Martin Treptow was Reagan's contribution to the inaugural address. Reagan knew the elements of Treptow's story possessed the restorative power to liberate sentimentality American style. He felt that Treptow's words had an almost cinematic quality, a quality that speechwriter Ken Khachigian reports "brought tears to his eyes and that he knew he could use to bring tears to the eyes of his audience."[22] Reagan's first presidential contribution to his administration's sustained retooling of the mimetic faculty was, as Benjamin wrote of the movies, "to teach those whom nothing moves or touches any longer to cry again."[23] To utilize Treptow's story in an affectively compelling performance, however, it was insufficient to have merely dug it up. Reagan's version of the story would require burying the body anew. Martin Treptow, it turns out, had not actually been interred under a white marker at Arlington. His final resting place was underneath a gray granite headstone eleven hundred miles away in Bloomer, Wisconsin. When this fact was revealed to Reagan before the inaugural, he was undeterred. According to Khachigian, who scripted the inaugural address, "Ronald Reagan has a sense of theater that propels him to tell stories in their most theatrically imposing manner. . . . He knew it would break up the story to say that Treptow was buried in Wisconsin." Arlington was where the nation buried its warriors. And so, on 20 January 1981, Ronald Reagan buried Martin Treptow at Arlington National Cemetery. The missing pieces performatively reproduced, the reborn actor staged a funeral for the absent soldier and a presidency began.

The Hauntology of Bitburg

In the Age of Reagan the cultural performer ceased to serve as the political leader's body double, becoming instead the principal actor in a variety of roles that mediated claims to political authority. And it was through the political and mimetic representations of bodies of memory that Ronald Reagan made his body politic and staked his claim as the mediator of cultural memory. With the raising of the dead, however, the taking up of bodies, there is always the possibility that these bodies will, as in *Hamlet,* elude the boundaries of their representation, that they will, in fact, re-present themselves. What specifically concerns me here in relation to the Reagan Era is the mimetic economy generated by the incessant performativity of corpses and the apparitions animated by the quickening of the dead. From one photo op to the next sound bite, Ronald Reagan played more memorials than any president in living memory, and it is perhaps here and there, speaking to and for the dead, that we might begin to map the contours of a haunting.

Jacques Derrida coined the term *hauntology* to describe a "logic of haunting" in which "a specter is always a *revenant.*" One cannot control the specter's comings and goings "because it *begins by coming back.*"[24] Beginning by coming back is another thing ghosts, kings, and players have in common. It is precisely this haunting paradox of the revenant (that it simultaneously manifests both similarity and difference, history and memory, tradition and transformation) that leads Marvin Carlson to identify "ghosting" as a constitutive component in the production and reception of theatrical performances.[25] It is this paradox that Hamlet seeks to conjure by having the players perform "something like" the murder of his father. Hamlet's script, the players' performance, and the pricking of Claudius's conscience all attest to the structural role of hauntology in the rites of national memory and mourning.

In her analysis of the rituals of mourning following the death of Princess Diana, Diana Taylor demonstrates the efficacy of the concept of hauntology for analyzing the cultural performances by which we represent the realm between that which is and that which was. These acts of mourning, she contends, reveal how "performance makes visible (for an instant, 'live,' 'now,') that which is always already there—the ghosts, the tropes, the scenarios that structure our individual and collective life."[26] Every new claim to power situates itself in relation to these performative structures. But the genealogy of political dominion is always up for grabs. And, as Claudius discovers, attempts to repress the constitutive acts on which a claim to power is predicated often fail. Bitburg was Reagan's mousetrap—The performance that exposed the political and theatrical verity that when what is is rotten what has been repressed returns . . . and with a vengeance.

Reagan's performances surrounding the Bitburg affair provide insight into the ways hauntology conditions performances and how acts of mourning embody political and cultural histories. As with *Hamlet,* the performances of the Reagan administration were dramatically enhanced by the hauntology that suffuses the theater of the state. "Hegemony," Derrida contends, "still organizes the repression and thus the confirmation of a haunting. Haunting belongs to the structure of every hegemony."[27] My use of the term *hauntology,* then, is predicated on its efficacy as an optic for analyzing the dramatization of the state as a means of rationalizing political power. In the theater of the state, the living speak of and for the dead. In the theater of memory, however, the dead talk back to the quick. To affectively engage the rites of memory, the political actor, like the stage counterpart, must balance the tasks of speaking for and listening to the dead. As Claudius discovered, representation cuts both ways. When the dead are exiled from the stage, the slippage of repetition and the congruence of representation and memory may result in a haunting performance of catastrophic proportions. Invited or not, specters always return to the scene of a crime. The reappearance of unwelcome specters—the return of the living dead—was so prevalent during Reagan's second term that the White House took on the appearance of a haunted house. Nowhere was this hauntology more clearly evidenced than in Reagan's encounters with the Holocaust and the Bitburg fiasco.

Act I: Purposes Mistook

> And let me speak to th'yet unknowing world
> How these things came about. So shall you hear
> Of carnal, bloody, and unnatural acts,
> Of accidental judgments, casual slaughters,
> Of deaths put on by cunning and forc'd cause,
> And, in this upshot, purposes mistook
> Fall'n on th'inventors' heads.
> —Horatio, *Hamlet*

At Bitburg, as in Elsinore, everything begins with the appearance of a specter. The specters at Bitburg were the first of the Furies to visit the administration during Reagan's second term of office, the first indication of ghosts in the memory machine. The thing about specters is that, like Old Hamlet, they only reveal themselves when absolutely necessary and only to those capable of acting in their name. Their hauntology, their capacity for coming and going, is predicated on their invisibility. "We literally could not see the pitfalls," writes Reagan's chief of staff of the advance team's visit to Kolmeshöhe cemetery in Bitburg. "It was February. The graves, most of the markers, were covered by blankets of snow."[28] Thus it began, with Michael Deaver, the vicar of visuals, snow-blind in a Nazi graveyard.

It was to be, as Deaver informs us in his memoirs, a "minor footnote," a sideshow, a photogenic preview in the provinces of historical memory en route to the feature presentation at a European economic summit in Strasbourg.[29] The trip to Bitburg had been conceived as a show of support for West German chancellor Helmut Kohl, who was facing important elections in North Rhineland Westphalia and was eager for the political capital that would accrue from a symbolic spectacle of German and American solidarity. Kohl had been personally and politically embarrassed by his exclusion from the Allied ceremonies in June of 1984 commemorating the fortieth anniversary of the D-day landings at Normandy. In September 1984, Kohl participated in a ceremony of reconciliation in which he stood hand in hand with French president François Mitterand at a French-German cemetery on the Verdun battlefield. Kohl suggested a similar commemoration to Ronald Reagan.

In a meeting in November, Kohl proposed that he and Reagan visit a German military cemetery and broached the idea of a trip to Dachau. Reagan's handlers were wary of Dachau. "There was a sense," Deaver writes, "of projecting an era of hope and a closing of the book on the past. This the camps could not do; they existed as a remembrance of the ghastly deeds that occurred there." If we listen carefully, we can hear the sound of six million bodies being traduced, dismembered, transformed into dematerialized signs of historical events. And there were still other reasons to reject Dachau. "I had the additional factor," Deaver continues, "of Ronald Reagan's nature. He was not at ease with, nor eager to confront scenes of unrelenting depression."[30] Dachau was rejected.

Finding a World War II site on German soil suitable for a ceremonial reconciliation without the depressing memory of the Holocaust was not an easy task. The fact that it was such a high priority for the administration speaks to the concern regarding the president's previous encounters with the death camps. On two separate occasions Reagan had told visiting dignitaries that his World War II assignments included filming concentration camps for the U.S. Army Signal Corps.[31] His moving accounts of the experience were marred only by history. Reagan never left the United States during the war. The only war footage Reagan shot was propaganda films at the Hal Roach studio in Culver City, California. Holocaust victims were not as easily embodied by the Reagan imaginary as were American war dead. Their foreign matter was not as easily assimilated into his domestic master narratives of rebirth and renewal.

Reagan's handlers settled instead on Kolmeshöhe, an obscure German military cemetery they mistakenly believed contained American soldiers. There was little cause for concern that Reagan would script a problematic war narrative from Bitburg's uneventful past: no Jews, no ovens, no problem. Bitburg, the Germans assured them, contained no surprises. Here Reagan could be trusted to put on a good show. "You put him near a flag, around uniforms, or in sight of a parade," Deaver enthused, "and he could lift anyone's spirits."[32] The plan was to build on the success of Reagan's D-day performances. Speaking at the Ranger Monument at Pointe du Hoc, France, Reagan had been in his element. Flags were flying; there were wreaths to lay and inspirational words to utter. The American survivors of the storming of the Normandy cliffs were there beside him. As he often did at ceremonies commemorating World War II, Reagan used the opportunity to compare the Soviet threat to the Nazi Holocaust. In asserting the moral superiority of the United States, he contrasted the "uninvited, unwanted, unyielding" Soviet occupation of Eastern Europe with the U.S. presence in Western Europe. "Today, as forty years ago," he said, "our armies are here for only one purpose—to protect and defend democracy. The only territories we hold are memorials like this one and graveyards where our heroes rest."[33] America need not occupy Western Europe, he implied. The nation's territorial claim—like the president's own—was staked in the domain of memorials and graveyards, on the historical fault line separating the living from the dead, along the frontiers of spectral memory.

Unlike Hamlet, whose curiosity about the dead is insatiable, Michael Deaver never bothered to find out for whom the bells tolled at Bitburg. The understanding Hamlet acquires over the course of the play of what it is *to be* is largely a product of the knowledge he gleans from the Ghost of what it is *not to be*. Hamlet is, in fact, obsessed with the dead: their ontology and injunctions, how they came to death, their type and place of burial, from where they have come and why. Knowledge of the dead forms the basis for Hamlet's decisions regarding the conduct of his life. As Bitburg demonstrates, the Reagan administration sought not to learn from the dead but to produce a spectacle of death to govern the conduct of the living. Unlike Hamlet, Deaver never sought out a grave digger to inquire about what bodies occupied this soil. He never understood that the plot of Bitburg, like that of *Hamlet,* would be sown in a plot of earth. Had

Deaver read his *Hamlet* he would have known that the earth covering those killed "for a fantasy and trick of fame" is never "tomb enough and continent to hide the slain."[34] When the dead lie un(re)marked beneath the soil, the nation suffers. These bodies must be accounted for or they will restlessly roam the earth, their anguished cries haunting the waking dreams of the living.

The problem with Bitburg was that, as it turned out, there were no American memorials inside its gates and no American heroes rested in its graves. Worse, it was discovered that forty-nine Waffen SS soldiers were buried alongside soldiers from the regular German army. What sort of spirits might Reagan uplift here? The outcry was deafening. Public opinion that the visit should be canceled was so intense, warned the presidential pollster Richard Wirthlin, that it had evoked emotions "stronger than we are able to measure in survey research."[35] Reagan's decision to go to Bitburg anyway, in uncharacteristic defiance of public opinion, his closest advisers, and his wife, has primarily been attributed to a stubborn unwillingness to reverse course and show weakness or to break a commitment to a vulnerable political ally. But there is another explanation for Reagan's recalcitrance: the personal and political capital he had invested in his role of memory doctor.

At the height of the controversy, Reagan presented the Congressional Gold Medal of Achievement to Elie Wiesel. Wiesel used the occasion to gently instruct the president on the moral geography of the Holocaust: "That place," he cautioned Reagan, "is not your place."[36] But to admit that Bitburg was not his place was to acknowledge a realm in which some bodies could not be redeemed. It would require conceding that Reagan was not, in Hamlet's words, "the king of infinite space," that here was a kingdom in which the president had no rights of memory.

Act II: Haunting the Boneyards

> If space has an air of neutrality and indifference with regard to its contents and thus seems to be "purely" formal, the epitome of rational abstraction, it is precisely because it has already been occupied and used, and has already been the focus of past processes whose traces are not always evident in the landscape.
>
> —Henri Lefebvre, *The Production of Space*

The dead, to paraphrase John Lennon, were only waiting for their moment to arrive. In the months between the appearance of the Waffen SS and Reagan's arrival at Bitburg, the moral and memorial authority of Doctor Feelgood began to wither on the vines creeping up the cemetery walls. On 21 March, by way of justifying his decision not to visit a concentration camp, Reagan warned against "reawakening the memories" of the Holocaust. To do so would be to "open up old wounds" and unnecessarily mar the celebratory event. He insisted that a mere forty years later "the German people have very few alive that remember even the war, and certainly none of them who were adults and participating in any way."[37] Through the foggy rhetoric and faulty reckoning we can discern the personal and political fortunes at stake in quieting the already recrudescent specters. "And," he might have added, "I alone am left to tell the tale."

To reawaken memory—to remember not wisely but too well—threatened to expose yet another old wound, the one hidden by the suture scar from Hinkley's bullet, the sign of Reagan's intimacy with death and his authority to speak to and for the dead. Bitburg threatened to revoke the sanction of death, the basis of Reagan's authority as the leading performer in the production of national rites of memory. On 18 April, he told an audience of broadcasters and editors that there was "nothing wrong with visiting that cemetery where those young men are victims of Nazism also. . . . They were victims, just as surely as the victims in the concentration camps."[38] By equating the dead German soldiers with Jews slaughtered in the camps, Reagan exposed the cynicism at the heart of his politics of resurrection: a corpse is a corpse is a corpse. The dead were interchangeable, simulacra to be deployed when politically expedient, remembered to be forgotten. The theologian Martin Marty coined the term *storycide* to describe the narratives Reagan spun around Bitburg. To commit "storycide," Marty laments, is to "distort, neglect, or mute" the story of the Holocaust. For a people sustained by stories, he concludes, this is the final act of genocide.[39]

Storycide, like the unmasking of regicide, threatens to expose the social fiction that constitutes the political theology of the state as a mere ideological construct. At times of political transition or crisis the scaffolding of the enabling fictions of state power are often laid bare and the ca-

pacity of the state to reproduce itself is called into question. The power of
the state is always contingent on the ability of its leaders to continuously
reproduce and convincingly perform the rites of memory because the
rights of memory are always in dispute among the living; they are only
held in perpetuity by the dead.

Again, *Hamlet* provides insight into the political significance of memory and mourning at Bitburg. Like the revelation of Claudius's murder of
Old Hamlet, Reagan's historical inventions around Bitburg threatened to
expose the invented traditions that comprise the architecture of state
power. In *Hamlet* the time is out of joint, and the rotting of both the
monarchal and spectral realms of Elsinore proceed apace until Hamlet
completes the political and filial rituals required "to set it right." The rites
Hamlet must perform to alleviate the suffering of his father's spirit, like
the performance of the players, link the rights of memory to the power of
the state through the connective thread and collective threat of
vengeance. Hamlet's tragedy is not simply that he must both remember
and revenge but that theatrical genre, the claims of inheritance, and the
political histories of Shakespeare's Denmark *and* England decree memory
and revenge to be inseparable.[40]

Fortinbras's arrival on the scene signals an end to a political economy
in which to remember is to be compelled to seek vengeance. "I have some
rights of memory in this kingdom," he asserts, taking in the dead, "Which
now to claim my vantage doth invite me." Fortinbras literally owes his
"vantage" to the carnage he surveys but also, by "rights of memory," to
the father slain by the father of the dead prince he eulogizes. His vantage
refers to the favorable opportunity he has stumbled on: to regain without
the threat of retribution the territory lost by his father to Hamlet's father
and to assume the throne of Denmark. Unlike Hamlet, Fortinbras successfully remembers and avenges his father, making the Norwegian state
whole again by reattaching its missing limb. But the rights of memory
multiply his vantages to include that of performing his claim to power
without spilling a drop of blood. Taking up the bodies, he restores the sta-
sis of stagecraft and statecraft by severing the link between the rights of
memory and the performance of revenge.

Bitburg, however, marks the outer limits of both Fortinbras's dominion and Reagan's capacity to perform the rites that constitute his rights of

memory. The Holocaust was catastrophe on an unprecedented scale. It was a scale too enormous to be tipped by the relatively insignificant weight of revenge. Only justice could balance these scales. Instead, unhinging memory from justice by insisting that the past and the dead lie buried in unmarked graves, Reagan struggled to retain his tenuous sway over a body politic increasingly resistant to embodiment.

In response to mounting pressure to distinguish between the dead, a camp was added to the itinerary. The choice of Bergen-Belsen as a stand-in for Dachau, however, only increased the storycidal impulse of the whole affair. "Both Dachau and Bergen-Belsen," writes Midge Decter, "were long ago cleaned up and converted to museums. But the Bergen-Belsen site consists only of plaques, monuments, and memorial displays."[41] It is what James Young has termed a "memorial camp," a site where the "icons of destruction seem to appropriate the very authority of the original events themselves."[42] Unlike Dachau, Bergen-Belsen would not force Reagan to confront the instruments of death, the material evidence of widespread complicity that gives the lie to his repeated denials of collective guilt and the dubious proposition that reconciliation was called for because only one man was responsible for the death of six million.

The ovens and gas chamber are still visible at Dachau. "The ovens," notes Decter, are "shockingly and instructively small." They are, she chillingly continues, "man-sized, requiring the constant, competent, daily attentions of reliable workmen."[43] The Holocaust was not a war movie in which Nazism could be personified as one man's totalitarian dictatorship or German soldiers and Jewish dead alike represented as "victims" of "the awful evil started by one man."[44] At Dachau, genocide was the visible product of an undeniable incarnation: the king was with the bodies, and the bodies were with the king. Dachau makes it clear that "this one man needed and received a fair amount of cooperation from others. It is better," Decter deadpans, "not to visit Dachau on a day one intends to embrace the Germans."[45]

Act III: Staring at Ruin

Reagan's visit to Kolmeshöhe cemetery lasted just eight minutes. He never spoke. He never looked at the graves of the Waffen SS. He never acknowledged the photographers and televison cameras. "During the wordless ceremony, a German bugler played '*Ich hatt einen Kameraden*' (I had a comrade) a song that predated the Nazi Regime."[46] Every effort was made to elide the historical specificity of the site.

Reviewing the videotapes of Reagan at Bitburg produced by the White House, it is astonishing to observe the transformation in Reagan's appearance. All the blood has left his famously rosy cheeks. His shoulders slump, and his body appears frail and shrunken under his raincoat. The furrows in his face have deepened, and his lips are tense, thin, and colorless. It is a vision of a man in need of a transfusion. He appears stiff, expressionless, wary, "like a wax figure," as one observer described him, "devoid of his usual Hollywood radiance."[47] He looks, in short, like a vampire or a zombie, a B-movie treatment of the undead surrounded by bodies from which no more blood can be sucked.

> *He stared at ruin. Ruin stared straight back.*
> *He thought they was old friends.*[48]

The subject and narrator of John Berryman's *Dream Songs* is an imaginary character named Henry who has suffered an irreversible loss. In "Dream Song #45," we learn of all the places where "ruin" has visited Henry. At the end of the poem, at the final visitation, Henry learns something.

> *. . . they were not old friends.*
> *He did not know this one.*
> *This one was a stranger, come to make amends*
> *for all the impostors, and to make it stick.*
> *Henry nodded, un—*[49]

"Un," indeed. Ronald Reagan had come face-to-face with ruin, and he was no friend.

At Bergen-Belsen, Reagan told the assembled audience that "the survivors carry a memory beyond anything that we can comprehend. The awful evil started by one man." Two hundred meters away a message inscribed on the memorial for those who could not escape ruin demanded a different performance of the rights of memory: EARTH CONCEAL NOT THE BLOOD SHED ON THEE.[50]

Act IV: Mourning in America

And what of mourning, one might ask. What does all this have to do with mourning? But I have spoken of nothing else. For it is the very possibility of mourning that the return of the specter both invokes and troubles. To invoke the troubling specter of Derrida: "Nothing could be worse for the work of mourning than confusion or doubt: one *has to know* who is buried where—and *it is necessary* (to know—to make certain) that, in what remains of him, *he remain there*. Let him stay there and move no more."[51] Deaver's inability to read the names of the dead through the snow, Kohl's blind pursuit of a ceremony of reconciliation, and Reagan's unwillingness to address the specters of the Holocaust all betrayed the victims of Nazism and the unacknowledged performance strategy of Bitburg, the ritual of mourning staged as a spectacle of forgetting.

For Reagan, the Holocaust was part of a larger political economy fueled by the traffic in corpses. The dead were hard currency, redeemable for political capital and transferable into cultural memory. In taking up the dead, they were born again as symbols, tropes, incarnations of a ruling ethos. In the mimetic regime of the Reagan presidency, memory was a floating signifier deployed to discipline unruly referents as required by political exigencies. The past was a boneyard to be scavenged for rhetoric, imagery, signs of life. The dead were dismembered, retrofitted, and re-membered in the political unconscious of a presidency that incessantly plundered history for, in Robert Lowell's words, "something imagined, not recalled."[52] Lowell's lines are from "Epilogue," the final poem in the last book of poetry he published before his untimely death in 1977. In the penultimate lines of the poem, he weighs in on the rites and rights of memory. "We are poor passing facts," he cautions, "warned by that to give each figure in the photograph his living name." Written on the cusp of the Reagan Revolution, Lowell's words speak to an understanding of the rights of memory and mourning in eclipse during the Reagan years.

Garry Wills has proposed that "the power of [Reagan's] appeal is the great joint confession that we cannot live with our real past, that we not only prefer but need a substitute."[53] Until Bitburg many Americans might have agreed with Michael Deaver that just because Reagan saw the Holocaust on film and not in person "that did not mean he saw it less."[54] But if mourning is to do its work, if mo(u)rning in America is to be something more than just a euphemism for four more years, we must acknowledge the specter. We must, as Derrida insists, speak to it not of revenge but of justice. And justice is impossible, unthinkable, "without the principle of some responsibility beyond all living present . . . without this responsibility and this respect for justice concerning those who *are not here,* of those who are no longer or who are not yet *present and living.*"[55] As in *Hamlet,* justice can only be achieved through knowledge gained from the revenant, the spectral performer of repetition and return. It is only in relation to ghosts that we come to know ourselves and others, that we can know any *thing* at all.

Act V: Epilogue

At the conclusion of the silent ceremony at Kolmeshöhe, Reagan was rushed to the American air force base nearby. Here, in the shadow of Air Force One, he answered his critics.

> Twenty-two years ago President John F. Kennedy went to the Berlin Wall and proclaimed that he, too, was a Berliner. Well, today, freedom-loving people around the world must say, I am a Berliner, I am a Jew in a world still threatened by anti-Semitism, I am an Afghan, and I am a prisoner of the Gulag, I am a refugee in a crowded boat foundering off the coast of Vietnam. I am a Laotian, a Cambodian, a Cuban, and a Miskito Indian in Nicaragua. I, too, am a potential victim of totalitarianism.[56]

The script was Ken Khachigian's, but the sentiment and performance were vintage Reagan. Invoking Kennedy just long enough to sweep him up in the wake of his other incarnations, Reagan took up the bodies of the Holocaust and placed them on the stage of the cold war drama in which he still played a leading role. Eschewing justice for yet another performance of that dependable old chestnut, Reagan recast the Jewish dead as first-act casualties in an enduring saga of memory and revenge. Re-membering the Holocaust as a mere *figura* of Soviet totalitarianism, deploying its victims as props for a more pressing engagement, Reagan took up the bodies and took his final bow to and as Fortinbras.

In the final moments of *Hamlet*, Fortinbras stares at ruin. He is cognizant of the political capital to be gained in laying claim to the nomination of Hamlet's "dying voice" and is eager to "call the noblest to the audience" to approve Horatio's tale of woe. Horatio's narrative will firmly establish Fortinbras's now uncontested rights of memory to the Danish throne.[57] But first Fortinbras must set the stage for his coronation. Horatio urges him to "give order that these bodies / High on a stage be placed to the view." Horatio's proposal is to display these bodies of memory as a *tableaux mori,* a staged image to illustrate the tale Horatio promises to tell "to th'yet unknowing world."[58] Fortinbras seemingly acquiesces to Horatio's blocking. In the end, however, Fortinbras eulogizes and stages only Hamlet's body. The other bodies are *taken up* only to be *taken off* the stage. In the manner in which he takes up the bodies, Fortinbras demonstrates the final paradox of the power of the state—that the production of the body politic through bodies of memory requires that some bodies be rendered invisible.

When is a thing not a thing?
When it is removed from the stage.

There is more to the ob/scene, however, than is dreamt of in the philosophy of Reaganism. As Terry Eagleton points out, Derrida's *toujours déjà* insists that "whenever we are confronted with a sign, object, or event something else must always already have happened for this to be possible, something that has not, moreover, simply gone away."[59] The logic of haunting, the hauntology of Bitburg, suggests that although the dead are often invisible to the living we cannot escape their gaze. As Derrida notes when the Ghost of Old Hamlet returns, "his apparition makes him appear still invisible beneath his armor."[60] That Barnardo on the battlements, Gertrude in her closet, or Deaver in the cemetery sees nothing is unsurprising. The only chink in the Ghost's armor, the only thing that makes of it something other than "vacancy" and "th'incorporal air," are the slits cut into the visor to permit the specter and actor to see and speak. These apertures give the Ghost a voice and the ability to see without being seen. Thus, the specter, through the actor, addresses the living and holds us accountable to the sanction of death and its bodies of memory.

The unacknowledged obscenity of Bitburg is that to observe the rights and perform the rites of memory require acknowledging the specter, looking it in the eye, and listening to its tale. In this regard both the state funeral's substitution of the empty boots for the shared burial of horse and rider and Bitburg's spectacle of mourning and forgetting are expressions of the futility of the modern impulse to enforce the strict separation of the quick and the dead. Whether deprived of a horse with which to ride into battle in the afterlife or consigned to an anonymous grave, the dead warrior, through the hauntology of performance, continues to exert its influence over the rights of memory and the conscience of kings.

Epilogue: Taking Up the Bodies

> Today abstraction is no longer that of the map, the double, the mirror or the concept. Simulation is no longer that of a territory, a referential being or a substance. It is the generation by models of a real without origin or reality: a hyperreal. The territory no longer precedes the map, nor does it survive it. It is nevertheless the map that precedes the territory—*precession of simulacra*—that engenders the territory. . . . It is the real, and not the map, whose vestiges subsist here and there, in the deserts that are no longer those of the Empire, but ours. The desert of the real itself.
>
> —Jean Baudrillard, *Simulacra and Simulation* (emphasis in the original)

To profess the intimate liaison between performance and the rites of memory is to nominate the actor as a surrogate for the rights of memory. Ronald Reagan claimed this prerogative in his performances on the political stage through the taking up of bodies of memory in the performative production of an imagined national past. These performances and their reception reflect a discursive shift in our contemporary understanding of political representation. During the Reagan years political representation becomes *sui generis,* fully liberated from its putative obligation to corre-

---

Epigraph: Jean Baudrillard, *Simulacra and Simulation,* trans. Sheila Faria Glaser (Ann Arbor; University of Michigan Press, 1995), 1.

Photo: Pedestrians in Times Square watch live video of the casket of former U.S. President Ronald Reagan in its procession to the National Cathedral in Washington for his state funeral in 2004. Photo © Peter Morgan/Reuters/Corbis.

spond to a material referent, historical precedent, or objective criteria of any kind. Political representation was an effect constituted through performative acts. Since the Reagan era, merely producing the bodies (empirical evidence, data, credentials, etc.) to support one's credibility as a candidate for surrogation is no longer sufficient and often irrelevant. The would-be king must *act* like a king. Fortinbras's claim to have some rights of memory in this kingdom is no longer evaluated as a verifiable truth. Instead it is assessed by criteria applied to the candidate's mimetic skill in performing the rites of memory.

The Reagan presidency was the catalyst for this paradigm shift. Reagan's inversion of the historical relationship between the performer and the political leader resulted in a mimetic regime in which the political leader derived authority from taking up the bodies the way an actor takes up a role. Under conditions of electronic mass mediation, government becomes increasingly dependent on the techne of the body electric for reproducing its body politic. In the postmodern state, the final arbiter of legitimacy for the statesman is television, and the critical standard for leadership is not veracity but belief. The greatest fan in the world had been trained to believe in belief. Equipped with the controllable and transferable skills of mechanical reproduction, Ronald Reagan's performances on the presidential stage were examples of Bram Stoker's characterization of "suggestive acting," which gave "strong grounds for belief, where the instinct can judge more truly than the intellect."[61] Reagan echoes *Dracula*'s author in his description of the knowledge his education before the camera has bestowed on him: "When you go on that TV tube and you're in a close-up—that happens to be my business. I came from the camera business and I know one rule we had in Hollywood and you can't break it—that camera knows when you're lying. That camera knows when an actor really doesn't feel the line he is saying."[62] That the content of the line is true or false, real or imagined is inconsequential. *Lying* is no longer the antonym of *truth telling* but of *believing*. Reagan was, as Peggy Noonan wrote of Oliver North, "not so much a liar as he was an actor acting out the truth; it never occurred to him not to act; it was his way of communicating; he is modern."[63] In contrast to the decidedly unmodern Henry Adams, Ronald Reagan's education prepared him to thrive in the new world that emerged from the steady remodeling of social and political habits, ideas, and institutions and the new scale and conditions generated by the fiat of electricity. Reagan's education made him an avatar for a thoroughly electrified and dramatized politics, equally adept at adapting his persona to fit the requirements of the scene or screen.

Writing during Reagan's first term, Norman Mailer lamented that Richard Nixon's amateur theatrical training had produced such a bad actor. He wonders "whether Nixon, if he had been somewhat better in those early years as an actor, would have become in later life, a politician more like Ronald Reagan." The occasion for Mailer's musings is the television broadcast of Nixon's interview with David Frost in which—much to Mailer's astonishment—Nixon gives a miraculous performance: "Watching Nixon it did not matter what the truth might be, any more than one would find fault with a great stage actor for bringing life and splendor and passion and the monumental echoes of tragic woe to lines that were not his own and that he could say in his sleep or while shaving, he had practiced them so well, yes, Nixon struck America with a miracle—a talentless actor had become a splendid actor—yes, Nixon now went to the root of good acting, where before he had lived in the center of bad acting."[64] After years of fruitless rehearsal, Nixon had somehow acquired the mimetic capacity that Reagan's training had instilled in him as second nature; the actor's belief in the script (the lines he speaks, the roles he performs) and the ability to generate the sympathetic magic by means of which the magician "infers that he can produce any effect he desires merely by imitating it."[65]

During the Bitburg affair, when Garry Wills asked a group of American businessmen and their wives their opinion of Reagan's fraudulent claim to have photographed the Nazi death camps, "they supported the President for expressing a 'higher truth' of concern for the persecuted. Heads nodded when one executive's wife said, 'Even Jesus spoke in parables.'"[66] By incorporation and incarnation the presidential performer legitimated his claims, authenticated his role, and captivated his audience. His performances were reviewed on the merits of the fit between actor and character and the affective power of the performance, not on the accuracy of the representation. Reaganism, to paraphrase Jean-François Lyotard, was constructed around the massive subordination of critical memory to the finality of the best possible performance.[67]

Perhaps it is true, as Michael Lynch and David Bogen contend in the context of the Iran-Contra hearings, that "Cynically understood, political actors are judged on the engrossing and inspiring qualities of their performances and not on whether the things they say are true, realistic, or acceptable as policy."[68] Or maybe it is more relevant (or at least more provocative) to appraise Ronald Reagan as a magician, a sorcerer or shaman, a practitioner of the healing arts whose real skill, as Michael Taussig writes of the magician, "lies not in skilled concealment but in the skilled revelation of skilled concealment." Faith, Taussig suggests, coexists with and may even require skepticism, and "magic is efficacious not despite the trick but on account of its exposure."[69] Could the common knowledge that Reagan's memories—the ones he made into stories and pictures—were recycled from motion pictures, radio programs, and television shows actually have contributed to his stature as caretaker of cultural memory? Were his mechanically reproduced memories instances of what Taussig finds in the shaman's performance of healing, "that most elusive trick of all, the magic of mimesis itself—at heart a fraud, yet most necessary for that ceaseless surfacing of appearances we defer to as truth"?[70] Electronic media, the progenitor of our society of common feeling, was the dynamo of the Reagan Revolution. The same mimetic machinery that ushered in the age of mechanical reproduction trained Ronald Reagan, the president electric who powered a new regime of political representation and ineradicably altered the course of American politics.

NOTES

Introduction

1. Brian Massumi and Kenneth Dean, "Postmortem on the Presidential Body," in *Body Politics: Disease, Desire, and the Family*, edited by Michael Ryan and Avery Gordon (Boulder: Westview, 1994), 158.

2. Michael Rogin, *Ronald Reagan the Movie and Other Episodes of Political Demonology* (Berkeley: University of California Press, 1987), 3.

3. Walt Whitman, "I Sing the Body Electric," in *Leaves of Grass* (Philadelphia: David McKay, [1855] 1900), 81.

4. David S. Reynolds, *Walt Whitman's America: A Cultural Biography* (New York: Vintage, 1996), 156.

5. Ibid., 154–93. See also Lawrence Levine, *Highbrow/Lowbrow: The Emergence of Cultural Hierarchy in America* (Cambridge: Harvard University Press, 1990).

6. Quoted in Reynolds, *Walt Whitman's America*, 161.

7. Dean Pitchford and Michael Gore, "I Sing the Body Electric," soundtrack from the movie *Fame*, 33 rpm and audio cassette, RSO Music, 1980.

8. Walt Whitman, "When Lilacs Last in the Dooryard Bloomed," in *Leaves of Grass* (Philadelphia: David McKay, [1855] 1900): 255.

9. Raymond Williams, "Drama in a Dramatized Society," in *Raymond Williams on Television*, edited by Alan O'Connor (London: Routledge, 1989), 3–4.

10. Ibid., 7, 11.

11. Lou Cannon, *President Reagan: The Role of a Lifetime* (New York: Simon & Schuster, 1991); Neil Gabler, *Life, the Movie: How Entertainment Conquered Reality* (New York: Vintage, 2000), 108.

12. Notable exceptions to this tendency are Cannon, *President Reagan*; Rogin, *Ronald Reagan the Movie*; Edmond Morris, *Dutch: A Memoir of Ronald Reagan* (New York: Random House, 1999); Peggy Noonan, *What I Saw at the Revolution: A Political Life in the Reagan Era* (New York: Random House, 1991); and Garry Wills, *Reagan's*

America: Innocents at Home (New York: Viking Penguin, 1988). Their accounts are indispensable, and I cite them throughout.

13. It was in his address to the 1988 Republican National Convention that Reagan declared, "[I]deas are stupid things."

14. Lawrence Grossberg, *We Gotta Get Outta This Place: Popular Conservatism and Postmodern Culture* (New York: Routledge, 1992), 255, emphasis in the original.

15. Ibid., 83–84.

16. Michael Denning, "The End of Mass Culture," in *Modernity and Mass Culture*, edited by James Naremore and Patrick Brantlinger (Bloomington: Indiana University Press, 1991), 256.

17. Karl Marx, *Capital*, vol. 1 (New York: International Publishers, 1967), 178.

18. Richard Dyer, "Entertainment and Utopia," in *The Cultural Studies Reader*, edited by Simon During (New York: Routledge, 1999), 373.

19. Raymond Williams, *Marxism and Literature* (Oxford: Oxford University Press, 1977), 128–35.

20. Quoted in Cannon, *President Reagan*, 51.

21. Quoted in Grossberg, *We Gotta Get Outta This Place*, 39–40.

22. Edward Bernays, "Engineering of Consent," *Annals of the American Academy of Political and Social Science* 250 (March 1947): 113–20.

23. Frederic Jameson, "Reification and Utopia in Mass Culture," *Social Text* (winter 1979): 139.

24. Frederic Jameson, *Postmodernism; or, The Cultural Logic of Late Capitalism* (Durham: Duke University Press, 1991), 48.

25. Michael McManus, undated memo to Michael Deaver, folder 1, box OA7624, 1982, Michael McManus files, Ronald Reagan Presidential Library.

26. Cannon, *President Reagan*, 156–57.

27. Noonan, *What I Saw at the Revolution*, 163.

28. Cannon, *President Reagan*, 53–54.

29. Quoted in Mark Hertsgaard, *On Bended Knee: The Press and the Reagan Presidency* (New York: Random House, 1988), 35.

30. Ibid., 35.

31. Ibid., 26–27.

32. Donald Regan, *For the Record: From Wall Street to Washington* (New York: Harcourt Brace Jovanovich, 1988), 248.

33. Cannon, *President Reagan*, 55.

34. Hertsgaard, *On Bended Knee*, 46–47.

35. Noonan, *What I Saw at the Revolution*, 159.

36. Henry Adams, *The Education of Henry Adams* (New York: Houghton Mifflin, 1961).

37. I refer throughout to *America* and *Americans* as the designation for a constellation of beliefs, ideas, and desires first enunciated by the Puritan clergy as "the errand in the wilderness" and echoed throughout the nation's history in terms such as *American Exceptionalism, Manifest Destiny,* and *myth of the frontier.* My use of

America is not meant to connote a geographically fixed place but rather a histori-cally contingent epistemological space. In the same vein, I use *Americans* to refer not to a group of individuals defined by a national boundary but to a mythic tribe. *Americans*, in this sense, does not describe the people born or living within the na-tional boundaries of the United States. Instead, like the term *Israelites*, it denotes the inheritors of a divinely sanctioned destiny.

38. Adams, *The Education of Henry Adams*, 381.

39. Ibid., 238.

40. Roland Barthes, "The Grain of the Voice," in *Image-Music-Text*, translated by Steven Heath (New York: Farrar, Straus and Giroux, 1993), 179–89.

41. Wills, *Reagan's America*, 155.

Chapter One

1. Michael Rogin, *Ronald Reagan, the Movie: and Other Episodes of Political De-monology* (Berkeley: University of California Press, 1987), 16.

2. Ibid., 5. See also Ernst Kantarowicz, *The King's Two Bodies: A Study in Medieval Political Theory* (Princeton: Princeton University Press, 1957).

3. Quoted in Rogin, *Ronald Reagan, the Movie*, 295.

4. Ibid., 5.

5. Thomas Hobbes, *Leviathan* (New York: Penguin Classics, [1651] 1982), 125, emphasis in the original.

6. Quoted in Joseph Roach, *Cities of the Dead: Circum-Atlantic Performance* (New York: Columbia University Press, 1996), 117. Roach is referring to Richard Steele's writings in the *Tatler.*

7. Ibid., 73–78.

8. Peggy Noonan, *What I Saw at the Revolution: A Political Life in the Reagan Era* (New York: Random House, 1991), 148, emphasis in the original.

9. Jon McKenzie, *Perform or Else: From Discipline to Performance* (New York: Rout-ledge, 2001), 18.

10. Seymour Martin Lipset, *The First New Nation: The United States in Historical and Comparative Perspective* (New York: Norton, 1963).

11. Christopher Looby, *Voicing America: Language, Literary Form, and the Origins of the United States* (Chicago: University of Chicago Press, 1996), 2–3.

12. I have borrowed these examples from Richard Sennett, *The Fall of Public Man* (New York: Norton, 1992), 34.

13. John Adams, *Diary and Autobiography of John Adams*, edited by L. H. But-terfield, 4 vols. (New York: Atheneum, 1964), 282.

14. In Sacvan Bercovitch, *The Rites of Assent: Transformations in the Symbolic Con-struction of America* (New York: Routledge, 1993), 40.

15. In Jay Fliegelman, *Declaring Independence: Jefferson, Natural Language, & the Culture of Performance* (Palo Alto: Stanford University Press, 1993), 93–94.

16. In Carol Smith-Rosenberg, "Dis-covering the Subject of 'The Great Constitutional Discussion,' 1786–1789," *Journal of American History* 79 (December 1992): 842.

17. Fliegelman, *Declaring Independence*, 3.

18. Ibid., 191.

19. In Michael Kammen, *Mystic Chords of Memory: The Transformation of Tradition in American Culture* (New York: Vintage, 1993), emphasis added.

20. Henry Adams, *The Education of Henry Adams* (New York: Houghton Mifflin, 1961), ix.

21. Ibid., 69.

22. Ibid., 64, 66, 37.

23. Ibid., 237–40, emphasis added.

24. Ibid., 434–35.

25. Ibid., 380.

26. Ibid., 382.

27. Ibid., 486.

28. Ibid., 478–79.

29. Ibid., 457.

30. Ibid., 380–81.

31. Ibid., 430.

32. Margaret Cleaver, "A Chair for the New Home," reprinted in the *Dixon Evening Telegraph*, 4 June 1928, 5.

33. Quoted in Lou Cannon, *President Reagan: The Role of a Lifetime* (New York: Simon & Schuster, 1991), 37.

34. Ronald Reagan, *An American Life* (New York: Simon & Schuster, 1990), 26; Ronald Reagan with Richard G. Hubler, *Where's the Rest of Me?* (New York: Duell, Sloan & Pearce, Best Books, 1965), 23.

35. Warren Sussman, *Culture as History: The Transformation of American Society in the Twentieth Century* (New York: Pantheon, 1984), 271–86.

36. Ibid., 274–75.

37. Ibid., 280.

38. Robert T. Handy, quoted in Charlotte Canning, *The Most American Thing in America: Circuit Chautauqua as Performance* (Iowa City: University of Iowa Press, 2005), 41.

39. Theodore Morrison, *Chautauqua: A Center for Education, Religion, and the Arts in America* (Chicago: University of Chicago Press, 1974), 31.

40. Hugh A. Orchard, *Fifty Years of Chautauqua: Its Beginnings, Its Development, Its Message, and Its Life* (Cedar Rapids, IA: Torch, 1923), 30.

41. Jesse Lyman Hurlbut, *The Story of Chautauqua* (New York: Putnam, 1921), 27.

42. Canning, *The Most American Thing in America*, 7–8.

43. Anne Edwards, *Early Reagan* (New York: Morrow, 1987), 60. While I have not uncovered any detailed accounts of Ronald Reagan's attendance at Chautauqua the circumstantial evidence connecting him to it is substantial. In 1928, when Dixon

was at risk of losing its place on the Chautauqua circuit, Rev. Ben Cleaver, Mugs's father and pastor of the Reagans' church, joined the committee formed to devise a plan to save it. That same year Nelle Reagan was placed on the committee in charge of selling tickets to Chautauqua events. The prominent role played by Nelle and Reverend Cleaver indicates a prior commitment to Chautauqua and the church's support for its mission and programs. Furthermore, the scope and influence of Dixon's assembly were pervasive during Reagan's childhood.

44. Anonymous, *The History of Rock River Assembly of Lutherans* (Dixon, IL: Committee of the Rock River Assembly of the Illinois Synod of the United Lutheran Church of America, 1923), 5.

45. Ibid., 12.

46. Ibid., 14.

47. Ibid., 18.

48. Ibid., 22–23.

49. Ibid., 32.

50. Quoted in Canning, *The Most American Thing in America,* 8.

51. Canning explains that while Theodore Roosevelt is most often credited with this characterization of Chautauqua it is far from clear that he actually said it. The attribution of the quote to Roosevelt is part of Chautauqua lore, however, and it has underwritten many of the claims for Chautauqua's status as emblematic of the best of what America has to offer. See ibid., 238, n. 100.

52. Ibid., 21.

53. Ibid., 1. Support for Chautauqua was by no means unanimous. Among the naysayers was William James who, after visiting the Chautauqua Institution in 1896, reported to his brother Henry that he found it "depressing from its mediocrity." Sinclair Lewis placed his opinion of Chautauqua in the mouth of Carol Kennicott, the heroine of *Main Street,* who finds the mixture of "vaudeville performance, Y.M.C.A lecture, and the graduation exercises of an elocution class" to be "nothing but wind and chaff."

54. Quoted in ibid., 131.

55. Ibid., 93.

56. Quoted in ibid., 14.

57. Cleaver, "A Chair for the New Home," 5.

58. Anonymous, "The Uplift of Chautauqua Week," *Literary Digest,* 18 October 1918, 684.

59. See Garry Wills, *Reagan's America: Innocents at Home* (New York: Viking Penguin, 1988), 21–25.

60. Ibid., 27.

61. Edwards, *Early Reagan,* 34.

62. Edmond Morris, *Dutch: A Memoir of Ronald Reagan* (New York: Random House, 1999), 19.

63. Neil Reagan, "Private Dimensions and Public Images: The Early Political

Campaigns of Ronald Reagan," interview conducted by Stephen Stern for the Oral History Program, University of California, Los Angeles, 1982, 110, Regional Oral History Office, UCLA Library.

64. *Dixon Evening Telegraph,* 21 March 1925, 28 March 1925.

65. Reagan, *An American Life,* 35.

66. Ibid., 35.

67. Reagan, *Where's the Rest of Me?* 17.

68. *Dixon Evening Telegraph,* 24 November 1923.

69. Wills, *Reagan's America,* 27; Edwards, *Early Reagan,* 59.

70. Edwards, *Early Reagan,* 35–36; Stephen Vaughn, *Ronald Reagan in Hollywood: Movies and Politics* (Cambridge: Cambridge University Press, 1994), 19.

71. Edwards, *Early Reagan,* 59.

72. Reagan, *An American Life,* 33; Reagan, *Where's the Rest of Me?* 7–8. Edmund Morris provides convincing evidence that the incident with Reagan's father had to have occurred in the three months prior to his reading *That Printer of Udell's.* See the unnumbered footnote in Morris, *Dutch,* 695.

73. Edwards, *Early Reagan,* 58–59.

74. Ibid., 60.

75. *Dixon Evening Telegraph,* 31 December 1923, 5 December 1924.

76. *Dixon Evening Telegraph,* 12 December 1923, 9 September 1927.

77. Shannon Jackson, *Lines of Activity: Performance, Historiography, Hull House Domesticity* (Ann Arbor: University of Michigan Press, 2000).

78. Cleaver, "A Chair for the New Home," 5.

79. Jane Harrison, *Themis: A Study of the Social Origins of Greek Religion* (New York: Humanities Press International, [1912] 1977).

80. Harry P. Harrison, as told to Karl Detzer, *Culture under Canvas: The Story of Tent Chautauqua* (New York: Hastings House, 1958), 201–2.

81. Canning, *The Most American Thing in America,* 204.

82. Victoria Case and Robert Case, *We Called It Culture: The Story of Chautauqua* (New York: Doubleday, 1948), 52–55.

83. Quoted in Canning, *The Most American Thing in America,* 189.

84. Benjamin McArthur, *Actors and American Culture, 1880–1920* (Philadelphia: Temple University Press, 1984), 130–31.

85. In Canning, *The Most American Thing in America,* 208–9.

86. McArthur, *Actors and American Culture,* 132.

87. Ibid., 123.

88. Ibid., 135.

89. Ibid., 339.

90. Ibid., 361.

91. Kiron Skinner, Annalise Anderson, and Martin Anderson, eds., *Reagan: A Life in Letters* (Boston: Free Press, 2003), 2.

92. Quoted in Canning, *The Most American Thing in America,* 53.

93. Ibid., 56.

94. Reagan, *Where's the Rest of Me?* 18.

95. Cleaver, "A Chair for the New Home," 5.

Chapter Two

1. Ronald Reagan with Richard G. Hubler, *Where's the Rest of Me?* (New York: Duell, Sloan & Pearce, Best Books, 1965), 1.

2. Michael Rogin, *Ronald Reagan, the Movie: and Other Episodes of Political Demonology* (Berkeley: University of California Press, 1987), 3.

3. Garry Wills, *Reagan's America: Innocents at Home* (New York: Viking Penguin, 1988), 80.

4. Roland Barthes, "The Grain of the Voice," in *Image-Music-Text,* translated by Steven Heath (New York: Farrar, Straus and Giroux, 1993), 182.

5. Ibid., 188.

6. James E. Murdoch, *A Plea for Spoken Language: An Essay upon Comparative Elocution* (Cincinnati and New York: Van Antwerp, Bragg, 1883), 133.

7. Quoted in Lawrence Grossberg, *We Gotta Get Outta This Place: Popular Conservatism and Postmodern Culture* (New York: Routledge, 1992), 268–69.

8. Quoted in Mathew Dallek, *The Right Moment: Ronald Reagan's First Victory and the Decisive Turning Point in American Politics* (New York: Free Press, 2000), 68.

9. Bercovitch began to develop his rhetorical history of "the idea of America" in Savcan Bercovitch, *The American Jeremiad* (Madison: University of Wisconsin Press, 1978). The arguments cited in this paragraph are from his *The Rites of Assent: Transformations in the Symbolic Construction of America* (New York: Routledge, 1993), 1–28.

10. Quoted in Dallek, *The Right Moment,* 68.

11. Christopher Looby, *Voicing America: Language, Literary Form, and the Origins of the United States* (Chicago: University of Chicago Press, 1996), 1–4, 18.

12. Thomas Sheridan, *A Course of Lectures on Elocution* (Menston, Eng.: Scolar, [1762] 1968), xii.

13. James Burgh, *The Art of Speaking* (Danbury, 1795), 7.

14. Paul Edwards, "Unstoried: Teaching Literature in the Age of Performance Studies," *Theatre Annual: A Journal of Performance Studies* 52 (fall 1999): 45.

15. Ibid., 103.

16. Ibid., 252.

17. Quoted in Sheridan, *A Course of Lectures on Elocution,* 28.

18. Isaac Kramnick, *Republicanism and Bourgeois Radicalism: Political Ideology in Late Eighteenth-Century England and America* (Ithaca: Cornell University Press, 1990), 64.

19. Ibid., 44.

20. Ibid., 215.

21. Quoted in Edwards, "Unstoried," 47–48.

22. Ibid., 46.

23. Ibid., 49.

24. Quoted in Morris, *Dutch,* 37.

25. Ronald Reagan, *An American Life* (New York: Simon & Schuster, 1990), 59.

26. Paul Starr, *The Creation of the Media: Political Origins of Modern Communication* (New York; Basic Books, 2005), 328.

27. Reagan, *Where's the Rest of Me?* 23; Anne Edwards, *Early Reagan* (New York: Morrow, 1987), 43.

28. Arjun Appadurai, *Modernity at Large: Cultural Dimensions of Globalization* (Minneapolis: University of Minnesota Press, 1996), 31.

29. Neil Reagan, "Private Dimensions and Public Images: The Early Political Campaigns of Ronald Reagan," interview conducted by Stephen Stern for the Oral History Program, University of California, Los Angeles, 1982, 3, Regional Oral History Office, UCLA Library.

30. Ironically, according to Neil Reagan, the reason the actor playing the Old Ranger had to be replaced was because he had gotten too old and couldn't remember his lines.

31. Reagan, *An American Life,* 59.

32. B. J. Palmer, *History in the Making* (Davenport, IA: B. J. Palmer, 1957), 22.

33. Wills, *Reagan's America,* 115, 119.

34. Gary D. Farr, "The Wisdom of B. J. Palmer," http://www.aucco.org/palmerbj .html, accessed October 2006.

35. Edmond Morris, *Dutch: A Memoir of Ronald Reagan* (New York: Random House, 1999), 114.

36. Ibid., 454.

37. George M. Beard, *American Nervousness, Its Causes and Consequences* (New York, 1881), 97–98.

38. Donald Meyer, *The Positive Thinkers: Popular Religious Psychology from Mary Baker Eddy, Norman Vincent Peale, and Ronald Reagan,* rev. ed. (Middletown, CT: Wesleyan University Press, 1988), 26; Farr, "The Wisdom of B. J. Palmer."

39. Wills, *Reagan's America,* 126.

40. Walter Benjamin, "The Work of Art in the Age of Mechanical Reproduction," in *Illuminations: Essays and Reflections,* translated by Harry Zohn, edited by Hannah Arendt (New York: Schocken, 1968), 243–44.

41. Quoted in Mark Hertsgaard, *On Bended Knee: The Press and the Reagan Presidency* (New York: Random House, 1988), 8.

42. Quoted in Lou Cannon, *President Reagan: The Role of a Lifetime* (New York: Simon & Schuster, 1991), 513.

43. Ibid.

44. Rogin, *Ronald Reagan, the Movie,* 8.

45. Wills, *Reagan's America,* 122.

46. Ibid., 115–17.

47. Quoted in Stephen Vaughn, *Ronald Reagan in Hollywood: Movies and Politics* (Cambridge: Cambridge University Press, 1994), 23.

48. Quoted in Wills, *Reagan's America,* 117–18.

49. Quoted in Paul Benedetti and Wayne MacPhail, "The Birth of Chiropractic," http://www.canoe.ca/ChiroYork/chiro_invented.html, accessed November 2006, capitalized words in original.

50. Edwards, *Early Reagan,* 57.

51. Starr, *The Creation of the Media,* 329.

52. Quoted in Austin Graham, "The Visitor in Your Living Room: Radio Advertising in the 1930s," http://xroads.virginia.edu/~CLASS/am485_98/graham/visitor.html, accessed June 2005.

53. Lee de Forest, *Father of the Radio: The Autobiography of Lee de Forest* (Chicago: Wilco and Follet, 1950), 4.

54. Mark McGurl, "Making It Big: Picturing the Radio Age in *King Kong,*" *Critical Inquiry* 22, no. 3 (1996): 422.

55. Quoted in ibid.

56. Quoted in Daniel Czitrom, *Media and the American Mind: From Morse to McLuhan* (Chapel Hill: University of North Carolina Press, 1982), 77.

57. Reagan, *An American Life,* 64, 70–71.

58. Quoted in Vaughn, *Ronald Reagan in Hollywood,* 24.

59. Morris, *Dutch,* 117–18.

60. Quoted in Stuart Ewen, *Captains of Consciousness: The Social Roots of Consumer Culture* (New York: Basic Books, 1976), 33.

61. See Edwards, *Early Reagan,* 52–53.

62. Reagan, *An American Life,* 44–45.

63. Ibid., 47.

64. Ibid., 60.

65. Bertolt Brecht, "Emphasis on Sport," in *Brecht on Theatre,* translated by John Willett (New York: Hill and Wang, 1977), 6.

66. Reagan, *An American Life,* 59.

67. Benjamin G. Rader, *In Its Own Image: How Television Has Transformed Sports* (Boston: Free Press, 1984), 30.

68. Video R33, Ronald Reagan Presidential Library.

69. Reagan, *Where's the Rest of Me?* 33.

70. Rader, *In Its Own Image,* 26. It was not until 1955 that a court ruling decreed that radio stations must compensate teams in exchange for the right to broadcast their games.

71. Reagan, *Where's the Rest of Me?* 48.

72. Ibid., 77.

73. Edwards, *Early Reagan,* 137.

74. Benjamin, "The Work of Art in the Age of Mechanical Reproduction," 225.

75. Reagan, *Where's the Rest of Me?* 77.

76. Edwards, *Early Reagan,* 137.

77. Benjamin, "The Work of Art in the Age of Mechanical Reproduction," 238.

78. Ibid., 223.

79. Ibid., 222.

80. Reagan, *Where's the Rest of Me?* 61, emphasis added.

81. Wills, *Reagan's America,* 142.

82. Reagan, *Where's the Rest of Me?* 61–62, emphasis added.

Chapter Three

1. Walter Benjamin, "The Work of Art in the Age of Mechanical Reproduction," in *Illuminations: Essays and Reflections,* translated by Harry Zohn, edited by Hannah Arendt (New York: Schocken, 1968), 247.

2. Unnamed newspaper editor, quoted in Robert J. Brown, *Manipulating the Ether: The Power of Broadcast Radio in Thirties America* (Jefferson, NC: McFarland, 1998), 126.

3. Peggy Noonan, *What I Saw at the Revolution: A Political Life in the Reagan Era* (New York: Random House, 1991), 53.

4. Quoted in Anne Edwards, *Early Reagan* (New York: Morrow, 1987), 119.

5. Quoted in ibid., 231.

6. Stuart Ewen, *PR! A Social History of Spin* (New York: Basic Books, 1996), 395.

7. Richard Whalen, quoted in Michael Rogin, *Ronald Reagan, the Movie: and Other Episodes of Political Demonology* (Berkeley: University of California Press, 1987), 33.

8. Roland Barthes, "The Grain of the Voice," in *Image-Music-Text,* translated by Steven Heath (New York: Farrar, Straus and Giroux, 1993), 181, emphasis in the original.

9. Betty Houchin-Winfield, *FDR and the News Media* (New York: Columbia University Press, 1990), 12.

10. Quoted in Stephen Fox, *The Mirror Makers: A History of American Advertising and Its Creators* (Urbana: University of Illinois Press, 1997), 117.

11. Hugh Gregory Gallagher, *FDR's Splendid Deception: The Moving Story of Roosevelt's Massive Disability and the Intense Efforts to Conceal It from the Public* (New York: Vandamere, 1985), 93–4, xiii.

12. Quoted in Brown, *Manipulating the Ether,* 9.

13. Robert Lynd and Helen Lynd, *Middletown: A Study in Contemporary American Culture* (New York: Harcourt, Brace, Jovanovich, 1929), 244.

14. Leonard J. Reinsch, *Getting Elected: From Radio and Roosevelt to Television and Reagan* (New York: Hippocrene, 1988), xii.

15. Brown, *Manipulating the Ether,* 2.

16. Quoted in Tom Lewis, "'A Godlike Presence': The Impact of Radio on the 1920s and 1930s," *Organization of American Historians Magazine of History* 6, no. 4 (1992): 26.

17. Quoted in Brown, *Manipulating the Ether,* 10.

18. Kenneth D. Yeilding and Paul H. Carlson, *Ah That Voice: The Fireside Chats of Franklin Delano Roosevelt* (Odessa, TX: Library of the Presidents, Presidential Museum, 1974), xiii.

19. Brown, *Manipulating the Ether,* 19–20.

20. Quoted in ibid., 19.

21. During Roosevelt's four presidential campaigns, endorsements from daily newspapers consistently declined from 38 percent in 1932 to 22 percent in 1944. One of the keys to Roosevelt's political mastery of radio was his crusade to prevent hostile newspaper magnates such as William Randolph Hearst from establishing significant ownership positions in radio networks. For an account of FDR's tactics in combating the incursion of newspaper publishers into radio, see Joon-Mann Kang, "Franklin D. Roosevelt and James L. Fly: The Politics of Broadcast Regulation, 1941–1944," *Journal of American Culture* 10, no. 2 (1987): 23–34.

22. Quoted in Ewen, *PR!* 251.

23. Samuel I. Rosenman, *Working with Roosevelt* (New York: Harper, 1952), 56.

24. Quoted in Brown, *Manipulating the Ether,* 19.

25. Quoted in ibid., 40–41.

26. Kang, "Franklin D. Roosevelt and James L. Fly," 24.

27. Quoted in Fred J. MacDonald, *Don't Touch That Dial! Radio Programming in American Life, 1920–1960* (Chicago: Nelson-Hall, 1979), 298.

28. Brown, *Manipulating the Ether,* 27.

29. Franklin Roosevelt, Inaugural Address, March 4, 1933, in *The Public Papers and Addresses of Franklin D. Roosevelt,* compiled by Samuel Rosenman, vol. 2, *The Year of Crisis, 1933* (New York: Random House, 1938), 11–16.

30. Frances Perkins, *The Roosevelt I Knew* (New York: Viking, 1946), 71–73.

31. Walter Benjamin, "One Way Street," in *Reflections: Essays, Aphorisms, Autobiographical Writings,* translated by Edmund Jephcott, edited by Peter Demetz (New York: Schocken, 1978), 86.

32. Ronald Reagan, *An American Life* (New York: Simon & Schuster, 1990), 66.

33. Benedict Anderson, *Imagined Communities: Reflections on the Origin and Spread of Nationalism* (London: Verso, [1984] 1991), 35–36.

34. A case could be made that radio was the single most important source for building the imagined communities of all the combatants in World War II, from Hitler and Mussolini's use of it to disseminate the national voice of fascism to the literal communities of anonymity constituted by resistance broadcasters and audiences throughout Western Europe. On the role of television in supplying an image repertoire for postcolonial imagi-nations, see Arjun Appadurai, *Modernity at Large: Cultural Dimensions of Globalization* (Minneapolis: University of Minnesota Press, 1996).

35. Quoted in Brown, *Manipulating the Ether,* 10.

36. Quoted in ibid., 18.

37. Perkins, *The Roosevelt I Knew,* 71–72.

38. Thomas Paine, *Common Sense,* edited by Isaac Kramnick (New York: Penguin Classics, 1982), 84.

39. Brown, *Manipulating the Ether,* 126.

40. Reagan, *An American Life,* 247.

41. Quoted in Edmond Morris, *Dutch: A Memoir of Ronald Reagan* (New York: Random House, 1999), 117.

42. Bill Boyarsky, *Ronald Reagan: His Life and Rise to the Presidency* (New York: Random House, 1981), 19.

43. Ronald Reagan, "The Creative Society," speech delivered at the University of Southern California, 19 April 1966, http://reaganlibrary.com/reagan/speeches/creative.asp, accessed September 2007.

44. Quoted in Ewen, *PR!,* 243. See also Mark Hertsgaard, *On Bended Knee: The Press and the Reagan Presidency* (New York: Random House, 1988), 52.

45. Quoted in Lou Cannon, *President Reagan: The Role of a Lifetime* (New York: Simon & Schuster, 1991), 60.

46. Fred J. MacDonald, *One Nation under Television: The Rise and Decline of Network TV* (New York: Pantheon, 1990), 221.

47. Haynes Johnson, *Sleepwalking through History: America in the Reagan Years* (New York: Doubleday, 1991), 141–42.

48. Pierre Bourdieu, *Outline of a Theory of Practice,* translated by Richard Nice (Cambridge: Cambridge University Press, 1977), 78, see also 93–94.

49. Benjamin, "The Work of Art in the Age of Mechanical Reproduction," 229.

50. See Garry Wills, *Reagan's America: Innocents at Home* (New York: Viking Penguin, 1988), 177; and Hortense Powdermaker, *Hollywood: The Dream Factory* (New York: Little, Brown, 1950), 209.

51. Reagan, *An American Life,* 96.

52. Howard Barnes quoted in Patrick McGilligan, *Yankee Doodle Dandy,* edited by Patrick McGilligan (Madison: University of Wisconsin Press, 1981), 60.

53. Quoted in Michael Rogin, *Blackface, White Noise: Jewish Immigrants in the Hollywood Melting Pot* (Berkeley: University of California Press, 1996). Rogin characterizes the ideological basis of American identity formation in the blackface film musical as one of "self-making through role-playing."

54. McGilligan, *Yankee Doodle Dandy,* 45.

55. In 1934, a Sacramento grand jury accused Cagney of being a communist. In 1940, a second grand jury labeled him a communist, a charge that was publicized by Los Angeles district attorney Buron Fitts in his reelection campaign.

56. McGilligan, *Yankee Doodle Dandy,* 15.

57. Ibid., 6, 16.

58. Stephen Vaughn, *Ronald Reagan in Hollywood: Movies and Politics* (Cambridge: Cambridge University Press, 1994), 89.

59. Ward Morehouse, *George M. Cohan: Prince of the American Theater* (New York: Lippincott, 1943), 229.

60. Ironically, the medal, which plays such a crucial ideological role in the film, was awarded in 1936. It sat in Roosevelt's desk for four years before Cohan, not a fan of FDR's, came to the White House to claim it.

61. Joseph Roach, *Cities of the Dead: Circum-Atlantic Performance* (New York: Columbia University Press, 1996), 117.

62. Morehouse subtitled his biography of Cohan *Prince of the American Theater*.

63. Quoted in Leo J. A. Lemay, "The American Origins of 'Yankee Doodle,'" *William and Mary Quarterly*, 3d ser., 33 (July 1976): 436.

64. Ibid. See also http://www.americanrevolution.com/YankeeDoodleDandy .htm, accessed March 2004.

65. Joseph Roach, "The Emergence of the American Actor," in *The Cambridge History of American Theatre*, vol. 1: *Beginnings to 1870*, edited by Don B. Wilmeth and Christopher Bigsby (Cambridge: Cambridge University Press, 1998), 344. For an in-depth account of how lines of business developed in an American context, see James C. Burge, *Lines of Business: Casting Practice and Policy in the American Theatre, 1752–1899* (New York: Peter Lang), 1986.

66. Homi K. Bhabha, *The Location of Culture* (London: Routledge, 1994), 86.

67. See McGilligan, *Yankee Doodle Dandy*, 47.

68. Rogin, *Blackface, White Noise*, 182.

69. McGilligan, *Yankee Doodle Dandy*, 147.

70. The quote is from Robert Buckner's "temporary" script for *Yankee Doodle Dandy*. "Apart from its story interest," he writes, "the purpose of this shot is largely historical," as it marked a milestone in Broadway stagecraft and "started George M. Cohan's fame for providing surprises." Quoted in ibid., 216.

71. Ronald Reagan, *Speaking My Mind* (New York: Simon & Schuster, 1989), 14.

72. Michael Taussig, *Mimesis and Alterity: A Particular History of the Senses* (New York: Routledge, 1993), 48.

73. Ronald Reagan with Richard G. Hubler, *Where's the Rest of Me?* (New York: Duell, Sloan & Pearce, Best Books, 1965), 9.

74. Noonan, *What I Saw at the Revolution*, 345–46.

Chapter Four

1. In James William Gibson, *Warrior Dreams: Violence and Manhood in Post-Vietnam America* (New York: Hill and Wang, 1994), 233.

2. Paige Baty, *American Monroe: The Making of a Body Politic* (Berkeley: University of California Press, 1995), 17.

3. Richard Schechner, *Between Theater and Anthropology* (Philadelphia: University of Pennsylvania Press, 1985), 36–37.

4. Arjun Appadurai, *Modernity at Large: Cultural Dimensions of Globalization* (Minneapolis: University of Minnesota Press, 1996), 54.

5. Arthur Bremer, *An Assassin's Diary* (New York: Harpers Magazine Press, 1973), 97.

6. Ibid., 79.

7. Ibid., 75.

8. Dietz's diagnosis is summarized in Lincoln Kaplan, *The Insanity Defense and the Trial of John Hinckley, Jr.* (Boston: Godine, 1984), 68–73, emphasis added.

9. Bremer, *An Assassin's Diary,* 40.

10. Ronald Reagan with Richard G. Hubler, *Where's the Rest of Me?* (New York: Duell, Sloan & Pearce, Best Books, 1965), 42.

11. Quoted in Gil Troy, *Morning in America: How Ronald Reagan Invented the 1980s* (Princeton: Princeton University Press, 2005), 103.

12. Quoted in Mark Hertsgaard, *On Bended Knee: The Press and the Reagan Presidency* (New York: Random House, 1988), 116–17.

13. Quoted in Mathew Dallek, *The Right Moment: Ronald Reagan's First Victory and the Decisive Turning Point in American Politics* (New York: Free Press, 2000), 235.

14. Abraham Lincoln, "First Inaugural Address, Final Text, March 4, 1861," in *The Collected Works of Abraham Lincoln,* edited by Roy P. Basler, vol. 4 (New Brunswick: Rutgers University Press, 1953), 271.

15. Quoted in Joseph Roach, "The Emergence of the American Actor," in *The Cambridge History of American Theatre,* vol. 1: *Beginnings to 1870,* edited by Don B. Wilmeth and Christopher Bigsby (Cambridge: Cambridge University Press, 1998), 370.

16. Reagan recorded his introduction on March 11. It aired during the Academy Awards broadcast, which was scheduled for the day Reagan was shot but was postponed to the following evening.

17. Anne Edwards, *Early Reagan* (New York: Morrow, 1987), 42; Edmond Morris, *Dutch: A Memoir of Ronald Reagan* (New York: Random House, 1999), 19.

18. Ronald Reagan, *An American Life* (New York: Simon & Schuster, 1990), 58.

19. Ibid., 57.

20. Ibid., 57–58.

21. For a description of the issues surrounding the student protest, see Garry Wills, *Reagan's America: Innocents at Home* (New York: Viking Penguin, 1988), 52–63.

22. Reagan, *Where's the Rest of Me?* 29, emphasis added.

23. Lou Cannon, *President Reagan: The Role of a Lifetime* (New York: Simon & Schuster, 1991), 33–35.

24. Morris, *Dutch,* 121.

25. Reagan, *An American Life,* 30.

26. Reagan, *Where's the Rest of Me?* 66–70. In *An American Life,* Reagan describes the scene he read for his screen test as being from Barry's *The Philadelphia Story.* However, this is highly unlikely since the play premiered at the Schubert Theatre in New York on 28 March 1939, two years after Reagan's screen test. *Holiday,* on the other hand, had its stage debut in 1928, the first film version was made by Warner Brothers in 1930, and the second, starring Cary Grant and Katherine Hepburn, was in production around the time of Reagan's screen test.

27. Reagan, *An American Life,* 80–82.

28. Robert P. Metzger, *Reagan: American Icon* (Lewisburg, PA: Center Gallery Publications, Bucknell University, 1989), 22.

29. Ibid., 22.

30. Reagan, *An American Life,* 83.

31. Morris, *Dutch,* 128.

32. Reagan, *An American Life,* 83.

33. P. David Marshall, *Celebrity and Power: Fame in Contemporary Culture* (Minneapolis: University of Minnesota Press, 1997), 50.

34. Baty, *American Monroe,* 18.

35. Ibid., 16.

36. Warren Sussman, *Culture as History: The Transformation of American Society in the Twentieth Century* (New York: Pantheon), 271–86.

37. Robert Sklar, *Movie-Made America: A Cultural History of American Movies* (New York: Vintage, 1994), 7–8.

38. Joshua Gamson, *Claims to Fame: Celebrity in Contemporary America* (Berkeley: University of California Press, 1994), 15–16.

39. Sklar, *Movie-Made America,* 14–33. See also Neil Gabler, *An Empire of Their Own: How the Jews Invented Hollywood* (New York: Anchor, 1989).

40. Gamson, *Claims to Fame,* 15–16.

41. Quoted in Richard Dyer, *Stars* (London: British Film Institute, 1979), 17.

42. Quoted in Sklar, *Movie-Made America,* 92. Bara was actually from Avondale, a largely Jewish suburb of Cincinnati, but Fox publicists supplied her with a new biography (and past life) for each new film role. Swathed in veils, furs, and silks, petting a python and nibbling on raw beef and lettuce, Bara deadpanned her various selves through hundreds of press conferences.

43. Richard Schickel, *Intimate Strangers: The Culture of Celebrity* (New York: Fromm International, 1985), 99.

44. Leo C. Rosten, *Hollywood: The Movie Colony, the Movie Makers* (New York: Harcourt, Brace, 1941), 3–4, 378–79.

45. Cathy Klaprat, "The Star as Market Strategy: Bette Davis in Another Light," in *The American Film Industry,* rev. ed., edited by Tino Balio (Madison: University of Wisconsin Press, 1985), 366.

46. Reagan, *An American Life,* 118.

47. Stephen Vaughn, *Ronald Reagan in Hollywood: Movies and Politics* (Cambridge: Cambridge University Press, 1994), 196.

48. Quoted in Gamson, *Claims to Fame,* 35, emphasis in the original.

49. John Adams, *Diary and Autobiography of John Adams,* edited by L. H. Butterfield, 4 vols. (New York: Atheneum, 1964), 282.

50. In his first three years at Warner Brothers, Reagan appeared in six films directed by Roy Enright, more than with any other director. Reagan acted in three films directed by Lloyd Bacon and three with Lewis Foster. None of these directors

was A-list or apparently left much of an impression on Reagan. Their absence from his memoirs suggests that they had little influence on his craft. In the remainder of his film career he never worked with the same director more than twice and thus never built a long-term relationship or body of work with any single director.

51. Thomas Schatz, *The Genius of the System: Hollywood Filmmaking in the Studio Era* (New York: Holt, 1996), 6.

52. Ibid., 136.

53. Dallek, *Ronald Reagan,* 10–11.

54. Michael Rogin, *Ronald Reagan, the Movie: and Other Episodes of Political Demonology* (Berkeley: University of California Press, 1987), 7.

55. Cannon, *President Reagan,* 116.

56. Reagan, *Where's the Rest of Me?* 37.

57. Reagan, *An American Life,* 42.

58. Reagan, *Where's the Rest of Me?* 17, 127.

59. Ibid., 3–8.

60. Brian Massumi and Kenneth Dean, "Postmortem on the Presidential Body," in *Body Politics: Disease, Desire, and the Family,* edited by Michael Ryan and Avery Gordon (Boulder: Westview, 1994), 159.

61. It has been brought to my attention by Peggy Phelan that the scene could have been rehearsed the way Reagan remembers and/or shot the way he describes it in a version left on the cutting room floor. Reagan, however, recalls begging the director, Sam Wood, not to rehearse the scene and "God rest his soul—fine director that he was, he just turned to the crew and said, 'Let's make it.'" Crucial to the ideological work of the anecdote and the line he utters is the integrity of a scene enacted without rehearsal or duplication: "There was no retake. . . . Perhaps I never did quite as well again in a single shot" (Reagan, *Where's the Rest of Me?* 9).

62. Wills, *Reagan's America,* 206–7.

63. Reagan, *An American Life,* 42.

64. James George Frazer, *The Golden Bough: A Study in Magic and Religion,* new abridgement by Robert Fraser from the second and third editions (Oxford: Oxford World Classics, 1998), 52.

65. Peggy Phelan, *Unmarked: The Politics of Performance* (New York: Routledge, 1993), 3.

66. Frazer, *The Golden Bough,* 52.

67. Reagan, *Where's the Rest of Me?* 9–10.

68. Warren Sussman, *Culture as History: The Transformation of American Society in the Twentieth Century* (New York: Pantheon, 1984), 200–201.

69. Reagan, *Where's the Rest of Me?* 10.

Chapter Five

1. Garry Wills, *Reagan's America: Innocents at Home* (New York: Viking Penguin, 1988), 126.

2. Guy Debord, *The Society of the Spectacle,* translated by Donald Nicholson-Smith (Detroit: Black and Red Press, 1970), chap. 1.

3. See Naomi Klein, *No Logo: No Space, No Choice, No Jobs* (New York: Picador, 2002), 7–8, 14.

4. Ibid., 1–14.

5. Sidney Blumenthal, *The Permanent Campaign* (New York: Simon & Schuster, 1980).

6. Samuel Kernell, *Going Public: New Strategies of Presidential Leadership* (Washington, DC: Congressional Quarterly Press, 1986).

7. Quoted in Mark Hertsgaard, *On Bended Knee: The Press and the Reagan Presidency* (New York: Random House, 1988), 15.

8. Harold Clurman quoted in Richard Nelson, *A Culture of Confidence: Politics, Performance, and the Idea of America* (Jackson: University of Mississippi Press, 1996), 113.

9. Thomas Ferguson and Joel Rogers, *Right Turn: The Decline of the Democrats and the Future of American Politics* (Chicago: Lawrence Hill, 1986), 24–25.

10. Colorado Congresswomen Patricia Schroeder coined the phrase "Teflon president."

11. Quoted in Hertsgaard, *On Bended Knee,* 35.

12. Donald Regan, *For the Record: From Wall Street to Washington* (New York: Harcourt Brace Jovanovich, 1988), 248.

13. Quoted in Hertsgaard, *On Bended Knee,* 48.

14. Quoted in ibid., 48.

15. Quoted in ibid., 46.

16. Michael Rogin, *Ronald Reagan, the Movie: and Other Episodes of Political Demonology* (Berkeley: University of California Press, 1987), 8.

17. Lizabeth Cohen, *A Consumer's Republic: The Politics of Mass Consumption in Postwar America* (New York: Vintage, 2003).

18. The Supreme Court decision in *U.S. v. Paramount Pictures, et al.* effectively brought to an end the Hollywood studio system. The Court ruled that movie studios must abolish the practice of block booking and sell their theater chains. The ruling would change the way Hollywood movies were produced, distributed, and exhibited.

19. Quoted in Dan Moldea, *Dark Victory: Ronald Reagan, MCA, and the Mob* (New York: Viking, 1986), 99–100.

20. Reagan's initial contract payed him 125,000 dollars a year. In 1959, MCA began paying him directly. By eliminating his agent's fee he received a 10 percent raise. The agency also negotiated a 25 percent stake for Reagan in the show's future proceeds, including reruns.

21. Quoted in Anne Edwards, *Early Reagan* (New York: Morrow, 1987), 42. See also Edmond Morris, *Dutch: A Memoir of Ronald Reagan* (New York: Random House, 1999), 446.

22. Ronald Reagan, *An American Life* (New York: Simon & Schuster, 1990), 125–26.

23. Mark McGurl, "Making It Big: Picturing the Radio Age in *King Kong*," *Critical Inquiry* 22, no. 3 (1996): 417.

24. Quoted in John Winthrop Hammond, *Men and Volts: The Story of General Electric* (New York: Lippincott, 1941), 387.

25. David Nye, *Image Worlds: Corporate Identities at General Electric, 1890–1930* (Cambridge: MIT Press, 1985), 35–36.

26. Quoted in Warren Sussman, *Culture as History: The Transformation of American Society in the Twentieth Century* (New York: Pantheon, 1984), 130.

27. Quoted in Nye, *Image Worlds*, 26.

28. Roland Marchand, *Creating the Corporate Soul: The Rise of Public Relations and Corporate Imagery in American Big Business* (Berkeley: University of California Press, 1998), 149.

29. Quoted in ibid., 162.

30. Ibid., 157.

31. Quoted in Nye, *Image Worlds*, 26.

32. Quoted in Stephen Fox, *The Mirror Makers: A History of American Advertising and Its Creators* (Urbana: University of Illinois Press, 1997), 117.

33. Larry Tye, *The Father of Spin: Edward L. Bernays and the Birth of Public Relations* (New York: Holt, 1998), 8.

34. Charles and Mary Beard quoted in Stuart Ewen, *PR! A Social History of Spin* (New York: Basic Books, 1996), 119.

35. Ivy Lee quoted in ibid., 132.

36. Quoted in ibid., 68.

37. Ibid., 71.

38. Quoted in Tye, *The Father of Spin,* 31.

39. Ibid., 65.

40. Quoted in ibid., 64–65.

41. Eric Lefcowitz, "Welcome to the Retro Future," 2002, http://www.retrofuture.com/futurama.html, accessed February 2003.

42. Quoted in Catherine Jurca, "Hollywood, the Dream House Factory," *Cinema Journal* 37, no. 4 (1998): 28.

43. Quoted in Tom Lewis, "'A Godlike Presence': The Impact of Radio on the 1920s and 1930s," *Organization of American Historians Magazine of History* 6, no. 4 (1992): 33.

44. Quoted in Ewen, *PR!* 386.

45. Cohen, *A Consumer's Republic,* 73.

46. Quoted in Jurca, "Hollywood, the Dream House Factory," 19.

47. Ibid., 20.

48. The use of model homes as a promotional tool was nothing new for GE, which during the 1930s had showcased its "magic home" at fairs and exhibitions. The company had also utilized film tie-ins as a vehicle for marketing its appliances as far back as 1933, when the Warner Brothers—GE Better Times Special, a train

filled with movie stars, traveled from Hollywood to the New York opening of *42nd Street,* and then to FDR's inauguration.

49. Norman Panama and Melvin Frank, *Mr. Blandings Builds His Dream House* (Los Angeles: Twentieth Century Fox, 1948), film.

50. Edward Bernays, "Engineering of Consent," *Annals of the American Academy of Political and Social Science* 250 (March 1947): 113–20.

51. Lynn Spigel, *Welcome to the Dream House: Popular Media and Postwar Suburbs* (Durham: Duke University Press, 2001), 386.

52. Quoted in Jurca, "Hollywood, the Dream House Factory," 20.

53. Earl B. Dunckel, "Ronald Reagan and the General Electric Theatre, 1954–1955," oral history conducted for the Ronald Reagan Gubernatorial Era Documentation Series, Regional Oral History Office, University of California, Berkeley, 1982, 4–7, typescript.

54. William L. Bird Jr., "General Electric Theater," Museum of Broadcast Communications, http://www.museum.tv/archives/etv/G/htmlG/generalelect/general-elect.htm, accessed April 2006.

55. Dunckel, "Ronald Reagan and the General Electric Theatre," 4–7; Bird, "General Electric Theater."

56. The statistics on the rise of television ownership, viewing, and advertising revenue in the 1950s can be found in Joshua Gamson, *Claims to Fame: Celebrity in Contemporary America* (Berkeley: University of California Press, 1994), 41; Fox, *The Mirror Makers,* 210–11; and Spigel, *Welcome to the Dream House,* 33.

57. Quoted in William Boddy, *Fifties Television: The Industry and Its Critics* (Urbana: University of Illinois Press, 1990), 155.

58. Ronald Reagan quoted in Moldea, *Dark Victory,* 189.

59. Wills, *Reagan's America,* 319.

60. Quoted in Moldea, *Dark Victory,* 189.

61. Ewen, *PR!* 389, emphasis in the original.

62. Quoted in Edwards, *Early Reagan,* 459.

63. Quoted in Ewen, *PR!* 390–91, emphasis in the original.

64. Quoted in Edwards, *Early Reagan,* 461.

65. Bird, "General Electric Theater."

66. Quoted in Edwards, *Early Reagan,* 459.

67. The segment ran during an episode titled "The Shadow Outside," *General Electric Television Theater,* aired 30 December 1956.

68. Thomas Hine, *Populuxe* (New York: Knopf, 1986).

69. Ibid., 6.

70. Quoted in Spigel, *Welcome to the Dream House,* 382–83.

71. Hine, *Populuxe,* 14.

72. "Too Good with A Gun," *General Electric Television Theater,* aired 24 March 1957.

73. "The Man Who Inherited Everything," *General Electric Television Theater,* aired 19 May 1957.

74. I viewed the lighting segment on an unmarked videotape at the Ronald Reagan Presidential Library. I am still trying to track down the airdate and other relevant information regarding the episode of which it was a part.

75. Quoted in Edmond Morris, *Dutch: A Memoir of Ronald Reagan* (New York: Random House, 1999), 304–5.

76. Quoted in Edwards, *Early Reagan*, 460.

77. Dennis McDougal, *The Last Mogul: Lew Wasserman, MCA, and the Hidden History of Hollywood* (New York: Crown, 1998), 191.

78. Gamson, *Claims to Fame*, 41.

79. Quoted in Wills, *Reagan's America*, 317.

80. Ibid., 317–18. For a detailed account of the scope and scale of MCA's competitive advantage, see Nat Henthoff, "The Octopus of Show Biz," *Reporter*, 23 November 1961, 41.

81. Quoted in Moldea, *Dark Victory*, 193.

82. Reagan, *An American Life*, 126–27.

83. Dunckel, "Ronald Reagan and the General Electric Theatre," 1.

84. Ibid., 6.

85. Reagan, *Where's the Rest of Me?* 229; Morris, *Dutch*, 305.

86. Kitty Kelley, *Nancy Reagan: The Unauthorized Biography* (New York: Simon & Schuster, 1991), 104.

87. Reagan, *Where's the Rest of Me?* 198.

88. Quoted in Wills, *Reagan's America*, 347.

89. Quoted in W. D. King, *Henry Irving's Waterloo* (Berkeley: University of California Press, 1993), 40.

90. Ibid., 41.

91. Ibid.

92. Ibid., 39.

93. See Lisa McGirr, *Suburban Warriors: The Origins of the New American Right* (Princeton: Princeton University Press, 2002), for an invaluable explanation of Reaganism's roots in the expanding southern and western professional middle class of the 1960s.

Chapter Six

1. William Shakespeare, *The Arden Shakespeare Hamlet,* edited by Harold Jenkins (London: Methuen, 1982), 4.3.27–30. All subsequent quotes from *Hamlet* are from this edition.

2. Joseph Roach, *Cities of the Dead: Circum-Atlantic Performance* (New York: Columbia University Press, 1996), 2–3.

3. Marita Sturken, *Tangled Memories: The Vietnam War, the AIDS Epidemic, and the Politics of Remembering* (Berkeley: University of California Press, 1997), 1.

4. Roach, *Cities of the Dead*, 2.

5. Judith Butler, *Bodies That Matter: On the Discursive Limits of Sex* (New York: Routledge, 1993), 2.

6. Ibid., 9, emphasis in original.

7. For the *TV Guide* rankings, see Lawrence Grossberg, *We Gotta Get Outta This Place: Popular Conservatism and Postmodern Culture* (New York: Routledge, 1992), 273. For a study that assesses the decade through television and the rubric of catastrophe, see Patricia Mellencamp, *High Anxiety: Catastrophe, Scandal, Age, and Comedy* (Bloomington: Indiana University Press, 1992).

8. *Hamlet*, 1.1.24–33.

9. The play's preoccupation with "things" that demand identification and nomination is established, prior to Horatio's question, in the opening dialogue between Barnardo and Francisco.

> BARNARDO: Who's there?
> FRANCISCO: Nay, answer me. Stand and unfold yourself.
> BARNARDO: Long live the King!
> FRANCISCO: Barnardo?

Barnardo's salutation ("Long live the King!") may indeed be the password that identifies him to Francisco, but it is hard not to hear in these lines—as Shakespeare's audience surely would have—a response to the unspoken cue that begins the phrase they traditionally complete: "The King is dead." The political imperative to penetrate the fog that engulfs Elsinore's midnight and question the Ghost is linked to both the possibility of regicide and the question of dynastic succession.

10. *Hamlet*, 2.2.520.

11. Ibid., 2.2.22.

12. Marvin Carlson, *The Haunted Stage: The Theater as Memory Machine* (Ann Arbor: University of Michigan Press, 2003), 4.

13. *Hamlet*, 2.2.600–601.

14. Ibid., 4.3.27–30.

15. Elizabethan jurist Edmund Plowden quoted in Ernst Kantarowicz, *The King's Two Bodies: A Study in Mediaeval Political Theory* (Princeton: Princeton University Press, 1957), 7.

16. *Hamlet*, 4.3.31–32.

17. Pierre Bourdieu, "The Social Space and the Genesis of Groups," *Social Science Information* 24, no. 2 (1985): 215–17.

18. *Hamlet*, 2.2.546–51.

19. Walter Benjamin, "The Storyteller: Reflections on the Works of Nikolai Leskov," in *Illuminations: Essays and Reflections,* translated by Harry Zohn, edited by Hannah Arendt (New York: Schocken, 1968), 94.

20. All the quotes from Reagan's first inaugural address are taken from the transcript published in Ronald Reagan, *Speaking My Mind* (New York: Simon & Schuster, 1989), 59–66.

21. Roach, *Cities of the Dead*, 73–78.

22. The Khachigian quotes are from Lou Cannon, *President Reagan: The Role of a Lifetime* (New York: Simon & Schuster, 1991), 99–100. The Treptow story was related to Reagan in a letter from Preston Hotchkiss, the chief executive officer of the Bixby Ranch in Saugus, California.

23. Walter Benjamin, "One-Way Street," in *Reflections: Essays, Aphorisms, Autobiographical Writings*, translated by Edmund Jephcott, edited by Peter Demetz (New York: Schocken, 1978), 85–86.

24. Jacques Derrida, *Specters of Marx: The State of the Debt, the Work of Mourning, and the New International*, translated by Bernd Magnus and Stephen Cullenberg (New York: Routledge, 1994), 10–11, emphasis in the original.

25. Carlson, *The Haunted Stage*.

26. Diana Taylor, "Dancing with Diana: A Study in Hauntology," *Drama Review* 43, no. 1 (1999): 64.

27. Derrida, *Specters of Marx*, 37.

28. Michael K. Deaver with Mickey Herskowitz, *Behind the Scenes: In Which the Author Talks about Ronald and Nancy Reagan . . . and Himself* (New York: Morrow, 1987), 81.

29. Ibid., 179.

30. Ibid., 180.

31. Reagan related this "story" to Israeli prime minister Yitzhak Shamir on 29 November 1983, and to Simon Wiesenthal and Rabbi Marvin Hier two months later. See Garry Wills, *Reagan's America: Innocents at Home* (New York: Viking Penguin, 1988), 199–200.

32. Deaver, *Behind the Scenes*, 180.

33. Reagan, *Speaking My Mind*, 221.

34. *Hamlet*, 4.4.61–65.

35. Quoted in Charles E. Silberman, "Speaking Truth to Power," in Ilya Levkov, *Bitburg and Beyond: Encounters in American, German, and Jewish History*, edited by Ilya Levkov (New York: Shapolsky, 1987), 346.

36. The full text of Wiesel's remarks can be found in *Bitburg and Beyond: Encounters in American, German, and Jewish History*, edited by Ilya Levkov (New York: Shapolsky, 1987), 42–44.

37. Presidential news conference, 21 March 1985, in *Bitburg and Beyond: Encounters in American, German, and Jewish History*, edited by Ilya Levkov (New York: Shapolsky, 1987), 34.

38. Quoted in Geoffrey H. Hartman, ed., *Bitburg in Moral and Political Perspective* (Bloomington: Indiana University Press, 1986), xii–xiv.

39. Martin Marty, "'Storycide' and the Meaning of History," in *Bitburg in Moral and Political Perspective*, edited by Geoffrey H. Hartman (Bloomington: Indiana University Press, 1986), 224–26.

40. My understanding of *Hamlet* has been vastly enriched by Stephen Green-

blatt's insights in *Hamlet in Purgatory* (Princeton: Princeton University Press, 2001) into how the play and its treatment of purgatory elucidate the cultural poetics of its age. But I think he is wrong to insist on "a shift of spectral obligation from vengeance to remembrance" (208), the primacy of memory at the expense of revenge. *Hamlet* is a revenge tragedy, albeit unique in many ways to the genre. The plot and much of the affective force of the play stems from Hamlet's struggle to avenge his father's murder. The rites of filial piety Hamlet, Laertes, and Fortinbras strive to perform derive from the same imperative: to both remember *and* revenge.

41. Midge Decter, "Bitburg: Who Forgot What?" in *Bitburg and Beyond: Encounters in American, German, and Jewish History,* edited by Ilya Levkov (New York: Shapolsky, 1987), 326.

42. James Young, "Memory and Monument," in Geoffrey H. Hartman, *Bitburg in Moral and Political Perspective* (Bloomington: Indiana University Press, 1986), 106.

43. Quoted in Decter, "Bitburg," 327.

44. This was Reagan's characterization in his "I am a Jew" speech delivered to U.S. soldiers at the Bitburg air base after visiting Kolmeshöe. The full text of this speech can be found in Levkov, ed., *Bitburg and Beyond,* 168–71.

45. Decter, "Bitburg," 328.

46. Raul Hilberg, "Bitburg as Symbol," in Geoffrey H. Hartman, *Bitburg in Moral and Political Perspective* (Bloomington: Indiana University Press, 1986), 23.

47. Walter Ruby, "Protesters in Bergen-Belsen: More Than Just Grandstanding," in Ilya Levkov, *Bitburg and Beyond: Encounters in American, German, and Jewish History,* edited by Ilya Levkov (New York: Shapolsky, 1987), 150.

48. John Berryman, "Dream Song #45," in *The Norton Anthology of American Literature,* edited by Ronald Gottesman, Francis Murphy, Laurence B. Holland, Hershel Parker, David Kalstone, and William H. Pritchard, vol. 2 (New York: Norton, 1979), 2319.

49. Ibid.

50. Quoted in Edmond Morris, *Dutch: A Memoir of Ronald Reagan* (New York: Random House, 1999), 529–30.

51. Derrida, *Specters of Marx,* 9.

52. Robert Lowell, "Epilogue," in *Day by Day* (New York: Farrar, Straus and Giroux, 1977).

53. Wills, *Reagan's America,* 458.

54. Deaver, *Behind the Scenes,* 177.

55. Derrida, *Specters of Marx,* xix, emphasis in the original.

56. "Remarks of President Reagan at Bitburg Air Base," in Geoffrey H. Hartman, *Bitburg in Moral and Political Perspective* (Bloomington: Indiana University Press, 1986), 261.

57. It is not until the fifth act, in the "perfect conscience" speech, and again when he casts his "dying voice" for the election of Fortinbras to the throne that Hamlet reveals Denmark to be an elective monarchy, providing a new and politi-

cally critical justification for killing Claudius and bequeathing Fortinbras the political authority and theological legitimacy to reincarnate the body politic (*Hamlet*, 5.2.63–70, 361–62). As Northrop Frye points out, the authoritative Elizabethan doctrine on tyranny, Bishop Thomas Bilson's *The True Difference between Christian Subjection and Unchristian Rebellion*, commissioned by Queen Elizabeth and issued three times between 1585 and 1595, rejected deposing a hereditary monarch who becomes a tyrant but endorses as lawful the unseating of an elected tyrant. Bishop Bilson justifies armed resistance to and restraint of a tyrannical hereditary monarch, "but he may not be deposed." Princes and nobles, however, may both lawfully resist an elected tyrant "or else repel him as a tyrant, and set another in his place by the right and freedom of their country." It is not only the Ghost's call for blood vengeance, then, but also the church's definition of political justice that sanctions Claudius's removal and Fortinbras's rights of memory. See Northrop Frye, *The Renaissance Hamlet: Issues and Responses in 1600* (Princeton: Princeton University Press, 1984), 265.

58. *Hamlet*, 5.2.382–84.

59. Terry Eagleton, *Against the Grain: Essays, 1975–1985* (London: Verso, 1986), 80.

60. Derrida, *Specters of Marx*, 7.

61. Quoted in W. D. King, *Henry Irving's Waterloo* (Berkeley: University of California Press, 1993), 4.

62. Quoted in Bill Boyarsky, *Ronald Reagan: His Life and Rise to the Presidency* (New York: Random House, 1981), 19.

63. Peggy Noonan, *What I Saw at the Revolution: A Political Life in the Reagan Era* (New York: Random House, 1991), 146.

64. Norman Mailer, "Of a Small and Modest Malignancy," in *Pieces and Pontifications* (Boston: Little, Brown, 1982), 79–80.

65. James George Frazer, *The Golden Bough: A Study in Magic and Religion*, new abridgement by Robert Fraser from the second and third editions (Oxford: Oxford World Classics, 1998), 52.

66. Wills, *Reagan's America*, 458.

67. Lyotard writes of capitalism's "massive subordination of cognitive statements to the finality of the best possible performance." See Jean-François Lyotard, *The Postmodern Condition: A Report on Knowledge*, translated by Geoff Bennington and Brian Massumi (Minneapolis: University of Minnesota Press, 1984), 45.

68. Michael Lynch and David Bogen, *The Spectacle of History: Speech, Text, and Memory at the Iran-Contra Hearings* (Durham: Duke University Press, 1996), 248.

69. Michael Taussig, "Viscerality, Faith, and Skepticism: Another Theory of Magic," paper presented at Northwestern University, 17 February 1997, typescript, 5.

70. Ibid., 61.

WORKS CITED

Adams, Henry. *The Education of Henry Adams*. New York: Houghton Mifflin, 1961.

Adams, John. *Diary and Autobiography of John Adams*. Edited by L. H. Butterfield. 4 vols. New York: Atheneum, 1964.

Adams, John. *John Adams's Earliest Diary*. Edited by L. H Butterfield. New York: Atheneum, 1966.

Anderson, Benedict. *Imagined Communities: Reflections on the Origin and Spread of Nationalism*. London: Verso, [1984] 1991.

Anderson, Martin. *Revolution: The Reagan Legacy*. Stanford: Hoover Institution Press, 1990.

Anonymous. "The Uplift of Chautauqua Week." *Literary Digest*, 18 October 1918.

Anonymous. *The History of Rock River Assembly of Lutherans*. Dixon, IL: Committee on Rock River Assembly of the Illinois Synod of the United Lutheran Church of America, 1923.

Appadurai, Arjun. *Modernity at Large: Cultural Dimensions of Globalization*. Minneapolis: University of Minnesota Press, 1996.

Barber, Rowland. "Just a Little List." *TV Guide*, 10 August 1974, 4–8.

Barnouw, Erik. *A Tower in Babel: A History of Broadcasting in the United States to 1933*. New York: Oxford University Press, 1966.

Barthes, Roland. "The Grain of the Voice." In *Image-Music-Text*, translated by Steven Heath, 179–89. New York: Farrar, Straus and Giroux, 1993.

Baty, Paige. *American Monroe: The Making of a Body Politic*. Berkeley: University of California Press, 1995.

Baudrillard, Jean. *Simulations*. Translated by Paul Foss, Paul Patton, and Philip Beitchman. New York: Semiotext(e), 1983.

Baudrillard, Jean. "Simulacra and Simulations." In *Selected Writings*, edited by Mark Poster, 169–87. Palo Alto: Stanford University Press, 1988.

Beard, George M. *American Nervousness, Its Causes and Consequences*. New York, 1881.

Benedetti, Paul, and Wayne MacPhail. "The Birth of Chiropractic." http://www.ca noe.ca/ChiroYork/chiro_invented.html. Accessed November 2006.

Benjamin, Walter. "The Storyteller: Reflections on the Works of Nikolai Leskov." In *Illuminations: Essays and Reflections*, translated by Harry Zohn, edited by Hannah Arendt, 83–110. New York: Schocken, 1968.

Benjamin, Walter. "The Work of Art in the Age of Mechanical Reproduction." In *Illuminations: Essays and Reflections*, translated by Harry Zohn, edited by Hannah Arendt, 217–52. New York: Schocken, 1968.

Benjamin, Walter. "Theses on the Philosophy of History." In *Illuminations: Essays and Reflections*, translated by Harry Zohn, edited by Hannah Arendt, 253–64. New York: Schocken, 1968.

Benjamin, Walter. "One Way Street." In *Reflections: Essays, Aphorisms, Autobiographical Writings*, translated by Edmund Jephcott, edited by Peter Demetz, 61–94. New York: Schocken, 1978.

Bercovitch, Sacvan. *The American Jeremiad.* Madison: University of Wisconsin Press, 1978.

Bercovitch, Sacvan. *The Rites of Assent: Transformations in the Symbolic Construction of America.* New York: Routledge, 1993.

Berlant, Lauren. *The Queen of America Goes to Washington City: Essays on Sex and Citizenship.* Durham: Duke University Press, 1997.

Bernays, Edward. "Engineering of Consent." *Annals of the American Academy of Political and Social Science* 250 (March 1947): 113–20.

Berryman, John. "Dream Song #45." In *The Norton Anthology of American Literature*, edited by Ronald Gottesman, Francis Murphy, Laurence B. Holland, Hershel Parker, David Kalstone, and William H. Pritchard, 2:2319. New York: Norton, 1979.

Bhabha, Homi K. "Introduction: Narrating the Nation." In *Nation and Narration*, edited by Homi K. Bhabha, 1–7. London: Routledge, 1990.

Bhabha, Homi K. *The Location of Culture.* London: Routledge, 1994.

Bird, William L., Jr. "General Electric Theater." Museum of Broadcast Communications. http://www.museum.tv/archives/etv/G/htmlG/generalelect/generalelect .htm. Accessed April 2006.

Blumenthal, Sidney. *The Permanent Campaign.* New York: Simon & Schuster, 1980.

Blyskal, Jeff, and Marie Blyskal. *PR: How the Public Relations Industry Writes the News.* New York: Morrow, 1985.

Boddy, William. *Fifties Television: The Industry and Its Critics.* Urbana: University of Illinois Press, 1990.

Bourdieu, Pierre. *Outline of a Theory of Practice.* Translated by Richard Nice. Cambridge: Cambridge University Press, 1977.

Bourdieu, Pierre. "The Social Space and the Genesis of Groups." *Social Science Information* 24, no. 2 (1985): 195–220.

Bourdieu, Pierre. *In Other Words: Essays towards a Reflexive Sociology.* Translated by Matthew Adamson. Stanford: Stanford University Press, 1990.

Boyarsky, Bill. *Ronald Reagan: His Life and Rise to the Presidency.* New York: Random House, 1981.

Brecht, Bertolt. "Emphasis on Sport." In *Brecht on Theatre,* edited and translated by John Willett. New York: Hill and Wang, 1977.

Bremer, Arthur. *An Assassin's Diary.* New York: Harpers Magazine Press, 1973.

Brown, Robert J. *Manipulating the Ether: The Power of Broadcast Radio in Thirties America.* Jefferson, NC: McFarland, 1998.

Burge, James C. *Lines of Business: Casting Practice and Policy in the American Theatre, 1752–1899.* New York: Peter Lang, 1986.

Burgh, James. *The Art of Speaking.* Danbury, 1795.

Butler, Judith. *Bodies That Matter: On the Discursive Limits of Sex.* New York: Routledge, 1993.

Canning, Charlotte. *The Most American Thing in America: Circuit Chautauqua as Performance.* Iowa City: University of Iowa Press, 2005.

Cannon, Lou. *Reagan.* New York: Putnam, 1982.

Cannon, Lou. *President Reagan: The Role of a Lifetime.* New York: Simon & Schuster, 1991.

Cantril, Hadley. *The Psychology of Radio.* New York: Harper, 1935.

Carlson, Marvin. *The Haunted Stage: The Theater as Memory Machine.* Ann Arbor: University of Michigan Press, 2003.

Carter, Dan T. *The Politics of Rage: George Wallace, the Origins of the New Conservatism, and the Transformation of American Politics.* Baton Rouge: Louisiana State University Press, 1995.

Carter, Jimmy. *Keeping Faith: Memoirs of a President.* New York: Bantam, 1982.

Case, Victoria, and Robert Ormond Case. *We Called It Culture: The Story of Chautauqua.* New York: Doubleday, 1948.

Cleaver, Margaret. "A Chair for the New Home." *Dixon Evening Telegraph,* 4 June 1928.

Cohen, Lizabeth. *A Consumer's Republic: The Politics of Mass Consumption in Postwar America.* New York: Vintage, 2003.

Connerton, Paul. *How Societies Remember.* Cambridge: Cambridge University Press, 1995.

Czitrom, Daniel. *Media and the American Mind: From Morse to McLuhan.* Chapel Hill: University of North Carolina Press, 1982.

Dallek, Mathew. *The Right Moment: Ronald Reagan's First Victory and the Decisive Turning Point in American Politics.* New York: Free Press, 2000.

Dallek, Robert. *Ronald Reagan: The Politics of Symbolism.* Cambridge: Harvard University Press, 1984.

Deaver, Michael K., with Mickey Herskowitz. *Behind the Scenes: In Which the Author Talks about Ronald and Nancy Reagan . . . and Himself.* New York: Morrow, 1987.

Debord, Guy. *The Society of the Spectacle*. Translated by Donald Nicholson-Smith. Detroit: Black and Red Press, 1970.

Decter, Midge, "Bitburg: Who Forgot What?" In *Bitburg and Beyond: Encounters in American, German, and Jewish History*, edited by Ilya Levkov, 318–30. New York: Shapolsky, 1987.

Denning, Michael. "The End of Mass Culture." In *Modernity and Mass Culture*, edited by James Naremore and Patrick Brantlinger, 253–66. Bloomington: Indiana University Press, 1991.

Derrida, Jacques. *Specters of Marx: The State of the Debt, the Work of Mourning, and the New International*. Translated by Bernd Magnus and Stephen Cullenberg. New York: Routledge, 1994.

D'Souza, Dinesh. *Ronald Reagan: How an Ordinary Man Became an Extraordinary Leader*. New York, Simon & Schuster, 1997.

Dunckel, Earl B. "Ronald Reagan and the General Electric Theatre, 1954–1955." Oral history conducted for the Ronald Reagan Gubernatorial Era Documentation Series, Regional Oral History Office, University of California, Berkeley, 1982. Typescript.

Dyer, Richard. *Stars*. London: British Film Institute, 1979.

Dyer, Richard. "Entertainment and Utopia." In *The Cultural Studies Reader*, edited by Simon During, 371–81. New York: Routledge, 1999.

Eagleton, Terry. *Against the Grain: Essays, 1975–1985*. London: Verso, 1986.

Edsall, Thomas Byrne, and Mary D. Edsall. *Chain Reaction: The Impact of Race, Rights, and Taxes on American Politics*. New York: Norton, 1992.

Edwards, Anne. *Early Reagan*. New York: Morrow, 1987.

Edwards, Paul. "Unstoried: Teaching Literature in the Age of Performance Studies." *Theatre Annual: A Journal of Performance Studies* 52 (fall 1999): 1–147.

Emerson, Ralph Waldo. *Representative Men*. Boston: Houghton Mifflin, 1988.

Englehardt, Tom. *The End of Victory Culture: Cold War America and the Disillusioning of a Generation*. New York: HarperCollins, 1995.

Erickson, Paul D. *Reagan Speaks: The Making of an American Myth*. New York: New York University Press, 1985.

Ewen, Stuart. *Captains of Consciousness: The Social Roots of Consumer Culture*. New York: Basic Books, 1976.

Ewen, Stuart. *PR! A Social History of Spin*. New York: Basic Books, 1996.

Farr, Dr. Gary D. "The Wisdom of B. J. Palmer." http://www.aucco.org/palmerbj .html. Accessed October 2006.

Ferguson, Thomas, and Joel Rogers. *Right Turn: The Decline of the Democrats and the Future of American Politics*. Chicago: Lawrence Hill, 1986.

Feuer, Jane. *Seeing through the Eighties: Television and Reaganism*. Durham: Duke University Press, 1995.

Fitzgerald, Frances. *Way Out There in the Blue: Reagan, Star Wars, and the End of the Cold War*. New York: Simon & Schuster, 2000.

Fliegelman, Jay. *Declaring Independence: Jefferson, Natural Language, and the Culture of Performance*. Stanford: Stanford University Press, 1993.

Forest, Lee de. *Father of the Radio: The Autobiography of Lee de Forest*. Chicago: Wilco and Follet, 1950.

Foucault, Michel. *The History of Sexuality*. Translated by Robert Hurley. Vol. 1. New York: Random House, 1978.

Foucault, Michel. "Body/Power." In *Power/Knowledge: Selected Interviews and Other Writings, 1972–77*, edited by Colin Gordon, 55–62. New York: Pantheon, 1980.

Foucault, Michel. "Conversation with Michel Foucault." *Threepenny Review* 1 (winter–spring 1980): 4–5.

Fox, Stephen. *The Mirror Makers: A History of American Advertising and Its Creators*. Urbana: University of Illinois Press, 1997.

Fraser, Steve, and Gary Gerstle, eds. *The Rise and Fall of the New Deal Order, 1930–1980*. Princeton: Princeton University Press, 1990.

Frazer, James George. *The Golden Bough: A Study in Magic and Religion*. New abridgement by Robert Fraser from the second and third editions. Oxford: Oxford World Classics, 1998.

Friedrich, Otto. *City of Nets: A Portrait of Hollywood in the 1940s*. New York: Harper and Row, 1987.

Frye, Northrop. *The Renaissance Hamlet: Issues and Responses in 1600*. Princeton: Princeton University Press, 1984.

Furtwangler, Albert. *Assassin on Stage: Brutus, Hamlet, and the Death of Lincoln*. Urbana: University of Illinois Press, 1991.

Gabler, Neil. *An Empire of Their Own: How the Jews Invented Hollywood*. New York: Anchor, 1989.

Gabler, Neil. *Life, the Movie: How Entertainment Conquered Reality*. New York: Vintage, 2000.

Gallagher, Hugh Gregory. *FDR's Splendid Deception: The Moving Story of Roosevelt's Massive Disability and the Intense Efforts to Conceal It from the Public*. New York: Vandamere, 1985.

Gamson, Joshua. *Claims to Fame: Celebrity in Contemporary America*. Berkeley: University of California Press, 1994.

Gibson, James William. *Warrior Dreams: Violence and Manhood in Post-Vietnam America*. New York: Hill and Wang, 1994.

Gitlin, Todd. *Inside Prime Time*. New York: Pantheon, 1983.

Gitlin, Todd. *Watching Television*. New York: Pantheon, 1986.

Golden, Eve. *Vamp: The Rise and Fall of Theda Bara*. Vestal, NY: Emprise, 1998.

Goldfarb, Jeffrey. *The Cynical Society: The Culture of Politics and the Politics of Culture in American Life*. Chicago: University of Chicago Press, 1991.

Gordon, Colin. "Governmental Rationality; An Introduction." In *The Foucault Effect*, edited by Graham Burchell, Colin Gordon, and Peter Miller, 1–52. Chicago: University of Chicago Press, 1991.

Graham, Austin. "The Visitor in Your Living Room: Radio Advertising in the 1930s." http://xroads.virginia.edu/~CLASS/am485_98/graham/visitor.html. Accessed June 2005.

Grandin, Thomas. *The Political Use of the Radio*. Newark: Arno, 1971.

Greenblatt, Stephen. *Hamlet in Purgatory*. Princeton: Princeton University Press, 2001.

Grossberg, Lawrence. *We Gotta Get Out of This Place: Popular Conservatism and Postmodern Culture*. New York: Routledge, 1992.

Halttunen, Karen. *Confidence Men and Painted Women: A Study of Middle-Class Culture in America, 1830–1870*. New Haven: Yale University Press, 1982.

Hammond, John Winthrop. *Men and Volts: The Story of General Electric*. New York: Lippincott, 1941.

Harrison, Harry P. (as told to Karl Detzer). *Culture under Canvas: The Story of Tent Chautauqua*. New York: Hastings House, 1958.

Hartman, Geoffrey H., ed. *Bitburg in Moral and Political Perspective*. Bloomington: Indiana University Press, 1986.

Hemphill, C. Dallett. *Bowing to Necessities: A History of Manners in America, 1620–1860*. Oxford: Oxford University Press, 1999.

Herries, John. *Elements of Speech and Vocal Music on a New Plan*. Menston, Eng.: Scolar, [1773] 1968.

Hertsgaard, Mark. *On Bended Knee: The Press and the Reagan Presidency*. New York: Random House, 1988.

Hilberg, Raul. "Bitburg as Symbol." In *Bitburg in Moral and Political Perspective*, edited by Geoffrey H. Hartman, 15–26. Bloomington: Indiana University Press, 1986.

Hine, Thomas. *Populuxe*. New York: Knopf, 1986.

Hobbes, Thomas. *Leviathan*. New York: Penguin Classics, [1651] 1982.

Houchin-Winfield, Betty. *FDR and the News Media*. New York: Columbia University Press, 1990.

Hurlbut, Jesse Lyman. *The Story of Chautauqua*. New York: Putnam, 1921.

Jackson, Shannon. *Lines of Activity: Performance, Historiography, Hull House Domesticity*. Ann Arbor: University of Michigan Press, 2000.

James, William. *The Varieties of Religious Experience: A Study in Human Nature*. New York: Macmillan, 1961.

Jameson, Fredric. "Reification and Utopia in Mass Culture." *Social Text* 1 (winter 1979): 130–48.

Jameson, Fredric. *Postmodernism; or, The Cultural Logic of Late Capitalism*. Durham: Duke University Press, 1991.

Jamieson, Kathleen Hall. *Packaging the Presidency: A History and Criticism of Presidential Campaign Advertising*. New York: Oxford University Press, 1984.

Jamieson, Kathleen Hall. *Dirty Politics: Deception, Distraction, and Democracy*. New York: Oxford University Press, 1992.

Johnson, Haynes. *Sleepwalking through History: America in the Reagan Years.* New York: Doubleday, 1991.

Jones, Alfred Haworth. *Roosevelt's Image Brokers: Poets, Playwrights, and the Use of the Lincoln Symbol.* Port Washington, NY: Kennikat, 1974.

Jurca, Catherine. "Hollywood, the Dream House Factory." *Cinema Journal* 37, no. 4 (1998): 19–36.

Kammen, Michael. *Mystic Chords of Memory: The Transformation of Tradition in American Culture.* New York: Vintage, 1993.

Kang, Joon-Mann. "Franklin D. Roosevelt and James L. Fly: The Politics of Broadcast Regulation, 1941–1944." *Journal of American Culture* 10, no. 2 (1987): 23–34.

Kantarowicz, Ernst. *The King's Two Bodies: A Study in Mediaeval Political Theology.* Princeton: Princeton University Press, 1957.

Kaplan, Lincoln. *The Insanity Defense and the Trial of John Hinckley, Jr.* Boston: Godine, 1984.

Kelley, Kitty. *Nancy Reagan: The Unauthorized Biography.* New York: Simon & Schuster, 1991.

Kernell, Samuel. *Going Public: New Strategies of Presidential Leadership.* Washington, DC: Congressional Quarterly Press, 1986.

Khachigian, Kenneth. Handwritten note, budget communications meeting, March 27, 1981, folder CFOA5, box 4689, Kenneth Khachigian files, Ronald Reagan Presidential Library.

King, W. D. *Henry Irving's Waterloo.* Berkeley: University of California Press, 1993.

Klaprat, Cathy. "The Star as Market Strategy: Bette Davis in Another Light." In *The American Film Industry,* edited by Tino Balio, rev. ed., 351–64. Madison: University of Wisconsin Press, 1985.

Klein, Naomi. *No Logo: No Space, No Choice, No Jobs.* New York: Picador, 2002.

Knoper, Randall. *Acting Naturally: Mark Twain in the Culture of Performance.* Berkeley: University of California Press, 1995.

Kramnick, Isaac. *Republicanism and Bourgeois Radicalism: Political Ideology in Late Eighteenth-Century England and America.* Ithaca: Cornell University Press, 1990.

Lefcowitz, Eric. "Welcome to the Retro Future," 2002. http://www.retrofuture.com/futurama.html. Accessed February 2003.

Lefebvre, Henri. *The Production of Space,* translated by Donald Nicholson Smith. Oxford: Oxford University Press, 1991.

Lemay, J. A. Leo. "The American Origins of 'Yankee Doodle'." *William and Mary Quarterly,* 3d ser., 33 (July 1976): 435–64.

Levine, Lawrence. *Highbrow/Lowbrow: The Emergence of Cultural Hierarchy in America.* Cambridge: Harvard University Press, 1990.

Levkov, Ilya, ed. *Bitburg and Beyond: Encounters in American, German, and Jewish History.* New York: Shapolsky, 1987.

Lewis, Tom. "'A Godlike Presence': The Impact of Radio on the 1920s and 1930s." *Organization of American Historians Magazine of History* 6, no. 4 (1992): 26–33.

Lincoln, Abraham. "First Inaugural Address, Final Text, March 4, 1861." In *The Collected Works of Abraham Lincoln,* edited by Roy P. Basler, 4:271–72. New Brunswick: Rutgers University Press, 1953.

Lipset, Seymour Martin. *The First New Nation: The United States in Historical and Comparative Perspective.* New York: Norton, 1963.

Looby, Christopher. *Voicing America: Language, Literary Form, and the Origins of the United States.* Chicago: University of Chicago Press, 1996.

Lowell, Robert. "Epilogue." In *The Norton Anthology of American Literature,* edited by Ronald Gottesman, Francis Murphy, Laurence B. Holland, Hershel Parker, David Kalstone, and William H. Pritchard, 2:2345–46. New York: Norton, 1979.

Lynch, Michael, and David Bogen. *The Spectacle of History: Speech, Text, and Memory at the Iran-Contra Hearings.* Durham: Duke University Press, 1996.

Lynd, Robert, and Helen Lind. *Middletown: A Study in Contemporary American Culture.* New York: Harcourt, Brace, Jovanovich, 1929.

Lyotard, Jean-François. *The Postmodern Condition: A Report on Knowledge.* Translated by Geoff Bennington and Brian Massumi. Minneapolis: University of Minnesota Press, 1984.

MacDonald, J. Fred. *Don't Touch That Dial! Radio Programming in American Life, 1920–1960.* Chicago: Nelson-Hall, 1979.

MacDonald, J. Fred. *One Nation under Television: The Rise and Decline of Network TV.* New York: Pantheon, 1990.

Mailer, Norman. "Of a Small and Modest Malignancy." In *Pieces and Pontifications,* 80–81. Boston: Little, Brown, 1982.

Marchand, Roland. *Creating the Corporate Soul: The Rise of Public Relations and Corporate Imagery in American Big Business.* Berkeley: University of California Press, 1998.

Marshall, P. David. *Celebrity and Power: Fame in Contemporary Culture.* Minneapolis: University of Minnesota Press, 1997.

Martin, Marty. "'Storycide' and the Meaning of History." In *Bitburg in Moral and Political Perspective,* edited by Geoffrey H. Hartman, 224–26. Bloomington: Indiana University Press, 1986.

Marx, Karl. *Capital.* Vol. 1. New York: International Publishers, 1967.

Massumi, Brian, and Kenneth Dean. "Postmortem on the Presidential Body." In *Body Politics: Disease, Desire, and the Family,* edited by Michael Ryan and Avery Gordon, 155–74. Boulder: Westview, 1994.

McArthur, Benjamin. *Actors and American Culture, 1880–1920.* Philadelphia: Temple University Press, 1984.

McDougal, Dennis. *The Last Mogul: Lew Wasserman, MCA, and the Hidden History of Hollywood.* New York: Crown, 1998.

McGilligan, Patrick. *Yankee Doodle Dandy.* Edited by Patrick McGilligan. Madison: University of Wisconsin Press, 1981.

McGirr, Lisa. *Suburban Warriors: The Origins of the New American Right.* Princeton: Princeton University Press, 2002.

McGurl, Mark. "Making It Big: Picturing the Radio Age in *King Kong.*" *Critical Inquiry* 22, no. 3 (1996): 415–45.

McKenzie, Jon. *Perform or Else: From Discipline to Performance.* New York: Routledge, 2001.

McManus, Michael. Undated memo to Michael Deaver, folder 1, box OA7624, 1982, Michael McManus files, Ronald Reagan Presidential Library.

Mellencamp, Patricia. *High Anxiety: Catastrophe, Scandal, Age, and Comedy.* Bloomington: Indiana University Press, 1992.

Metzger, Robert P. *Reagan: American Icon.* Lewisburg, PA: Center Gallery Publications, Bucknell University, 1989.

Meyer, Donald. *The Positive Thinkers: Popular Religious Psychology from Mary Baker Eddy, Norman Vincent Peale, and Ronald Reagan.* Rev. ed. Middletown, CT: Wesleyan University Press, 1988.

Moldea, Dan. *Dark Victory: Ronald Reagan, MCA, and the Mob.* New York: Viking, 1986.

Morehouse, Ward. *George M. Cohan: Prince of the American Theater.* New York: Lippincott, 1943.

Morris, Edmond. *Dutch: A Memoir of Ronald Reagan.* New York: Random House, 1999.

Morrison, Theodore. *Chautauqua: A Center for Education, Religion, and the Arts in America.* Chicago: University of Chicago Press, 1974.

Murdoch, James F. *A Plea for Spoken Language: An Essay upon Comparative Elocution.* Cincinnati: Van Antwerp, Bragg, 1883.

Nelson, Richard. *A Culture of Confidence: Politics, Performance, and the Idea of America.* Jackson: University of Mississippi Press, 1996.

Noonan, Peggy. *What I Saw at the Revolution: A Political Life in the Reagan Era.* New York: Random House, 1991.

Nye, David. *Image Worlds: Corporate Identities at General Electric, 1890–1930.* Cambridge: MIT Press, 1985.

Orchard, Hugh A. *Fifty Years of Chautauqua: Its Beginnings, Its Development, Its Message, and Its Life.* Cedar Rapids, IA: Torch, 1923.

Paine, Thomas. *Common Sense.* Edited by Isaac Kramnick. New York: Penguin Classics, 1982.

Palmer, B. J. *History in the Making.* Davenport, IA: B. J. Palmer, 1957.

Panama, Norman, and Melvin Frank. *Mr. Blandings Builds His Dream House.* Los Angeles: Twentieth Century Fox, 1948. Film.

Perkins, Frances. *The Roosevelt I Knew.* New York: Viking, 1946.

Phelan, Peggy. *Unmarked: The Politics of Performance.* New York: Routledge, 1993.

Powdermaker, Hortense. *Hollywood: The Dream Factory.* New York: Little, Brown, 1950.

Rader, Benjamin G. *In Its Own Image: How Television Has Transformed Sports.* Boston: Free Press, 1984.

Reagan, Nancy. *My Turn: The Memoirs of Nancy Reagan.* New York: Random House, 1989.

Reagan, Neil. "Private Dimensions and Public Images: The Early Political Campaigns of Ronald Reagan." Interview conducted by Stephen Stern for the Oral History Program, University of California, Los Angeles, 1982. Regional Oral History Office, UCLA Library.

Reagan, Ronald, with Richard G. Hubler. *Where's the Rest of Me?* New York: Duell, Sloan & Pearce, Best Books, 1965.

Reagan, Ronald. "The Creative Society." Speech delivered at the University of Southern California, 19 April 1966. http://reaganlibrary.com/reagan/speeches/creative.asp. Accessed September 2007.

Reagan, Ronald. Interview with Vin Scully, 27 November 1980. Videotape R33, Video Archive, Ronald Reagan Presidential Library.

Reagan, Ronald. *Speaking My Mind: Selected Speeches.* New York: Simon & Schuster, 1989.

Reagan, Ronald. *Ronald Reagan: An American Life.* New York: Simon & Schuster, 1990.

Reagan, Ronald. *Reagan: A Life in Letters.* Edited by Kiron Skinner, Annalise Anderson, and Martin Anderson. Boston: Free Press, 2003.

Regan, Donald. *For the Record: From Wall Street to Washington.* New York: Harcourt Brace Jovanovich, 1988.

Rein, Irving J., Philip Kotler, and Martin R. Stoller. *High Visibility.* New York: Dodd, Mead, 1987.

Reinsch, J. Leonard. *Getting Elected: From Radio and Roosevelt to Television and Reagan.* New York: Hippocrene, 1988.

Reynolds, David S. *Walt Whitman's America: A Cultural Biography.* New York: Vintage, 1996.

Roach, Joseph. *Cities of the Dead: Circum-Atlantic Performance.* New York: Columbia University Press, 1996.

Roach, Joseph. "The Emergence of the American Actor." In *The Cambridge History of American Theatre,* vol. 1: *Beginnings to 1870,* edited by Don B. Wilmeth and Christopher Bigsby, 338–72. Cambridge: Cambridge University Press, 1998.

Rogin, Michael. *Ronald Reagan, the Movie: and Other Episodes in Political Demonology.* Berkeley: University of California Press, 1987.

Rogin, Michael. "'Make My Day': Spectacle as Amnesia in Imperial Politics." *Representations* 29 (winter 1990): 99–124.

Rogin, Michael. *Blackface, White Noise: Jewish Immigrants in the Hollywood Melting Pot.* Berkeley: University of California Press, 1996.

Roosevelt, Franklin. Inaugural Address, March 4, 1933. In *The Public Papers and Addresses of Franklin D. Roosevelt,* compiled by Samuel Rosenman, vol. 2, *The Year of Crisis, 1933,* 11–16. New York: Random House, 1938.

Rosenman, Samuel I. *Working with Roosevelt.* New York: Harper, 1952.

Rosten, Leo C. *Hollywood: The Movie Colony, the Movie Makers.* New York: Harcourt, Brace, 1941.

Ruby, Walter. "Protesters in Bergen-Belsen: More Than Just Grandstanding." In Ilya Levkov, *Bitburg and Beyond: Encounters in American, German, and Jewish History,* edited by Ilya Levkov, 141–51. New York: Shapolsky, 1987.

Schatz, Thomas. *The Genius of the System: Hollywood Filmmaking in the Studio Era.* New York: Holt, 1996.

Schechner, Richard. *Between Theater and Anthropology.* Philadelphia: University of Pennsylvania Press, 1985.

Schickel, Richard. *Intimate Strangers: The Culture of Celebrity.* New York: Fromm International, 1985.

Schudson, Michael. *Watergate in American Memory: How We Remember, Forget, and Reconstruct the Past.* New York: Basic Books, 1992.

Sennett, Richard. *The Fall of Public Man.* New York: Norton, 1992.

Shakespeare, William. *Hamlet.* Arden Shakespeare ed. New York: Methuen, 1982.

Sheridan, Thomas. *A Course of Lectures on Elocution.* Menston, Eng.: Scolar Press, [1762] 1968.

Sherwood, Robert. *Roosevelt and Hopkins: An Intimate History.* New York: Gosset and Dunlap, 1950.

Silberman, Charles E. "Speaking Truth to Power." In *Bitburg and Beyond: Encounters in American, German, and Jewish History,* edited by Ilya Levkov, 344–49. New York: Shapolsky, 1987.

Skinner, Kiron, Annalise Anderson, and Martin Anderson, eds. *Reagan: A Life in Letters.* Boston: Free Press, 2003.

Sklar, Robert. *Movie-Made America: A Cultural History of American Movies.* New York: Vintage, 1994.

Slotkin, Richard. *Gunfighter Nation: The Myth of the Frontier in Twentieth-Century America.* New York: Macmillan, 1992.

Speakes, Larry, with Robert Pack. *Speaking Out: The Reagan Presidency from within the White House.* New York: Scribner's, 1985.

Spigel, Lynn. *Welcome to the Dream House: Popular Media and Postwar Suburbs.* Durham: Duke University Press, 2001.

Starr, Paul. *The Creation of the Media: Political Origins of Modern Communication.* New York: Basic Books, 2005.

Steele, Richard W. *Propaganda in an Open Society: The Roosevelt Administration and the Media, 1933–1941.* Westport, CT: Greenwood, 1985.

Sturken, Marita. *Tangled Memories: The Vietnam War, the AIDS Epidemic, and the Politics of Remembering.* Berkeley: University of California Press, 1997.

Sussman, Warren. *Culture as History: The Transformation of American Society in the Twentieth Century.* New York: Pantheon, 1984.

Taussig, Michael. *Mimesis and Alterity: A Particular History of the Senses.* New York: Routledge, 1993.

Taussig, Michael. "Viscerality, Faith, and Skepticism: Another Theory of Magic." Paper presented at Northwestern University, 17 February 1997. Typescript.

Taylor, Diana. "Dancing with Diana: A Study in Hauntology." *Drama Review* 43, no. 1 (1999): 59–78.

Taylor, Paul. *See How They Run: Electing the President in an Age of Mediaocracy.* New York: Knopf, 1990.

Troy, Gil. *Morning in America: How Ronald Reagan Invented the 1980s.* Princeton: Princeton University Press, 2005.

Turner, Victor. "Frame, Flow, and Reflection: Ritual and Drama as Public Liminality." In *Performance in Postmodern Culture,* edited by Michel Benamou, 33–55. Madison: University of Wisconsin Press, 1977.

Tye, Larry. *The Father of Spin: Edward L. Bernays and the Birth of Public Relations.* New York: Holt, 1998.

Vaughn, Stephen. *Ronald Reagan in Hollywood: Movies and Politics.* Cambridge: Cambridge University Press, 1994.

Walker, Alexander. *Stardom: The Hollywood Phenomenon.* New York: Stein and Day, 1970.

Warner, Michael. *The Letters of the Republic: Publication and the Public Sphere in Eighteenth-Century America.* Cambridge: Harvard University Press, 1990.

Walt Whitman. "I Sing the Body Electric." In *Leaves of Grass.* Philadelphia: David McKay, [1855] 1900, 81–86.

Whitman, Walt. "When Lilacs Last in the Dooryard Bloomed." In *Leaves of Grass,* 255–62. Philadelphia: David McKay, [1855] 1900.

Williams, Raymond. *Marxism and Literature.* Oxford: Oxford University Press, 1977.

Williams, Raymond. "Drama in a Dramatized Society." In *Raymond Williams on Television,* edited by Alan O'Connor, 3–13. London: Routledge, 1989.

Wills, Garry. *Reagan's America: Innocents at Home.* New York: Viking Penguin, 1988.

Wills, Garry. *Lincoln at Gettysburg: The Words That Remade America.* New York: Simon & Schuster, 1992.

Winfield, Betty Houchin. *FDR and the News Media.* Urbana: University of Illinois Press, 1990.

Yeilding, Kenneth D., and Paul H. Carlson. *Ah That Voice: The Fireside Chats of Franklin Delano Roosevelt.* Odessa, TX: Library of the Presidents, Presidential Museum, 1974.

Young, James. "Memory and Monument." In *Bitburg in Moral and Political Perspective,* edited by Geoffrey H. Hartman, 103–13. Bloomington: Indiana University Press, 1986.

INDEX